American Lives

Volume One: To 1876

American Lives

Volume One: To 1876

Willard Sterne Randall

John Cabot University, Rome

Nancy Nahra

John Cabot University, Rome

 LONGMAN

An imprint of Addison Wesley Longman, Inc.

New York • Reading, Massachusetts • Menlo Park, California • Harlow, England
Don Mills, Ontario • Sydney • Mexico City • Madrid • Amsterdam

Executive Editor: Bruce Borland
Developmental Editor: James Strandberg
Text Design and Project Coordination: Ruttle Graphics, Inc.
Cover Designer: Paul Lacy
Cover Illustration: War news from Mexico. Richard C. Woodville courtesy of the
                Manoogian Foundation.
Photo Researcher: Carol Parden
Electronic Production Manager: Angel Gonzalez Jr.
Manufacturing Manager: Willie Lane
Electronic Page Makeup: Ruttle Graphics, Inc.
Printer and Binder: RR Donnelley & Sons Company
Cover Printer: The Lehigh Press, Inc.

Library of Congress Cataloging-in-Publication Data
Randall, Willard Sterne.
    American lives/ Willard Sterne Randall, Nancy Nahra.
        p.   cm.
    Includes bibliographical references and index.
    Contents: v. 1. To 1876.
    ISBN 0–673–46986–7
    1. United States—Biography. I. Nahra, Nancy Ann. II. Title.
CT214.R36   1996   96–11929
920.073—dc20   CIP

ISBN 0–673–46986–7

345678910-DOC-999897

To Lucy
so full of
American life

Contents

Preface

History is about people.

It is impossible to write or to study history without considering the lives of people. Perhaps nowhere is this more true than in studying the history of America, where diversity has encouraged individualism. Even great social, economic, intellectual, and political forces took shape in the minds of individual Americans. The record of their lives documents their personal actions.

All of these forces and the great ideas of these individuals are bound up in the fortress of memory called history. But how is the interested student to approach this great mass of ideas, actions, and struggles? Too often, the historical record has been rendered impenetrable. There must be some accessible way, some pathway or bridge to approach the study of history. Biographies, especially short biographies, provide one such approach.

The idea of using biography—the study of human lives—to teach is certainly not new. Plutarch's forty-six *Parallel Lives*, written in the second century, long remained the model for others who sought to teach by showing a system of ethics, by recording the exploits, the virtues, and the maxims of kings and generals. As late as the mid-nineteenth century, biography was considered an all-male business for author and subject alike. The English historian Thomas Carlyle pronounced it "the story of the great men." It was only in the past century that a significant number of biographies written by and about women began to appear.

Writing about great men and great women prompts discussions of leadership, of charisma, and of relationships between leadership and power, between leaders and the people. But the lives of the not-so-great more and more are attracting biographers who use them to show how people in everyday life react to the same events and problems. Short biographies of the great and not-so-great also serve as case studies of the periods in which people live, using individuals to study ideas.

Each of these lives puts us in another time and place. Each one shows what we can and cannot comprehend about the past. And each life invites us to remember these remarkable people and the problems they faced, and to see, in their memories, links to history, their past and ours.

Acknowledgments

The authors think that the collective subject of this book helped inspire a constructive spirit of cooperation that left many people encouraged and hopeful. In a project like this, different kinds of assistance made a crucial difference at moments when we needed help. Here are some of the people who have our gratitude. At Addison Wesley Longman, we owe thanks to Bruce Borland, Executive Editor, who listened to the idea for the book and boldly signed it up. James Strandberg, Development Editor, did many jobs meticulously and cheerfully to transform the idea into bound pages. Ray Lincoln, agent and friend, gave exactly the suggestions and opinions that we would have asked for. Ruth Gminski helped a great deal with the early library searches. Dr. Vincent Naramore, emeritus professor of mathematics at St. Michael's College, helped us with many useful observations. Diann Varricchione helped us, as usual, in her competent and unflappable way as she prepared the many drafts of the manuscript. And our thanks, too, to Kimberly Thompson at Ruttle Graphics for her thoroughgoing copyediting.

The manuscript got better as it passed through the hands of a team of careful historians whose expertise sharpened points and refined factual distinctions at different stages. These include: Anne B. Harris, Old Dominion University; Philip H. Vaughan, Rose State College; Theresa Kaminski, University of Wisconsin-Stevens Point; Hilliard J. Goldman, Meramec Community College; Jerry Thompson, Texas A&M International University; Timothy Koerner, Oakland Community College-Royal Oak Campus; B. B. McCool, Arkansas Tech University; David Dixon, Slippery Rock University; Michael Weiss, Linn-Benton Community College; Mark C. Herman, Edison Community College; David A. Walker, University of Northern Iowa; Deborah M. Jones, Bristol Community College; Tommy Stringer, Navarro College; Kenneth H. Williams, Alcorn State University; Ellen Shockrow, Pasadena City College; Valeen T. Avery, Northern Arizona University; and David Godshalk, Shippensburg University. Errors that may remain, of course, can be attributed not to them but to us. For the photos that illustrate our book, we thank Carol Parden, who saw to that aspect of the research.

Willard Sterne Randall
Nancy Nahra

1

Christopher Columbus

For five hundred years, European mariners had sought new trade routes. Hampered by crude navigational tools, they could only edge along the European land mass. Boldest of all were the Norsemen, steering by memory of myriad elements—shoreline profiles, water color, starscapes, the angle of the sun from the horizon—passing on their lore by ballad and saga as they reached farther west to Iceland, Greenland, and the north shore of Newfoundland by the eleventh century. But their settlements did not last and their attempts at trading textiles were not welcomed by warlike natives. Soon they concentrated their efforts on wars of conquest from England to Russia. By 1410, famine ended their last colony on Greenland.

By the thirteenth century, venturesome Italian merchants feeding new appetites for luxuries whetted by the Crusaders had stolen a march all the way to China, India and Indonesia. In an age before refrigeration, spices helped not only the palate but the nose. Pearls, gold, coffee, decorative tiles and sumptuous Persian rugs adorned the cold stone houses of a growing wealthy clientele—offering rich rewards for the courageous merchant voyager. Competition for trade routes along with raw materials for manufacture and trade set off a rage for exploration and discovery by the mid-fifteenth century.

JUST WHAT DAY and in what place Christopher Columbus was born is unknowable. These are two of the many hundreds of disputes about this stubborn, courageous man of controversy who, at the very least, brought the Old and New Worlds together, giving birth to modern times. Sometime between August 25 and October 31, 1451, Christoforo Colombo was born to Domenico Colombo, a wool weaver, sometime petty official and tavernkeeper, in Savona, which today is a suburb of the port city of Genoa. His father, from the wool-weaving enclave of this city of skilled artisans, had married Susanna Fontanarossa, the daughter of a woolweaver. However, he was never content and when Christopher—as Americans call him—was two, Domenico left Susanna's family home in Savona, where he had bought a tavern, and moved back to his native Genoa to take up the minor public office of city gatekeeper. Eventually, he would also set up a wineshop and dabble, unsuccessfully, in local politics, making and losing the money. He once went to jail briefly after he aligned himself with the local faction that backed the French in a war against the Spaniards of Aragon.

When Christopher was not quite two, disaster befell the rich city-state of Genoa as it did to a lesser extent all of Christian Europe. In 1453 after a century-long struggle, the Ottoman Turks conquered Constantinople. The trade crossroads for the ten-thousand mile caravan network that brought silk, spices, pearls, and gold from China, India, and Japan overland to the eastern rim of the Mediterranean. Ships from Genoa and Venice had vied for four centuries, since the First Crusade, to enrich the tables and wardrobes of Europe's wealthy. The fall of Constantinople was an especial tragedy for the Genoese who, hedging their bets, had lost six hundred soldiers among the defenders of the walls of the beautiful eastern Christian capital of the Greco-Byzantine Empire. Meanwhile in the Genoese suburb of Pera, merchants who monopolized the trade in grain, caviar, and many other goods gave covert assistance to the advancing Turkish armies in hopes of receiving future favors. When Constantinople fell, the Genoese opened their gates to the Turks and their colony became a Turkish town. This was a psychological calamity for all Genoese, who would long live under the shadow of being considered traitors to Christianity.

Nevertheless, Genoa remained a great banking, shipping and mapmaking center which sent trading vessels as far away as Iceland and West Africa. It was also a famous religious center which had built the Crusaders' ships and then, in black and white checkerboard marble the Cathedral of San Lorenzo to hold in its crypt the relics of the Holy Lands, including the fabled silver casket of John the Baptist and the green plate, the Holy Grail, that supposedly held his head. Columbus would grow up under the spell of powerful religious legends, developing a crusading sense of mission.

Growing up tall, blue-eyed, red-haired, and fair skinned, Christopher was the oldest of five children, which was a modest family for the time. He was close to his brothers, Bartholomeo and Diego; all three boys were probably sent to a monastery school to learn basic Latin and mathematics. After his formal education ended at fourteen, Christopher went to work in his father's wineshop in Savona, where the family had settled. There he learned about buying, selling, and book-keeping. His father, an ambitious man, pushed him into business, but Christopher yearned to go to sea. With his growing knowledge of trade, the tall, strong youth was able to combine the two. He began to sail as the agent for Genoese mercantile families, the Spinolas, Di Negros and Centuriones. He was in his early twenties when he made his first documented voyage in the mid–1470s, joining a trading expedition to Chios, the Genoa-owned island in the Aegean Sea. There, Genoa held the monopoly on mastic, the medieval equivalent of chewing gum which is derived from the resinous sap of an evergreen shrub called the lentisk. A popular trade item with the Turks, mastic was used as a breath-freshener for their harems. It was also traded as far away as England, where it was used as a painkiller, the fifteenth Century equivalent of aspirin.

Each year Columbus sailed out of Genoa and away from the tedium of his father's shop. He made a second trip to Chios and took part in a minor naval campaign in a continuing war between Genoa—backed by the French—and the Kingdom of Aragon in Spain. In the summer of 1476, at twenty-five, Columbus shipped out with a Genoese fleet of five vesse_s bound for Lisbon and England with a cargo of Chios mastic. He saw the Atlantic Ocean for the first time. He felt its strong tradewinds in his face as they passed through the Straits of Gibraltar. On August 13, 1476, the fleet was attacked by booty-hunting French and Portuguese ships. Three ships caught fire and sank, many Genoese drowning. Columbus, possibly wounded and clinging to an oar, struggled to shore, landing near Lagos, Portugal, where villagers nursed the survivors.

Making his way to Lisbon, the stranded Columbus settled into the community of Genoese merchants and shipowners in the Alfama section beside the Tagus River. This remained his home for the next eight years from 1476 to 1484. During long hours of conversations with mariners and mapmakers, he began to form his ideas of westward exploration. No single inspiration came to him; it was all around him in late fifteenth-century Portugal.

Since 1419, when Prince Henry the Navigator had begun his lifelong support of exploration, Portugal (ideally situated on the tip of the European landmass where it jutted into the Atlantic) had pioneered an age of discovery. Navigators, cartographers and cosmographers—many of them Italians whose trade to the East was now blocked by the Turks—gathered as Portugal launched far-ranging Renaissance explorations. These explorations amounted to planned discoveries and brought Europe out of the Middle Ages. New knowledge and vast new wealth that further whetted the thirst for new discoveries, new markets, and new conquests were the results of these discoveries. Prince Henry was the first rational organizer of explorations. His program of exploration gave tiny Portugal the first European overseas empire.

Many of the early explorers had been Italian like Columbus and had great credibility at the Portuguese court. Columbus owned, read, and annotated a copy of Marco Polo's *Il Millione*, which detailed his travels to China. He may have heard in Lisbon of the Vivaldi brothers of Genoa, the first to set out to find a route around southern Africa to the Indian Ocean, only to be lost at sea. By 1434, Portuguese mariners were probing south along the African coast, despite medieval superstitions that anyone who tried to cross the equator would die in boiling waters. Before Prince Henry's death in 1460, when Columbus was a boy of nine, Portuguese mariners had charted the African coast as far as modern Dakar and were bringing back regular shipments of gold, ivory—and slaves. By 1457, when Columbus was six and living nearby, a Genoese mapmaker commissioned by Prince Henry drew a map showing for the first time the Spice Islands. These islands were detailed in the travel writings of Venetian merchant Nicola de Conti, who had spent twenty-five years in the Far East, not only retracing Marco Polo's travels but visiting Sumatra, Borneo, and Java.

By 1472, when Columbus was twenty-one, Portuguese forts guarded gold and slave-trading centers in present-day Ghana. The new king, John II, continued the single-minded Portuguese search for water routes around and through Africa and for natural resources to mine, thus increasing the fabulous new wealth pouring into his kingdom. Portugal's state policy of exploration drew on the traveler's reports, new maps, and the geographical theories of early Italian Renaissance humanists, particularly those from Florence, who were intent on reversing the thousand year old belief that only one-seventh of the earth was covered by water and six-sevenths by land.

Half a century before Columbus's first voyage of exploration, Portuguese theoreticians agreed with Florentines that the ocean could be used as an intercontinental waterway. However, the Portuguese ignored the Florentines' contention that there was a shorter route to the Asian landmass and that thousands of miles could be saved by sailing west. The rediscovery of the writings of the second century Roman, Ptolemy's *Geography,* offered a textbook for debates among mariners and theoreticians in Portugal, where, between voyages as far as England, Ireland and Iceland, the young Columbus steeped himself in accounts and theories of exploration. But he was not always the careful student. He preferred theories based on the mariner's anecdote, his own observations from growing experience, and intuition. As the idea of sailing west to China and Japan took hold of him during his eight years in Portugal, he ignored well-known calculations of distances. He became obsessed with the idea that Japan was only about three thousand miles west of Portugal. If he had been a better student, he might not have discovered a new world to the West.

As early as 1477, a twenty-six-year-old Columbus began to think of sailing west to find the East. He sailed with a Genoese fleet to Bristol, England and may, as his son later insisted, have taken a ship to Iceland. Hernando Columbus, quoting his father's letters, years later wrote, "In February 1477, I sailed my self [sic] an hundred leagues [300 miles] beyond Thule [Greenland]." Had Columbus heard stories of Norsemen, sailing from this advanced base, sailing to North America nearly five hundred years earlier?

The next year, 1478, Columbus gained more knowledge of the currents and winds of the Atlantic by sailing to Madeira to buy sugar as an agent for Italian merchants. And the next year, he sailed to Genoa to testify in a lawsuit arising from the Madeira run. It was his last visit to Genoa.

When he came back to Portugal, he married Felipa Perestrello Moniz, whom he had met at a convent school for Portuguese noblewomen. He saw her at Mass, which was a favorite way to begin the courting ritual. Was it a love match? Columbus never wrote about any of his family. But Felipa's family were nobles and the prosperous young Genoese merchant mariner was an eligible bachelor. Besides, Felipa's father came from an Italian seafaring family and had been appointed by Prince Henry as hereditary governor of the Portuguese island of Porto Santo in the Madeiras. The ambitious Columbus married her in 1479 and moved into her family home in the Madeiras.

It was probably in the next two years that Columbus worked out in detail his plan to put together an expedition to seek a western route to Asia. Columbus's mother-in-law apparently gave him her late husband's books, journals, and sea charts. Here, historians believe, he systematically studied Ptolemy, the French Cardinal Pierre d'Ailly's *Imago Mundi,* the ancient pronouncements of Seneca and Aristotle, the latest edition of Marco Polo's *Il Millione,* and the Florentine,

Toscanelli's, 1474 letter and map. These studies furthered his belief that it was possible to sail west to the Indies. Columbus wrote to Toscanelli, who wrote back urging him to sail west to find China, which Toscanelli believed to be only 4,000 miles west of Portugal. Columbus's taste for adventure and wealth was further whetted in 1481, when he shipped aboard a Portuguese fleet to the Guinea coast of West Africa. There at the new fortress of El Mina for the first time he saw gold and slaves being traded.

But by the 1480s, the Portuguese were firmly committed to a policy of sailing east around Africa to reach the Indies (now India, China, the East Indies and Japan). When, sometime in 1483, Columbus gained an audience with King John II and proposed his westward voyage, the king turned his plan over to his council of advisors. The advisors turned it down ostensibly because they believed, and correctly so, that he had greatly underestimated the length of the journey. But they probably would have rejected his proposal anyway, believing with the king that all Portugal's resources should be devoted to pursuing the route around Africa.

In 1485, Columbus, now thirty-four and a widower, took his young son to Spain, the bitter rival of Portugal. He arrived at the height of King Ferdinand and Queen Isabella of Aragon's war to drive the Muslims out of their last Iberian stronghold of Granada. Although Columbus was able to win the support of two wealthy Spanish dukes for his plan, he still needed royal permission. It took another year to win this royal audience. Meanwhile Columbus cleverly put himself into the hands of a Franciscan friar close to the deeply religious queen. While his first conference with the monarchs was less than a complete success, Columbus did win a royal allowance from Isabella while he pursued his pleadings before her advisors. The Spanish rulers, in truth, could ill afford his expedition yet they were reluctant to yield such an opportunity to any of their subjects.

Following the Spanish court from castle to castle for nearly seven years, the doggedly persistent Columbus won a wide following of converted Jewish merchants and bankers, including the royal treasurer. Columbus also had to overcome diplomatic objections. Spain and Portugal had recently settled disputes over islands off Africa. But it was the eloquent and persuasive vow by Columbus to use the rewards of his expedition to recapture Jerusalem from the Muslims, to rebuild the Jews' Temple there, and begin an "Age of the Holy Spirit," that captivated Isabella. This won the support of Franciscan friars and also Jews who were being forced to convert to Christianity or leave Spain.

In 1486, Isabella ordered Columbus's plan studied by a commission of experts headed by her priest-confessor, Hernando de Falavera. The commission in 1490 flatly rejected his plan partly on grounds that he was underestimating the distance, but also because he was now demanding not only ships, crews, and cash for provisions but a noble title, the rank of admiral, hereditary rights to land, and a percentage of the riches he found in his explorations. Refusing to give up, Columbus sent his brother, Bartholomeo, a mapmaker, to England and France to seek support, where he, too, was turned down.

When Granada fell early in 1492, Columbus's friend, converted Jewish financier Luis de Santangel, finally convinced Queen Isabella she was losing a great opportunity. Suddenly, that April, Columbus won royal approval. The Crown ordered the seaport of Palos to wipe out a royal debt by providing Columbus with two caravels. He rented a third with borrowed money and its owner, Juan de la Cosa, came along as captain. Columbus, a seaman for nearly twenty years, had never been master of a ship himself.

With combined crews of about ninety men, the three small wooden ships, including the *Niña* and the *Pinta*, captained by experienced sailing masters Martin and Vincente Pinzón behind the slightly larger mother-ship, *Santa Maria*, with Columbus and the supplies on board, left Palos on August 3, 1492. They arrived in the Canary Islands after six days, took on fresh food and water, then sailed due west. Columbus followed the twenty-eighth degree of latitude, using a technique called dead reckoning, which he had mastered during his years at sea. This technique takes advantage of strong trade winds which, at that latitude, always blow to the west. He held to his course using only a crude navigational tool called a quadrant that plots the ships' position by sighting the North Star. He guessed his speed, had cabin boys constantly watch and turn the half-hour glass, and used a compass to keep to his course. It was, in fact, the perfect course: any other could have brought disaster. In a month of fast, smooth sailing, the flotilla crossed the Atlantic and was approaching Cuba when his crews became panicky. Only the promise of turning back if they didn't find land in three days averted all-out mutiny.

It was at this point that Columbus made another fateful decision. He had begun to notice signs of land, including seaweed on the water's surface that must have come from a shore nearby. When he spotted a flight of land-based birds, he ordered a change in course to the southwest and followed them. (Had he gone straight ahead, he would have come ashore at what is now Cape Kennedy, Florida.) Just before dawn on October 12, 1492, a sailor aboard *Pinta* yelled, "*Terra, terra!*" ("Land, land!") Columbus fired a cannon to notify the *Niña* of the sighting of one of the Bahama Islands. Just before noon, Columbus climbed into a launch with his officers and a hand-picked crew and went ashore (on just which island is in sharp dispute). They planted the flags of Ferdinand and Isabella, claiming the islands for Spain, not bothering to consult with their inhabitants. Believing he had reached the East Indies, he called the tall, long-haired, semi-nude natives who came to greet him Indians, a name that stuck to these Tainos and all other natives of the uncharted hemisphere he had stumbled onto by mistake.

On that first of four voyages, Columbus explored the Bahamas, the northeastern coast of Cuba, and the northern shore of Hispaniola (present-day Haiti and the Dominican Republic) before his flagship ran aground on a reef on Christmas Day. Establishing a post he called La Navidad to mark the date, he left forty volunteers in grass-roofed huts inside a fort armed and reinforced by the ship's cannon and timbers. He promised to return within a year. His voyage home aboard *Niña* was stormwracked, very nearly ending in disaster when he had to seek the aid of the Portuguese king who had refused to help him make the voyage. Finally, arriving at Palos, Spain on March 15, 1493, Columbus received a grand reception from the king and queen at Barcelona. He had little to show but some gold trinkets he had bartered away from natives—seven of whom he had kidnapped.

Yet Columbus's voyage and the widely published letter he wrote on his voyage home electrified all of Europe. He maintained, and until his dying day believed,

The Bettmann Archive

Mariner Christopher Columbus studied Atlantic currents for twenty years before seeking a water route to China.

that the West Indies he had found were actually the East Indies, just off the Asian mainland. He wrote that the small fort he had built on Hispaniola was convenient for all kinds of trade with "the Great Khan" of China. The natives he described as "artless and free with all they possess." They were not black, as Europeans of the time expected "as in Guinea [West Africa] but with flowing hair." And, he promised his monarchs, he could "give them as much gold as they want" as well as "slaves, as many as they shall order."

Deciding to exploit Columbus's discoveries, Ferdinand and Isabella quickly applied to Pope Alexander VI for authority to Christianize the lands Columbus had visited as well as control over all lands west of a line nine hundred miles west of the Azores. Eventually, by the Treaty of Tordesillas of 1494, Spain received the right to preach (and by inference conquer) all of the Western Hemisphere except Brazil and Newfoundland, which were awarded to Portugal.

Columbus sailed west three more times. With seventeen ships and 1,200 men on the second voyage, he found La Navidad burned to the ground and its garrison dead; its settlers had fought over native women and shot some native men. Undeterred, he planted the colony of Isabella on Santo Domingo in January 1494, using it as a base for inland exploration. In 1496, he left his brother, Bartholomeo, in command while he returned to Spain. In 1498, this time with a fleet of seven ships, he sailed a more southerly route, touching the Cape Verde Islands and reaching Trinidad. This was the first time he saw the South American continent and it was on this trip that he discovered the mouth of the mighty Orinoco River.

Returning to Santo Domingo, despite his new identity as Don Cristoforo Colon, he was a poor administrator and a foreigner unable to maintain control over the noble-born Spanish *hidalgos*. A new governor arrived in August 1500 and sent Columbus and his two brothers back to Spain in chains. Cleared of charges of misconduct in office, Columbus was honored by the queen, but he would never again be given any authority. All his discoveries and their income were taken over by the Crown.

Allowed to make a final voyage with four ships in 1502, Columbus made landfalls in the Canaries and Martinique before exploring the coast of Honduras and sailing southward as far as Panama. He arrived off the Isthmus of Panama on April 15, 1503. Exhausted and dispirited, he ignored hints from the natives that there was a great body of water only a few days' march to the west. Thus, he lost the opportunity to see the Pacific Ocean and to discover just how wrong he had been about the true distance from Spain to Asia. En route home, he was shipwrecked and marooned on Jamaica for a full year. A loyal follower rowed to Hispaniola in a dugout canoe and, eventually, authorities there grudgingly sent a ship to take him back to Spain for the last time.

The death of Queen Isabella, his steadfast friend and protector, doomed Columbus's last wish—to lead a Christian crusade to reconquer Jerusalem. He wandered the streets of Valladolid, often dressed in a Franciscan friar's robes and cowl. At a final audience with Ferdinand, the king offered to trade in all the gold and privileges still due Columbus for a great ducal estate in north-central Spain, far from the court, but Columbus stubbornly refused to give up his demands for restoration of his authority and an increased income.

On May 20, 1506, at age fifty-four, Columbus died in his modest house in Valladolid, suffering terribly from Reiter's syndrome, a crippling form of spinal arthritis common among seamen. He died a wealthy man. He took to his grave a stubborn set of beliefs that had helped him succeed in his single-minded search for a westward route to Asia. His persistence, his courage, and his great maritime achievements forever changed the views of Europe toward the rest of the world. By bringing Old and New Worlds irreversibly into contact, he helped to change forever how the entire world lived. The two hemispheres exchanged their resources, their diseases, their customs, and finally, their political systems. Columbus's quest for God and gold had brought him first glory, and then shame: after half a millennium, historians are still arguing how to apportion the shares. In the next century, gold and silver from the New World opened up by Columbus's voyages would make Spain the wealthiest imperial power in the world. Meanwhile European diseases, military campaigns, and the introduction of slave labor would so depopulate Latin America that only the introduction of millions of African slaves could keep the mines and plantations producing the riches Europe had come to expect from overseas possessions. Eventually, the American colonies would revolt, bringing down the European monarchies and creating in their place a new world of democratic governments.

QUESTIONS FOR THOUGHT AND DISCUSSION

1. What caused Christopher Columbus to dedicate his life to seafaring? Is there a negative side to his thirst for adventure and discovery?

2. What methods did Columbus use to finally secure financing for his initial voyage in 1492? What does his ultimate success in winning financing suggest about his abilities?

3. Given the fact that he never found the shorter trade route to the Orient which had been the purpose of his voyages, was Columbus really a hero?

4. The 500th anniversary of Columbus' 1492 arrival in the Americas saw a raging controversy over whether Columbus should be honored or condemned in the historical memory. Native Americans in particular offered the opinion that Columbus had unleashed greed, violence, racism, and disease on the so-called "New World." How should history treat Columbus?

SUGGESTED READINGS

Columbus, Christopher. *Diaries of First Voyage to America.* Ed. by Oliver Dunn and James E. Kelley, Jr. Norman: U of Oklahoma P, 1989.

Dor-Ner, Zvi. *Columbus and the Age of Discovery.* New York: Morrow, 1991.

Dyson, John. *Columbus: For Gold, God and Glory.* New York: Simon, 1991.

Fernández-Armesto, Felipe. *Columbus.* New York: Oxford UP, 1991.

Lunenfeld, Marvin. 1492: *Discovery, Invasion, Encounter.* Lexington, Mass.: D. C. Heath, 1991.

Morison, Samuel Eliot. *Admiral of the Ocean Sea: A Life of Christopher Columbus.* Boston: Little, 1942.

_____. *The European Discovery of America: The Northern Voyages.* New York: Oxford UP, 1971.

Taviani, Paolo Emilio. *Columbus: The Great Adventure.* Trans. by Luciano Farina and Marc Beckwith. New York: Orion, 1991.

Wilford, John Noble. *The Mysterious History of Columbus.* New York: Knopf, 1991.

2

Anne Marbury Hutchinson

The last European power to enter the race for New World territories and riches was England. While Portugal and Spain expanded their imperial possessions rapidly at the turn of the fifteenth century, England's monarchs were slowly turning from civil wars to wars on the European mainland. Not until Elizabeth I came to the throne did an English monarch think about competing with her mainland rivals—and then she was satisfied with commissioning marauders to poach the wealth of the New World from treasure ports and fleets. James I, who came to the throne in 1603, launched the first for-profit English settlement at Jamestown and also chartered the Plymouth Plantation (half the passengers on the Mayflower were merchants). By the time the spread of religious persecution in Europe sent a large English contingent toward Massachusetts Bay in 1629, prospective English colonists had their choice of colonial destinations—and the managers of colonies had to compete with each other for settlers.

FOR NEARLY A DECADE in the early years of New England's history, women enjoyed more rights and respect, less abuse, and the promise of a progressively better way of life than in their homeland Old England. They emigrated happily to Boston with their husbands, brothers, and fathers. Although relieved as they were to escape the tightening noose of religious persecution, until 1637 there were only two women in Massachusetts Bay colony for every three men, the highest ratio in the American colonies. Then, as a democracy led by a woman, the colony began to call into question many church-state arrangements. Questions were raised including the differences between the sexes. A harsh crackdown put an end to this brief outbreak of equality between men and women.

The Puritan fathers at first outdid themselves pampering, as they saw it, female colonists, and probably did not see where it could lead. In tracts such as William Wood's *New England's Prospect*, written to promote immigration to the edge of the wild American continent, women were told that their gender had already taken several upward steps. In England, wife beating was commonly used to keep women in their place; in New England, it was forbidden. Furthermore, men were forbidden to treat their wives as servants. Heavy fines punished infractions of either offense. In the early years after Boston's founding in 1630, New England authorities took pains to make women happy so that they would write glowing letters back to England to lure more of their sisters.

One of the more eager recipients of this good news from America was Anne Marbury Hutchinson, the cheerful middle-aged wife of a prosperous silk manufacturer and the mother of fourteen children. Married to a man who believed in the equality of sexes, Anne Hutchinson was also a devoted follower of a charismatic Puritan divine. As it became apparent that Puritans would have to flee intensifying persecution by the English government, Anne, her husband, and their seven younger children left behind the comfortable life of English gentry to become pioneers on the edge of the American wilderness.

Greater equality for women did not seem a distant prospect or a hypothetical philosophical concept when Anne Hutchinson was born in England in 1591. A woman was on the throne of England. Queen Elizabeth I was not just a time-serving stand-in between male rulers, she was the second queen in a row to rule England. She spent much of her forty-four year reign contending not only with less successful male European kings but with other powerful and ambitious women, including the cousin she would put to death, Mary Queen of Scots. It was, in fact, an age of queens in Europe, but the specter of enduring female power alarmed many Protestant rulers, including Henry Knox, a founder of the Presbyterian Church and spiritual father of English Puritanism. Knox had denounced government by women in his treaties, *The First Trumpet Blast Against the Monstrous Regiment of Women* (1558). Elizabeth established herself as the unchallenged magnate of Europe by defeating the Spanish Armada three years before Anne Hutchinson's birth, and remained, all through Anne's childhood, the figure of a brilliant woman towering over England.

While Anne never met the queen, she saw all around her evidences of her authority. Her mother's uncle, Sir Anthony Cope, a Puritan member of Parliament, was repeatedly jailed for opposing Queen Elizabeth's middle-of-the-road church policies. One incarceration included a one month visit to the Tower of London for sponsoring Cope's Bill and Book, which would have authorized a Puritan revision to the official Book of Common Prayer. When Elizabeth had come to the throne, it had been widely assumed that she would push ahead the radical Reformation agenda of the Puritans, who wanted to "purify" the Church of England of all remaining traces of the Church of Rome, including vestments, incense, and bishops. But her Act of Settlement suppressed zealous reformers: she preferred to downplay religious contention and made it clear from time to time by exemplary execution that she would tolerate neither criticism on the subject of religion or any open opposition either by Puritan reformers or Catholics.

The daughter of a Church of England preacher and a Puritan mother who was descended from a noble Lincolnshire family, Anne grew up in the small market town of Alford, 114 miles northeast of London, in a houseful of books, daughters, and religious disputation. Her father, Francis Marbury, was master of Alford Grammar School and preacher at 250-year-old St. Wilfrid's Church, hub of Alford's religious, social and political life. Francis Marbury was frequently in trouble with the bishops for loudly denouncing the lazy, uneducated clergy of the Church of England. Twice, he was tried by church courts and stripped of his living for his outspoken views. His pet targets were the "self-seeking, soul-murdering" bishops and the low preaching standards of the country priests. In virtual house arrest through much of Anne's childhood, her father had plenty of time to instruct his eager daughter (often his only appreciative audience), whom he treated as a son.

A born bookworm with a retentive memory, Anne, a kinswoman of playwright John Dryden on her mother's side, spent more time reading than sewing. She also learned midwifery by helping with several of her mother's deliveries, and learned to be a skilled nurse and herbalist. These qualities made her a figure respected by other women. Inspired no doubt by a queen who had mastered Latin, read Plato in the original Greek, and could argue in French, Spanish, Portuguese, Italian and Welsh, Anne grew up at a time when female literacy in England was higher than ever before or again until the late nineteenth century. One widely read London educator, Richard Mulcaster, argued "that young maidens can learn, nature doth give them, and that they have learned, our experience doth teach us." "What," asked Mulcaster, headmaster of St. Paul's School, "can more assure the world than our diamond [Queen Elizabeth] at home?"

At times, Francis Marbury was the sole voice advocating Puritan reforms to the Church of England. On trial, he argued bravely and disrespectfully against grillings by powerful bishops. Anne could not help but mark the lesson. She also must have been aware that, after Elizabeth I died and even as the misogynist King James I ascended the throne, more Puritan women were beginning to lecture publicly across England. They, too, were persecuted. When Anne was thirteen, her father was knighted and made pastor of the vast parish of St. Martin in the Vintry, London, in the shadow of St. Paul's Cathedral.

It was in London that Anne first imbibed the ideas of Familism, a radical sect that preached direct communication between each individual, male and female, and God. Its teachings rejected the Calvinist doctrine of predestination, which precluded individual free will and Original Sin, and which denounced Eve and blamed women for all sin. Young Anne began to listen closely to women's voices in the nonconformist sects sprouting in London—she was attracted at various times by Familism, Separatism, and Puritanism, to which her mother subscribed. London women took active roles in the Puritan movement and some 200 of them were hauled before the bishop of London in Star Chamber ecclesiastical trials. A majority of these women were tried. They suffered heavy fines and imprisonment for, among other offenses, keeping secret the locations of clandestine Puritan printing presses. London women not only supported the Puritan underground but held the equivalent of salons in their parlors to preach and lead religious discussions.

At James I's accession in 1603, he, too, was expected to unleash a Puritan reform movement, but at the Hampton Court conference of church leaders, he proclaimed that Puritanism "agrees as well with a monarchy as God and the Devil." He not only attacked Puritans, but also women, several times digressing from his prepared speech to disparage them. His bishops took his cue, and among other strictures imposed a ban on infant baptism by midwives, even when no priest was available and the baby was dying. As James took every opportunity to reverse Elizabeth's policies toward women, he introduced a stiff new anti-witchcraft law and, in his bestselling witch book, *Demonology*, declared that for every twenty-one witches, twenty were women. James argued that all women were weak and lustful and easy prey to "the snares of the Devil as was ever well proved to be true by the Serpent's deceiving of Eve at the beginning." In his first speech to Parliament, James lashed out at women, paraphrasing Scripture: "The head of every man is Christ and the head of the woman is man." In a widely printed letter to his son, the king instructed his son, "Teach your wife that it is your office to command, hers to obey. Women must never be allowed to meddle in the government."

By the time Anne was seventeen, Separatists who had given up on reforming the Church of England were trying to escape, first to Holland. Anne had her first glimpse at persecuted Englishwomen driven from their homeland as the Pilgrims fled.

When Anne was twenty, her father, her soul mate and intellectual companion, died. He left his wife as the sole executrix of his will, an uncommonly liberal gesture for the time, and left each of his twelve children 200 marks, a tidy sum. One year later, Anne, twenty-one, married William Hutchinson, twenty-six, a wealthy textile merchant. The first of their fourteen children was born soon after they moved back to their childhood home, Alford.

Along the English Channel, in the shadow of Dutch windmills, new religious winds were blowing. Women were appearing in pulpits as preachers, a practice originating across the Channel in Holland. Soon, there were women ministers all over England, many of them preaching the reform doctrines of Familism. This sect held that the spirit was superior to the Bible, that women and men could return to the innocence that preceded the Fall, advocated the election of the clergy by the people, and put reason above ritual.

The rapid spread of this radical agenda by women preachers brought intensifying persecution by the state church. In January 1620, the Bishop of London told all his clergy to preach vehemently against the insolence of women and to condemn their "wearing of broad-brimmed hats, pointed doublets, hair cut short or shorn," and their carrying of daggers and swords. One Londoner recorded, "Our pulpits ring continually of the insolence and impudence of women."

In rural Alford, Anne had little contact for many years with persecution until the mid–1620s, when Charles I succeeded James and even further stepped up persecution of dissenters. Anne flirted at first with Separatism but then seems to have rejected the idea of leaving her father's church after she heard of the preaching of a charismatic Puritan preacher, John Cotton, at Boston, located twenty-four miles away on the English Channel. Frequently, she and her husband journeyed there to hear him preach his gentle version of Puritanism. Cotton had won a reputation all over England as a Biblical scholar and, as the leading nonconforming minister in the Church of England, for his evangelical preaching of the Covenant of Grace, which he described as a covenant between God and man whereby God drew the soul to salvation. He preached that there was nothing a man—or woman—could do to acquire this covenant. If Anne Hutchinson was predestined to salvation, God would endow her with faith and fulfill the covenant. This doctrine differed somewhat from the version that the founders of Massachusetts Bay Colony demanded as orthodox when they sailed to Boston in 1630. The faithful were expected to "prepare" themselves for God's saving grace by good works, especially following the laws of the New England church state. Anne espoused John Cotton's evangelical preaching of divine omnipotence and human helplessness. She believed with him that to draw comfort from doing good works was presumptuous, that God acted alone and that humans had no way of preparing for it.

In the winter of 1629, as the persecution of Puritans worsened, John Winthrop, a Cambridge-educated London barrister, was elected governor of a company of a thousand Puritans preparing to establish a permanent settlement in New England. The company made strong overtures to women, strongly implying that the New World would have no use for Old World women-trammeling traditions. One leader wrote of "the kind usage of the English [in Massachusetts Bay] to their wives" and of households where "equals gather with equals." The 1620s had been years of severe restrictions and heavy taxes on English businessmen and of drought and famine in the English cities and towns. Reports from the New World emphasized abundant game, seafood, fruit, berries, and pumpkins for the taking. In the sermon John Cotton preached to the Puritans departing on the four ships commanded by Governor Winthrop, he emphasized the economic opportunities for merchants like Anne's husband:

> Nature teaches bees [that] when the hive is too full, they seek abroad for new dwellings.... [so it is] when the hive of [England] is so full that the tradesmen cannot live one by another, but eat up one another ....

What may have pushed the Hutchinsons off the fence to decide to emigrate was the latest policy of King Charles I, who combined unparalleled taxation and religious persecution by exacting forced loans from Puritans. Anne's uncle, seventy-year-old Erasmus Dryden, owner of Canons Ashby, one of England's great houses, was jailed when he refused to lend the king money. William Hutchinson believed it was only a matter of time before his turn came. A second assault on her family circle came when her brother-in-law, the Puritan preacher John Wheelwright, was arrested. Anne also learned that John Cotton was on the run, in disguise from Archbishop Laud's agents, and using an assumed name. He was living in hiding in a series of Puritan houses. In July 1633, Reverend Cotton boarded the *Griffin* and escaped to New England. Two members of the Hutchinson family sailed with him to begin transferring the family business to Boston. Shortly after their twelfth child was born, Anne and William began giving away their belongings and selling their home of twenty years.

From almost the moment she stepped on board the *Griffin*, bound for Boston on Massachusetts Bay, Anne Hutchinson spoke her mind, perhaps feeling she was safely away from the inhibiting atmosphere of England's church spies. She almost immediately incurred the wrath of two Puritan ministers who, along with a hundred head of cattle, were crowded in among the voyagers to the New World. The Reverends Zechariah Symmes and William Bartholomew reported to Boston authorities that Anne had confided to Bartholomew "that she had never had any great thing done about her but it was revealed to her beforehand." To claim that she communicated directly with God through revelations was heretical enough for

The Bettmann Archive

Anne Hutchinson, preaching in her Boston home, found there was less freedom in the New World than at home in England.

the two ministers: that a *woman* claimed direct contact with God smacked of witchcraft.

To make matters worse, Anne had quickly grown tired of Reverend Symmes' five-hour, nonstop, shipboard sermons, especially his constant belittling of women. Anne announced that once in Boston she would expose them as a tissue of errors and she began holding shipboard women's meetings, as she had done for years unmolested in Alford. She was surprised that some of the men aboard objected, confronting her with a quote from the Bible (1 Corinthians 14:35), "And if they [women] will learn anything, let them ask their husbands at home."

Anne was shocked at the mean, uncouth look of Boston, a flat, swampy backwater town of crowded, unpaved streets with pigs rooting in the filth. Its hundred-odd houses were dominated by the square barnlike Puritan meetinghouse. Inside, she received another shock: instead of automatic admission to membership, she was subjected to an all-day hearing by Governor Thomas Dudley, her old pastor, Reverend Cotton, the pastor of her new Boston church, the Reverend John Wilson, and Reverend Symmes, one of the shipboard clergymen she had openly criticized. Finally "satisfied that she held nothing different from us," Governor Dudley urged her admission to the church. But if Anne Hutchinson expected freedom of expression or the right to dissent in Massachusetts, she must have been sadly disappointed.

For the next two years, Anne and William Hutchinson were busy with building and furnishing a spacious, thatch-roofed wattle-and-daub house in Boston's Cornhill section right across the street from former Governor John Winthrop. He had recently been displaced as governor because many country clergy thought he had been too lenient with dissenters and had closed an eye to sharp business practices. Demoted to the colony's council, Winthrop was waiting for the next election to prove his toughness: he had received a copy of Anne's hearing record and had already put her down as someone to watch. All oblivious, Anne was busy building her practice as one of only four midwives in all of Boston, and if that and her large family were not enough, she began holding weekly meetings in her home to discuss with other women the finer points of Mr. Cotton's sermons.

In these meetings, soon so popular that sixty or seventy people packed in and stood for an hour or two as Anne elaborated Cotton's teachings, she began to take Cotton's principles of divine omnipotence and human helplessness in a new direction. Her first principle was "that the person of the Holy Ghost dwells in a justified person [predestined for salvation]." This threatened the fundamental doctrine on which Puritans had built their church-state, that God's will could only be fathomed in the pages of the Bible. She further claimed that a good life—"sanctification"—offered no proof of salvation, or "justification." This undermined the whole Puritan belief that good works were necessary to "prepare" for salvation. Her emphasis on personal revelation minimized the role of the clergy. She also maintained that "justified" people knew by revelation from the Holy Spirit that they were already "justified." On the basis of this mystical insight, "justified" people could tell whether other people were "under a covenant of grace" (saved) or "under a covenant of works" (damned because they were depending on good works instead of divine grace). How damaging this set of beliefs could be to the stable clergy-dominated society of Boston began to become clear by October 1636 to now re-elected Governor Winthrop when Anne hinted to her admirers that in all of Massachusetts there were only two churchmen, John Cotton and her brother-in-law, John Wheelwright, who were under a covenant of grace and therefore were fit to preach. If she had given this opinion to only a handful of listeners she might have only been censured by her pastor. But by late 1636, up to eighty eager auditors were jamming her house three times a week. Many of the listeners were merchants disgruntled with clergy controls on trade and profits, and members of other congregations who trekked great distances from all over the colony to see and hear this bold woman speaking out against the black-robed, all-male power structure. As historian Edmund Morgan has put it, "more was at stake here than the welfare of the Boston church."

When Anne's mentor, John Cotton, had applied to become teacher of First Church of Boston, which had the largest congregation in the colony, Winthrop couldn't stop him. But when Anne's brother-in-law, John Wheelwright, whose views were no different from Cotton's nor from Anne's, was proposed as a teacher at a church meeting on October 30, 1636, Winthrop saw his chance to block Anne's growing influence. Most recent among her followers was Sir Henry Vane, the new Puritan governor from England. Winthrop opposed Wheelwright's appointment as the church's third minister, "whose spirit they knew not and [who] seemed to dissent in judgment." Despite the fact that Wheelwright had the support of most of the congregation, Winthrop was even more popular as the man who had led and formed the Puritan colony over the years. And now he was putting all that influence on the line to rouse the entire colony to the threat posed by Anne Hutchinson.

By early 1637, the colony was divided into two hostile factions, the town of Boston versus the surrounding countryside. In January, the worried General Court, the colony's ruling body, declared a day of fasting and prayer, a compulsory holiday. John Cotton preached and when he finished, Wheelwright rose from his bench and criticized anyone adhering to the Covenant of Works: "The more holy they are, the greater enemies they are to Christ .... We must kill them with the word of the Lord." Speaking figuratively, Wheelwright no doubt thought that most of the clergy and magistrates were dead wood, but someone took down his words and at its next session, the General Court charged him with sedition, convicting him but deferring sentence until after the annual May election. When the Court sat again, John Winthrop was back in power. He had moved the Court and the elections out of Boston into the countryside, to remote Cambridge, where he had the support of orthodox country clergy who had ousted Governor Vane from office (Vane soon sailed back to England). To further buttress his position, Winthrop again put off sentencing Wheelwright, calling a synod of ministers in late summer to examine the doctrines his informants told him were coming from Anne Hutchinson's parlor. In the meantime, to keep their numbers from swelling further, Winthrop sponsored a General Court order forbidding anyone to entertain strangers for more than three weeks without permission of the magistrates. The order was pointed at new immigrants from England whose views accorded with Mrs. Hutchinson's. America's first immigrant-screening law, aimed at stifling religious dissent, had been enacted.

On August 30th, ministers converged from all over Massachusetts and Connecticut, for twenty-four days defining orthodox Puritan doctrines and spelling out for each other the implications of some eighty-two "erroneous" doctrines they heard from witnesses were coming from Anne Hutchinson's parlor. Anne's old mentor, John Cotton, fell into line with the orthodox majority; only her brother-in-law, John Wheelwright, dissented. When the General Court reconvened in November, Wheelwright refused to recant and was banished from the colony. The Court then summoned Anne Hutchinson.

The year 1637, the ninth year of Massachusetts Bay colony, was the year when Puritan New England lost its innocence. Massachusetts troops used the murder of a New England trader to destroy the main stronghold of the Pequot Indians near Stonington, Connecticut, and slaughtered the escaping remnants near New Haven. Wheelwright was banished, and was expected to go off to Rhode Island to join Roger Williams, who had been banished the year before and was starting a new colony among the Indians. Then, on November 12, 1637, the General Court, its collective mind already made up that Anne Hutchinson must be silenced, tried the five-month-pregnant, forty-six-year-old midwife and lay teacher on charges of sedition and contempt.

The New Town (as Cambridge was then called) Courthouse was unheated, stark, and crowded. Some two hundred persons had crowded into the courthouse when Anne, dressed in black, was escorted in and told to stand facing the bench, a long table at which gowned and wigged General Court officials sat flanking Governor Winthrop. There was no jury, although this was a civil case. Only the judges had footwarmers with hot coals inside. Anne heard the charges read to her for the first time. She was accused of eighty-two "errors in conduct and belief," including "consorting with those that had been sowers of sedition." Did they mean her own brother-in-law Wheelwright? In England, all Puritans were nonconformists by definition; in New England, nonconformity had just become an indictable offense. She was also accused of breaking the Fourth Commandment. The Bible was the lawbook and "Honor thy father and thy mother" now meant that the governors of the colony were the fathers and all women were their dutiful children, to honor and obey. Her third offense was to claim revelation of God's Word directly and her fourth that she had misrepresented the conduct of the ministers.

Legally, the Court was on slippery ground, handicapped by Anne Hutchinson's carefulness. She had written nothing down and never spoken in public. Furthermore, Winthrop could only accuse her of "countenancing and encouraging" Wheelwright's seditious circulation of a petition to reform the clergy: she had not actually signed it. To hold home meetings had never been a crime in England or New England before: it was the bedrock of the persecuted underground Puritan tradition. Only the charge of traducing the authority of the ministers seemed serious.

Without a lawyer, Anne ably conducted her own defense. Standing and parrying the Governor's questions for seven uninterrupted hours, with a devastating combination of nerve, logic, and an expert knowledge of the Bible, she often reduced lawyer Winthrop to exasperated outbursts of pique: "We do not mean to discourse with those of your sex." Called on to justify teaching crowds in her home, she quoted the Bible to show older women were required to teach younger women. When Winthrop would not accept two Biblical sources as grounding for her meetings, she answered sarcastically, "Must I show my name written therein [in the Bible]?" One clergyman after another paraded to testify that she had belittled and insulted the ministers. Winthrop seemed to prevail on this charge, but only after introducing notes from an off-the-record pre-trial meeting with Anne.

The first day's grilling only paused when the pregnant Anne fainted after not being allowed to sit, eat, drink, or leave the courtroom for natural relief. That night, she found discrepancies in the testimony of her principal accuser, her pastor, Reverend Wilson, after a supporter slipped her notes. The next day, she insisted that all witnesses be put under oath, including the clergy, nearly setting off a riot. One final witness was her old friend, John Cotton, who rebutted the testimony of Reverend Wilson that Anne had admitted accusing the clergy of being "under a covenant of works" (unsaved). The case against Anne Hutchinson collapsed.

In her moment of unexpected triumph, Anne blurted out that she had known from a revelation at the start of her trial that she would prevail. And then she went even further: "And see this scripture fulfilled this day in mine eyes .... Take heed what ye go about to do unto me ... God will ruin you and your posterity and this whole state." This public challenge was too much for Winthrop and his all-male panel of judges and clergy. Winthrop asked Anne how she knew "that it was God that did reveal these things" and Anne, condemning herself under the colony's Biblical laws against claiming immediate revelation, replied, "By the voice of his own spirit to my soul."

Deliberating only briefly, the Court agreed Anne's words were enough grounds for banishment. And when Anne asked to "know wherefore I am banished," Winthrop gave her only a curt, highhanded answer: "Say no more, the court knows wherefore and is satisfied."

Ordered held under house arrest in the isolated manse of a clergyman safely away from Boston all winter, when Anne still refused to recant, she was excommunicated in March 1638 and ordered to leave the colony. At her sentencing, the Reverend Hugh Peter told her that her principal offense was that "you have stepped out of your place, you have rather been a husband than a wife." And Reverend John Wilson, her nemesis, noting that "you have so many ways troubled the church" added, "I do cast you out and deliver you up to Satan." Immediately after her November 1637 hearing, the Court went on to strip Captain John Underhill, hero of the Pequot War, of his militia rank and disfranchised him for supporting Wheelwright and Hutchinson. Twelve days after sentencing Anne Hutchinson, the court ordered fifty-eight Bostonians (William Hutchinson was third on the list) stripped of their guns, powder, lead, and their right to vote—seventeen others from other towns were punished similarly. Six more women were tried and expelled in 1638.

With eighteen inches of snow still in the woods, Anne, now nine months pregnant, and her children traveled sixty-five miles from Boston to Aquidneck by horse, canoe, and on foot over Indian paths in a journey that took eight days. Her husband had gone ahead with twenty of her faithful adherents to build log cabins. By March 1639, Anne was preaching again, her following growing. As excommunications continued in Boston, John Winthrop raged that Massachusetts would soon seize Rhode Island: Anne could not stay there. After her husband died in 1642, Anne moved to New York Province with several other families. Far from the reach of John Winthrop, she built a house on Pelham Bay on the outskirts of the Dutch settlements. She did not believe in war or firearms, and her Boston adherents had refused to fight in the Pequot Wars. Now, on the frontier, she steadfastly refused to defend herself as a new war against the Indians broke out in 1643. She opened her gate one day to a group of young Indians who asked her for cold water from her well. They rushed in and killed Anne Hutchinson and all but one of her daughters, who was taken into captivity. Unsympathetic even at the hour of her tragic death, the Reverend Thomas Weld, in whose house she had been held under arrest, gleefully reported her death back to England: "Thus the Lord heard our groans to heaven, and freed us from this great and sore affliction."

QUESTIONS FOR THOUGHT AND DISCUSSION

1. Anne Marbury Hutchinson's father treated her "as a son." What effect did this have on her?

2. How did Hutchinson's voyage aboard the *Griffin* to start a new life in America foreshadow the controversies that overtook her in Boston?

3. Was Hutchinson too quick to judge Boston authorities or simply speaking her beliefs? Why were so many in Boston ready to listen to and concur with her opinions?

4. Should Massachusetts Bay have tolerated Hutchinson's radical beliefs, or were they right in banishing her as a dangerous threat to public order? To what degree do you think her banishment was due to her breaking the boundaries set for her gender?

SUGGESTED READINGS

Battis, Emery. *Saints and Sectaries: Anne Hutchinson and the Antinomian Controversy.* Chapel Hill: Institute of Early American History and Culture, 1962.

Crawford, Deborah. *Four Women in a Violent Time.* New York: Crown, 1970.

Hall, David D. *The Antinomian Crisis, 1636–1638: A Documentary History.* 2nd ed. Durham: Duke UP, 1990.

Lang, Amy Scrager. *Prophetic Women: Anne Hutchinson and the Problem of Dissent in the Literature of New England.* Berkeley: U of California P, 1987.

Miller, Perry. *The New England Mind: The Seventeenth Century.* Cambridge, Mass.: Belknap, 1959.

Morgan, Edmund. *The Puritan Dilemma: The Story of John Winthrop.* Boston: Little, 1958.

Newcomb, Wellington. "Anne Hutchinson versus Massachusetts." *American Heritage,* June, 1974, pp. 12–15, 78–81.

Pettit, Norman. *The Heart Prepared.* New Haven: Yale UP, 1966.

Rimmer, Robert H. *The Resurrection of Anne Hutchinson.* Buffalo: Prometheus, 1987.

Williams, Selma R. *Divine Rebel: The Life of Anne Marbury Hutchinson.* New York: Rinehart, 1981.

3

${\it Teedyuscung}$

The struggle for dominion over New World territory, raw materials, and markets sparked three-quarters of a century of confrontation and armed conflict between France and her Canadian colonies on the one hand, and England and its Atlantic Seaboard settlements. Four intercolonial wars broke out between 1689 and 1763. The competing networks of European forts and trading stations gradually entangled most Native Americans south of Hudson's Bay and east of the Mississippi River. Natives became dependent even for the weapons they needed to hunt for food and hides. They became habituated to factory-made kettles, knives, hatchets, coats, trousers, trinkets, liquor—all provided in exchange for the furs so much in demand in Europe.

When intermittent colonial wars broke out, only pacifist Pennsylvania had seemed immune to the bloodshed. Founded by Quaker William Penn, this sylvan island of tranquility was a magnet for European as well as English pacifists. Some 250 sects of German pietists alone settled in the fertile valleys between the Quaker settlements on the Delaware River and Susquehannah River, 100 miles to the west.

As the European struggle to control North America intensified in the mid-eighteenth century, Native Americans were forced to take sides. Treaty alliances and bribes of trade goods corrupted older Native American power relationships. The Delawares of New Jersey and Pennsylvania, for instance, became pawns of the Six Nations Iroquois Confederacy of New York in its lucrative dealings with their military allies, the English. Not all Native Americans were willing to sit still for the new arrangements.

SURROUNDED BY A graceful ring of hills, the Lehigh Valley had become the heartland of Moravian settlements in eastern Pennsylvania. Even in the drought-ridden 1750s, it was rich in corn and wheat, and thick with dairy herds. The Moravians, German forerunners of the Methodists, had purchased most of the valley from William Penn's sons. They established unarmed towns with Biblical names—Bethlehem, Nazareth—built missions, and preached to the Indian "heathen" of Christian salvation. They alone among the peaceful Pennsylvanians methodically studied the Native American cultures and dialects.

At the heart of their wilderness utopia was Bethlehem, including a hospital, colleges for men and women, woolen mills, shops, grist mills that served surrounding valleys, running water from the first waterworks in America, apothecary gardens, and a cocoonery for producing silk. The Moravians were housed in dormitories according to age, sex, marital status, occupation. For recreation, they loved to sing in *a cappella* choirs, the well-scrubbed women in long black dresses and white caps, and the brethren in starched white linen roundabouts and linen trousers. On summer evenings, violin and French horn, oboe and trombone music floated out to the Delaware Indians who came to visit and pray.

On November 25, 1755, there was no music. In the chilly early dawn, Bethlehem awakened to the doleful tolling of the town bells. The Moravian bishop told his people of the massacre at Gnadenhütten, the principal Moravian mission twenty miles up the Lehigh River. There, on the west bank, was the principal Moravian language school, a church, dormitories, stores, and barns. On the east bank, the Indians had recently been given separate quarters in a new village of stone cottages. About 100 Delaware Indians, mostly women and children, remained in the village; the older boys and the men were away on the annual winter hunt. Even with the men gone, the mission was crowded.

There were sixteen Moravians at the old mission as the last glow of twilight had disappeared on November 23. When the dinner bell rang, they stopped their chores and gathered in the main mission house. After asking for grace, they passed the food around and spoke German softly. John and Susanna Partsch, who had recently arrived, ate together. Martin Kiefer, the blacksmith, sat next to linguist George Fabricius. Martin Nitschmann, a missionary, sat with his wife, Susanna. Gottlieb Anders was serving his wife, Johanna, who was nursing their infant daughter. Five single men sat near the front door.

One of them, seventeen-year-old Joseph Sturgis, was the first to hear footsteps on the snow-crusted ground outside. As he unlatched the door and swung it wide, he saw black, blue, brown, and green-painted faces of Munsee and Shawnee warriors. He heard the first shrieking war cry and saw the flash of muskets. He fell, shot in the face. Another ball hit Nitschmann, killing him instantly. A dozen Native Americans burst into the room and fired. Three men were hit; Susanna Nitschmann was wounded as she shoved other women ahead of her up the stairs into the women's dormitory. When she fell, two Native Americans dragged her outside. She cried out, "Oh, brethren! Brethren! Help me!" The other Indians dragged out the three bleeding, dying men and scalped them.

In the dormitory upstairs, Anna Sensemann sank to the edge of a bed, sobbing, "Dear Savior, this is what I expected!" Johanna Anders wrapped her baby in her apron and bent down over her as the warriors pounded on the trapdoor. All the women could do was scream for help through the garret window in the hope of attracting Native Americans on the other side of the river. Downstairs, the surviving men looked for makeshift weapons—they had no guns. Suddenly, it was quiet outside. It seemed the Indians had gone. When Joachim Sensemann came out and ran toward the new Indian village, he saw the attacking Indians had surrounded the mission house with bundles of brush and were setting them afire.

From a second-story window of the single men's house nearby, Peter Worbas, who was ill, watched helplessly. He saw the Indians drag Susanna Nitschmann away and scalp the three men. His horror increased when he saw a half-dozen warriors ignite the piles of dry wood. Joseph Sturgis, bleeding from wounds in the face and arm, jumped from a window, landed safely, and ran into the woods. Susanna Partsch jumped next: she also made it to the woods. George Fabricius was less fortunate: when he stepped through the window, four Indians fired. The Indians scalped him. As the flames burned higher, seven more Moravians died. Martin Presser was the last to get out: four months later, he was found and identified by his clothing. He had died lying on his back, his hands folded in prayer.

The twelve Indian raiders stripped the food from the stores, butchered sixty cattle, set the other buildings afire, and then cooked a feast before making off with their plunder and the wounded Susanna Nitschmann. She died at the Munsee Indian stronghold of Tioga several weeks later. Captain Jachebus, her pro-French captor and the leader of the raid, was strangled to death a year later by a Delaware Indian chief who had been baptized by the Moravians. His name was Teedyuscung.

Born east of Trenton in the New Jersey Pine Barrens around 1700, he was one of six sons of an outspoken Indian known to his white neighbors as Old Captain Harris. He called himself a Lenni Lenape, One of the Original People. The colonists named his tribe the Delawares after Lord De Le Warr, who had been granted much of the region by the King of England and had its principal river and inhabitants named after him. Teedyuscung's father spoke English and could remember the arrival of thousands of English Quakers in the 1680s, steadily hemming in his people and forcing them to alter their ancient way of life from being farmers and fishermen to hunters. As game became scarce, they had to range farther and farther from their longhouse villages to find food and pelts for clothing. Long absences were killing the old native skills of pottery turning, stone cutting, and making leather garments, bows and arrows, utensils of bark and bone, and ornaments made with oyster and clam shells from the annual summer migration to the Jersey shore. Instead, the Delawares had become dependent on white traders to supply their guns and ammunition for the hunt that gave them hides and furs to barter for copper kettles and steel knives and shoddy factory-made blankets and clothing. And after the long hunting trips there was always rum, drunken brawls, and trouble with the resented white neighbors.

Little is known of Teedyuscung before age thirty except that he married, had a son, and considered himself one of his tribe's natural leaders. He was tall, powerful, and terribly fond of rum. He could drink a gallon of rum and stay sober enough to make eloquent speeches, but became known as indiscreet and totally lacking in the decorum that his tribe prided itself on in official councils if he had anything to drink. By the time he was thirty, friction between whites and Delawares in West Jersey Province had grown so acute that Teedyuscung's family, which never did get along well with the white neighbors, decided to leave their homeland and cross the Delaware River to the Lehigh Valley, sixty miles north of Philadelphia, a rugged country of mountains and fast rivers where no whites lived.

Teedyuscung's family was welcomed by native Delawares and his father became the chief man of Pocopoco in the Lehigh Gap near present-day Nazareth.

But in only three years, white settlers began to intrude here, too. There were so many of them by the mid-1730s that the Delawares protested to the Penns in Philadelphia. Teedyuscung was present when they met at Durham in 1734; James Logan, lawyer and secretary to the Penns' proprietary government, claimed the Penns had already bought the land. He would never forget when Secretary Logan warned the Delawares to leave the forks of the Delaware and the Lehigh and stop impeding the white settlers. If they did not go peaceably, they would be cut off from trading with Philadelphia. Logan followed up his threat by circumventing the Delawares and sending emissaries to the Six Nations Iroquois, in western New York State, who considered themselves the overlords and powerful protectors of the Delawares. Logan's maneuver divided the Indians: the Iroquois were staunch allies of the English; the Delawares were increasingly hostile. The Iroquois sent a chief to berate the Delawares and ordered them to leave and go to rental lands they owned to the north that they had set aside for dispossessed Indians.

When more white settlers came, the Delawares refused to move away from the Forks. By 1740, more than one hundred white families had moved in, ignoring the Delawares' protests. On November 21, 1740, the Delawares sent a petition to Bucks County justices of the peace, denying they had sold their lands and warning that intruders would be met with force. When the next white man tried to settle at the Forks, a recently dispossessed New Jersey Indian attacked and nearly killed him.

But Pennsylvania officials were determined. That same year, as evangelist George Whitefield preached his Great Awakening revival from Boston to Savannah, the Pennsylvania Land Office sold his agents 5,000 acres as the site of a school for freed blacks. But the project failed and was abandoned. Whitefield's agents resold the land to Moravian immigrants seeking to establish an American religious colony, an asylum from decades of persecution by Protestants and Catholics. When their leader, Count von Zinzendorf of Saxony, visited the Forks, he did not consult with the Delawares. Instead, on Christmas Eve, 1741, he founded the Moravian settlement called Bethlehem. When the Count visited Teedyuscung's father's village, Teedyuscung heard a white man preaching for the first time and admired it. There, the German-speaking pietists lived lives of spiritual simplicity that Teedyuscung came to admire. For the rest of his life, he would be inextricably tied up with the Moravians in a turbulent twenty-year relationship. The communal Moravian life resembled the tribal native ways: Indians did not believe in ownership but in sharing. Anything produced on church-owned lands was contributed to the common good. Meals were taken at common tables; there were dormitories for sleeping.

As the first whites had moved into the Lehigh Valley in 1740, Teedyuscung had moved his family deeper into the hills farther south to a place called Memolagomeka. When the Moravian Frederick Hoeth and his family moved into the valley in 1750, Teedyuscung and his relatives were forced to evacuate. This time, he did not resist: he decided to join the whites. In the spring of 1750, homeless for the third time, he moved to the new Moravian mission to the Indians at Gnadenhütten ("The Huts of Grace"). At age fifty, on March 12, 1750, wearing a white robe, he was baptized a Christian and took a new name, Gideon. In the mission journal,

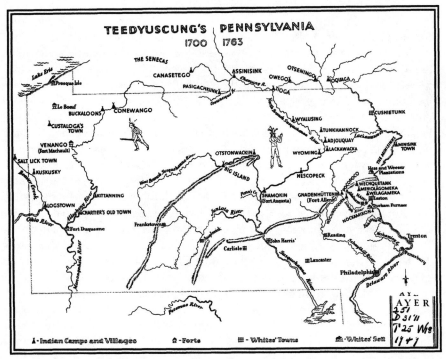

TEEDYUSCUNG'S | PENNSYLVANIA
1700 | 1763

The Newberry Library, Chicago

While no picture of Teedyuscung survives, this map shows the large number of Indian camps and villages in Pennsylvania in his era.

Bishop Spangenburg noted, "Today I baptized Tatiuskundt, the chief among sinners." One week later, Teedyuscung's Munsee Indian wife was baptized, taking the new name of Elizabeth. Within a year, his eldest son joined them as Christians: his wife's sister married a leading Moravian missionary.

As Christian Indians, the Delawares wore distinctive garb. They stopped shaving their heads and wore their hair shoulder length, donning caps and long shirts and trousers. Instead of carrying their guns under their capes Indian style to keep the priming dry, they slung them over their shoulders as they went off to hunt for the game needed by the mission. For the next four years, Teedyuscung and his followers lived as whites at Gnadenhutten. Styling himself a sachem, he had emerged as the spokesman and leader of the Forks Delawares, even in self-imposed exile among the Moravians.

There was a canny side to Teedyuscung; his people remained among the Moravians through a long drought that brought famine, weakness, and disease to the natives of Pennsylvania. During this period, thousands of Delawares, unhappy with Pennsylvania land policies and seeking a surer supply of game, migrated four hundred miles west to the Ohio Valley. By April 1754, Teedyuscung, too, had had enough of Moravian life: with seventy followers, he led an exodus from the Moravian mission, where 500 Indians now lived, to the Wyoming Valley, the site of present-day Wilkes Barre.

Shortly after Teedyuscung staked out the new town in the Wyoming Valley, Iroquois chiefs representing the Great Council of the Iroquois signed a deed giving the Penns a vast new territory west of the Susquehanna River encompassing the Wyoming Valley. Only five days later, several of the same Iroquois chiefs secretly sold a large tract between the Delaware and Susquehanna Rivers, also including the Wyoming Valley, to the rival Susquehannah Company of Connecticut. To further confuse matters, the Iroquois encouraged Teedyuscung and his kinsmen to stay in the valley to act as a buffer between white settlers and the southeastern rim of Iroquois lands. Briefly that summer of 1754 there was peace in the valley. When four Moravian missionaries visited Brother Gideon, they found his people once again living their ancient farming way of life. They had horses, hogs, cattle, grew corn, fished in the river, and hunted the abundant game in the woods.

But the bucolic interlude was shattered when a twenty-two-year-old Virginian, Colonel George Washington, bent on claiming thousands of acres of Pennsylvania land for veterans of King George's War, triggered the longest and bloodiest struggle between the French and English. Within a year, a British army commanded by General Edward Braddock marched toward present-day Pittsburgh. After its rout, French-led Indians from the Ohio Valley—including one of Teedyuscung's sons—raided English settlements all over the settled eastern half of Pennsylvania. From the Delaware Water Gap to Maryland, men, women, and children were killed as hundreds of farms were burned. The destruction of the Moravian mission at Gnadenhutten brought the raids within twenty miles of the Delaware River. Almost all of Pennsylvania had fallen to the French.

In this climactic power struggle, every Indian was forced to take a side. The Iroquois, traditional allies of the English, expected Teedyuscung and his Delawares to side with the English, too, and hold the Wyoming Valley against French-instigated Indians. Until the massive raids in Northampton County in November 1755, Teedyuscung had tried to stay neutral, tending to side with the English. But he had every reason to fear attack by the French-led Shawnees from the Ohio Valley. For more than a dozen years, he had tried to accommodate the whites; now he became a native leader. When he appealed to Pennsylvania authorities in Philadelphia for help, he received no answer. He waited a tense month, meanwhile sending a series of requests for advice and aid to the Iroquois. He met with Scaroyady, a Six Nations Indian acting as go-between from Pennsylvania to the Iroquois, giving him a black wampum belt. "This I am now going to send to the Six Nations," he told the old chief. "If they send an answer, well and good. If they do not, I shall know what to do." When no answer came, he decided to break with the English and cast his lot with the apparent victors, the French-led Indians. He sent a large belt of wampum to the Ohio Valley with the message, "I am in exceeding great danger, the English will kill me, come and help me."

Teedyuscung began in his messages to assert himself as "sachem," "King of the Delawares." He needed the prestige that came from battle to enhance his claims. For the first time in his life, at age fifty-five, he became a warrior. On December 10, 1755, he led the first Wyoming Delaware war party of thirty men, defying the Six Nations and seeking English scalps. In his party were three of his sons, three half-brothers, and a nephew. The Delaware Indian family once called Harris was out to avenge half a century of indignities and humiliation at the hands of the white settlers.

Skirting German settlements north of Kittatinny Mountain near the Delaware River on New Year's Eve, Teedyuscung and his three sons surrounded four whites working on the isolated farm of the Weiser family, shooting down the elder Weiser and Hans Adam Hess. Two younger men, Leonard and William Weeser, were captured by Indians in a second party led by Teedyuscung's son, Amos. The next morning they attacked two more farms, killing two hired men on the farm of Peter Hess and taking him and his son, Henry, captive. Next they attacked the farm of Hess's brother, killing two more laborers and taking two more prisoners. Taking a few horses, they torched the farmhouses and barns and slaughtered the livestock. As they led their prisoners back toward the Wyoming Valley the next day, old Peter Hess was lagging: they killed him, stabbed him to death, stripped off his clothes, and took his scalp while his son looked on. On January 3, 1756, Teedyuscung and his war party reached their homes with their prisoners and scalps.

This was Teedyuscung's only act of war but it made him the most respected of the eastern Delawares, the leader of a community of about one hundred. As a chieftain, he did not allow the torture or slow killing of prisoners. He continued to send out small raiding parties of half a dozen warriors to take scalps and prisoners, whom he needed for diplomatic bartering with the whites when peace came. His daring raids briefly brought him honor among the natives and even attracted runaway slaves to his ranks. At one point he considered persuading one runaway to foment a slave insurrection: he was one of the first native leaders to see the plights of natives and African Americans as linked.

After the erection of forts along the Pennsylvania frontier in 1756 protected settlers from further Indian raids, a series of conferences between natives and Pennsylvania government representatives began at Easton in July 1757 and lasted off and on for nearly five years. Teedyuscung enjoyed the solid support of the Quakers and their anti-Proprietary group in the Pennsylvania Assembly. The Quakers blamed the Indian attacks on the avarice of the Penn family, and especially on their fraudulent claims to have deeds proving they had bought the area around the Forks of the Delaware in the late seventeenth century.

When the Easton talks began, Teedyuscung arrived with one hundred of his followers, warriors, and councilors. The English officers and Philadelphia Quaker merchants saw a tall, heavyset man, his face painted bright red, wearing a suit of English tailored clothes complete with vest and shiny buttons and English riding boots, stand and address them in English in a speech a Quaker schoolteacher quickly took down:

> We desire you will look upon us with eyes of mercy. We are a very poor people. Our wives and children are almost naked. We are void of understanding and destitute of the necessaries of life. Pity us!

As usual, Teedyuscung had been drinking a considerable quantity of rum, but it only seemed to make him more logical and eloquent. In the course of the Easton treaty talks, the most elaborate in the history of Pennsylvania, he insisted that land disputes were not the principal cause of the alienation of natives from whites but "had caused the stroke to come harder than it otherwise would have come." What he and his people wanted, he said, was a permanent Indian reservation in the Wyoming Valley of northeastern Pennsylvania,

> and we want to have certain boundaries fixed between you and us and a certain tract of land fixed which it shall not be lawful for us or for our children ever to sell, nor for you or any of your children ever to buy.

Teedyuscung asked for help building white men's houses at the Wyoming reservation and missionaries to teach his people "the Christian religion," reading, and writing (which he had never learned). He also asked that "a fair trade be established between us."

His visionary appeal only met with derision from Iroquois emissaries and resistance from the Penns, who demanded the return of all white prisoners before peace could be concluded. Teedyuscung, on August 3, 1757, rose again, stating "They should certainly be restored, but [the Governor] must remember, they [the Indians] must first be satisfied for their lands."

The upshot of the conference was an agreement to allow the British government to investigate and mediate the conflicting claims. The Quaker-controlled Pennsylvania Assembly sent Benjamin Franklin to London on the mission. Pennsylvania authorities in turn sent Teedyuscung on an embassy to the Ohio Valley.

The five years after the cessation of fighting was the high point of Teedyuscung's life. After he returned from his first visit to Indian country along the Ohio in the summer of 1757, he stopped off at Bethlehem for a few days. Moravian archives show that Bishop Spangenburg invited "the Apostate, who had raised himself to a King" and his family to have coffee with church leaders. The Bishop recorded that "the King was animated and strictly attentive." Teedyuscung had begun refusing liquor before and during high-level meetings. "He is naturally quick of apprehension and ready of reply." Bishop Spangenburg tried once more to buy the Wyoming Valley for the Moravians. Teedyuscung refused.

After a year of almost ceaseless traveling and negotiating on behalf of the Delawares, Teedyuscung had the satisfaction of seeing fifty Philadelphia carpenters sent to present-day Wilkes-Barre to build a white man's village of ten solid log cabins for his kinsmen. All but one cabin was ten by ten by fourteen feet. His own house, built of squared and dovetailed logs, measured a substantial sixteen by twenty-four feet, larger than the average white settler's home. The settlement was also fenced and gardens plowed around it. For the first time since they had been dispossessed by the whites nearly thirty years earlier, Teedyuscung and his family could look forward to traditional Lenni Lenape lives of farmers—ensconced in the modern homes of whites.

It appeared for about five years that Teedyuscung had succeeded in his dream of bridging the white man's world and the Indian's but the building of the new Delaware town at Wyoming only aroused the jealousy of the Six Nations, who still claimed the valley, and whites from already overcrowded settlements in Connecticut.

In the summer of 1762, Teedyuscung attended his last conference with the whites at Lancaster. He had come to hate Indian treaty conferences: his wife had died in a dysentery outbreak after a 1762 parley brought natives and whites together during an epidemic. He had the great satisfaction to receive orders from the Six Nations to remain in the Wyoming Valley. Tom King, a Seneca chief, handed Teedyuscung's band a belt of wampum and said, "By this belt I make a fire for Teedyuscung at Wyoming." Pennsylvania authorities had something for him, too, presents valued at £200 sterling (about $200,000 today). Most of the Wyoming Delawares had traveled all the way from Wilkes-Barre to Lancaster on foot for the great peace conference.

Only seven Native Americans remained at home, not enough to resist the force of 119 armed settlers from the Susquehannah Company who chose this moment to assert their claim to the Wyoming Valley deeded to them by the Six Nations Iroquois. They ignored the handful of Delawares and cut down their hay and began building three blockhouses and made huts for themselves and sowed grain. On September 22, 1762, Tom King and the Six Nations delegation arrived on their way home to New York and surprised the Connecticut workmen. The angry Iroquois warned off the Yankees: he had just told the Lancaster conferees that the Six Nations would never permit the Susquehannah Company to have the Wyoming Valley. The workmen had finished their tasks and agreed to leave. The next spring, they said, they would be back with a thousand armed men and cannons.

When Teedyuscung and his entourage arrived a week later, the Iroquois chieftain advised him to "be quiet" while the Six Nations conferred with Connecticut authorities to prevent the Susquehannah settlers from returning. But all that autumn, more Connecticut settlers came, fourteen to build a sawmill near Teedyuscung's house, then eight more who stole Teedyuscung's horse. Teedyuscung received a gift horse in return and rode it to Philadelphia, where he received assurances of government protection. He then returned home.

On the evening of April 19, 1763, as he lay asleep in his cabin, someone set it afire. Simultaneously, all twenty houses in the growing Delaware settlement went up in flames. In minutes, the Delaware village of Wyoming burned to the ground. The survivors fled to Moravian settlements. Teedyuscung died in the lodge his Pennsylvania brethren had built for him. Two weeks later, the first permanent settlers from Connecticut arrived, bringing herds of cattle. Planting fields of corn and arming massive blockhouses, they named the place Wilkes-Barre. Their descendants wrote local history, which claimed that Teedyuscung had been drunk and that it was the Iroquois who burned his settlement. But the Iroquois officially condemned the act, accusing the Connecticut men.

The Delawares had no doubt who murdered Teedyuscung. Six months later, under cover of Pontiac's War, his son, Captain Bull, led a Delaware war party from their new home on the Ohio River all the way to the Wyoming Valley and killed twenty-six Connecticut settlers. By the end of 1763, no white men and no Indians remained alive amid the ruins of Teedyuscung's experiment in assimilation in the Wyoming Valley.

QUESTIONS FOR THOUGHT AND DISCUSSION

1. How did the way of life practiced by the Delaware Indians differ from that of the majority of white settlers who streamed into colonial Pennsylvania in the 1700s?

2. How had Teedyuscung's contacts with white settlers and the Pennsylvania colonial government exacted a cost in his personal life?

3. Why did Teedyuscung's efforts to assimilate his people into white society ultimately fail?

4. What larger truth does Teedyuscung's ultimate fate suggest about relations between white settlers and Indian peoples in the late colonial era?

SUGGESTED READINGS

Boyd, Julian P., ed. *Indian Treaties Printed by Benjamin Franklin, 1736–1762*. Philadelphia: Historical Society of Pennsylvania, 1938.

Brinton, D. G., ed., *The Lenape and Their Legends*. New York: AMS Press, 1969.

Jennings, Francis. *The Ambiguous Iroquois Empire*. New York: Norton, 1983.

_____. *Empire of Fortune: Crowns, Colonies, and Tribes in the Seven Years' War in America*. New York: Norton, 1988.

Josephy, Alvin M., Jr. *500 Nations: An Illustrated History of North American Indians*. New York: Knopf, 1994.

Randall, Willard Sterne. *A Little Revenge: Benjamin Franklin and His Son*. Boston: Little, 1984.

Reichel, William C. ed. *Memorials of the Moravian Church*. Philadelphia: Lippincott, 1870.

Sullivan, James, ed. *Papers of Sir William Johnson*. 9 vols. Albany: University State of New York, 1921–1939.

Wallace, Anthony F. C. *Teedyuscung: King of the Delawares*. Philadelphia: U of Pennsylvania P, 1949.

Wallace, Paul A. W. *Conrad Weiser: Friend of Colonist and Mohawk*. Philadelphia: U Pennsylvania P, 1945.

Weslager, C. A. *The Delaware Indians*. New Brunswick: Rutgers UP, 1972.

4

Tom Quick

As the European settlements in America expanded, they put pressure on Native Americans and their food supply, often changing ways of life and patterns of hunting. The natives, in turn, were pitted against each other and relied on the whites increasingly for their weapons. The Six Nations Iroquois, for instance, became the loyal allies of the English; the Hurons depended on the French.

Some tribes, like the Tuscarora and the Delaware, who once lived from present-day southern New York to northern Virginia, became so decimated by disease, war and encroachment that they fought each other and then were appended to the Six Nations Iroquois for protection. But many of the Delawares resented the tricky deals and endless treaty-making conferences that only stripped them of their traditionally communal lands. They headed west and shifted their allegiance to the Hurons and their French allies. When the French and Indian War of 1754–63 came, it struck deep into their old homelands. For one thing, this desperate effort only gave whites such as Tom Quick the excuse he needed to launch his own campaign of extirpation.

TOM QUICK GREW up, strong and agile and cunning as any Native American in the elm forest of northeastern Pennsylvania. From his infancy, he played with Native-American children around his father's house in Matchepeconck ("beautiful valley" in the Lenni-Lenape dialect), near present-day Milford. His closest friend was Mushwink, son of a Delaware chieftain. While Tom's father ground grain or cut up timber that floated to his sawmill where the creek called the Van de Mack met the Delaware River, Tom explored neighboring hills and woods with Mushwink. He learned to track like the Native Americans, with great skill and daring. He trapped bears, snared partridges, and hunted elk and deer with either bow or musket.

Tom's parents, who were Dutch, had come from New York in 1733 to build their first log house at Milford. By then the Delaware Indians, a defeated tribe paying tribute to the Iroquois, had settled into a rather sophisticated civilization, living side by side with their allies, the English. Their peace was marred only by periodic depredations by French-led renegade warriors. The population of the six-tribe Iroquois Confederacy was never more than 12,000. This included the estimated 2,000 coastal Delawares, who hunted and fished from the top of the river after which they were named, to the bottom of the bay given the same name. They spent their winters in the forests of Pennsylvania and New Jersey, migrating to the shore each summer to gather shellfish for food and from which to make wampum.

The Delawares and their cousins were well organized in battle, moved quickly and quietly, struck with ferocity, and did unspeakable things to their prisoners. Before the English arrived, they were generally left alone to till their corn and squash, dry their fish, string their beads, and puff their calumets in the smoke-filled, elm-bark longhouses in their stockaded towns. They could afford to be generous and hospitable: The land they inhabited was unimaginably rich, producing tender ears of corn up to twenty-four inches long and squashes the size of pumpkins.

Thanks to the Delawares' hospitality, the colony of Pennsylvania, peopled by pacifist English Quakers, had grown up without a shot fired in anger in its first three-quarters of a century. Shortly after the first hundred shiploads of immigrants had arrived in 1682, William Penn, leader of these political and religious refugees, wrote back to potential colonists in London:

> The soil is good, air serene from the cedar, pine and sassafras with the wild myrtle of great fragrance ... I have had better venison [here], bigger, and more tender, as fat as in England. Turkeys of the wood I have had of 40 and 50 pound weight ... flowers for color, largeness and beauty excel.

Penn's promotional literature and his policy of religious toleration packed Philadelphia with immigrants of every faith. Nevertheless, his judgment in appointing governors to rule in his place was less than wise. One governor distinguished himself chiefly as a barroom brawler; accompanied by friends, including William Penn, Jr., he severely beat up the town constable. His successor bickered with the Assembly so regularly they refused to pay his salary. Infuriated, this governor left the province, but not before kicking a judge. Fifty years were to elapse, however, before Pennsylvania politicians caused any lasting problem.

The Delaware Indians were generous to the New Yorkers migrating into their domain, among whom were the Quicks. As their children came—ten of them, which was enough to make the elder Quick hustle about his gristmill and later his sawmill—the neighboring Delawares taught the family how to farm and hunt, brought them presents of fur, and taught them their language. Young Mushwink, son and heir of the local chieftain, virtually grew up at the Quick homestead, eating, playing and sleeping with the eldest Quick boy, Tom, Jr.

Young Tom was only three when William Penn's sons, hard-pressed by creditors, sought to add to their real estate inventory by invoking an old promise made to their late father: He could extend his settlements "as far as a man can walk in a day and a half." In the first "Walking Purchase" in 1701, the elder Penn—strolling along with the Delaware chieftains, pushing branches aside, stopping often, smoking the calumet, and exchanging pleasantries in their native tongue—had covered fifteen miles. This was the distance that the Delawares expected his sons to cover.

But now, in 1737, the Delawares were dealing with lawyers. The bargain did not specify which man should make the walk or exactly what route he should follow. The young Penns ordered a wide pathway cleared through the underbrush. They hired and trained the three fleetest white couriers in the colony and provided relays of horses and riders to take them food, drink, and fresh moccasins. Leaving Wrightstown in Bucks County at dawn on September 19, 1737, the colonists, heeling and toeing furiously, quickly outdistanced their Native-American escorts.

By noon, the fastest woodsman had already covered twenty-one miles and had crossed the Lehigh River. Halting only fifteen minutes for a meal, he set off briskly and duly reached the end of the prepared road. After a short night's sleep, he was handed a compass, and he struck off to the northeast, taking a well-worn warrior path along the Delaware River to Milford at the current border with New York. By the time he stopped at midday, he had covered nearly seventy-two miles and had virtually doubled the Penn real estate holdings.

The Delawares honored their pledge. Slowly, mournfully, and resentfully, they began to move farther west, many of them migrating over the next twenty years to the Ohio River Valley. There they mixed with other displaced tribes and waited to take revenge on the English. Only at the top of the Delaware River, near the Quick homestead, did they linger in any significant numbers, around their family burial grounds.

The cycle of revenge and reprisal called the French and Indian War broke out in its final and bloodiest spasm in 1754, when a detachment of Virginia militia led by young George Washington tried to construct Fort Necessity at the forks of the Ohio, Allegheny, and Monongahela Rivers, only to clash with the French and be driven, humiliated, from the area.

In July 1755, seventy-five years of peace between colonists and Native Americans in Pennsylvania ended when a British army, led by General Edward Braddock, trudged into a bloody three-hour crossfire at the Monongehela. The Indians, annoyed by the Penn land deals, had begun to listen to the promises of food and clothing made by the French Canadians building the massive Fort Duquesne—now Pittsburgh—close to the site of Braddock's defeat. Chief Logan, the Iroquois Six Nations' representative to the Pennsylvania government, had warned a few months earlier.

> Whosoever of the white should venture to settle any land belonging hitherto to the Indians will have his creatures killed first, and then if they do not desist, they themselves would be killed, without distinction, let the consequence be what it would.

When no retaliation came from the pacifist Quakers for the defeat of Braddock's army, the French and their new Indian allies sent out small raiding parties to attack isolated targets. Then they became bolder. By October, bands of up to 250 Delawares were ranging east from Fort Duquesne. One large party struck at Penn's Creek on the Susquehanna River, within 100 miles of Philadelphia. Postmaster Benjamin Franklin relayed word to London:

> Just now arrived in town an express from our frontiers with the bad news that eight families of Pennsylvanians were cut off last week ... Thirteen men and women were found scalped and dead and twelve children missing.

On October 11, in the first raid east of the Susquehanna, 120 warriors attacked farms just west of Reading. After killing fifteen men and women and scalping three children (who survived), they set fire to scores of houses and destroyed large numbers of cattle and horses, as well as quantities of grain and fodder. The Quick family and their neighbors fled across the Delaware to a fortified stone house in New Jersey's Sussex County. There, in December, Thomas Quick and his eldest son, now twenty-one, joined Captain John Van Etten's company of militia.

Colonel Benjamin Franklin, chairman of the Pennsylvania Assembly's Defense Committee, ordered Van Etten to help build a series of small forts in the fifty-mile stretch of the Pocono Mountains between Milford and the Delaware Water Gap, the area ceded after the 1737 Walking Purchase. The company stayed on active duty for about a year and a half, basing itself in the Minisink Valley just south of Milford. Each man would be paid six dollars a month plus one dollar for the use of his musket and blanket, since pacifist Pennsylvania had no munitions to issue.

In their flight, the Quicks and their neighbors had managed to carry off only enough grain for a month. After the militia had built stockades and cut gun slits, they stood guard as the settlers harvested and threshed their corn. The Quicks milled it and stuffed it into heavy grists before hauling the sacks to canoes to transport them to the Sussex fort. On Colonel Franklin's orders, most of the militia then began patrolling the five miles of hills to the outpost of the next fort to the southeast. Among Franklin's orders, which carried the authority of Governor Robert Hunter Morris, was permission to scalp Indians:

> You are to acquaint the men that, if in their ranging, they meet with, or are at any time attacked by the enemy, and killing any of them, forty dollars [the equivalent of six months' pay] will be allowed and paid by the government for each scalp of an Indian Enemy so killed, the same being produced with proper attestations.

Under a new moon at the end of November, the Delawares attacked all along the line of settlements planted since the Walking Purchase. In the Minisink region alone, scores of farms were laid waste, houses and barns burned, and at least twelve farmers killed. At Easton, Franklin was rallying and training them with the help of his son, William, a captain in King George's War of the 1740s. On Christmas Day the elder Franklin described the devastation in a report to the governor:

> The Country all above this town for fifty miles is mostly evacuated and ruined ... The people are chiefly fled into the Jerseys ... The enemy made but few prisoners, murdering almost all that fell into their hands, of all ages and both sexes. All business is at an end ... The few remaining starving inhabitants ... are quite dejected and dispirited.

Inside the stockade on the Delaware River, hunger and illness grew worse as the weeks dragged. Late one afternoon in early February 1756, Thomas Quick, his son Tom, and a son-in-law strapped on snowshoes, hoisted heavy grists of corn onto their shoulders and headed for the mill, about a mile away across the frozen Delaware. All night they labored, at dawn recrossing the ice. The elder Quick fell behind under the weight; when he was at midriver, shots rang out and he dropped. Indians yelled and rushed toward him. Young Tom reached him first and began to drag him away.

"I'm a dead man," whispered his father. "I can go no farther. Leave me. Run for your lives."

The Newberry Library, Chicago

Under cover of the Revolutionary War, thousands of Washington's best troops were dispatched to destroy the Iroquois confederacy.

Reluctantly, Tom and his brother-in-law escaped across the river and stumbled up the bank. They could hear the chilling cries of the Indians and make out their faces. Tom recognized his boyhood companion, Mushwink, bending over his father.

Mushwink, now a full-fledged chief, had been selected at a tribal council to lead the attack on his native Matchepeconck. He had given the Milford settlers a single warning to leave, kidnapping Tom Quick's young niece and then freeing her unharmed. Now Mushwink and his warriors scalped Tom's father, rifled his pockets, and cut off his silver sleeve buttons and shoe buckles.

The shooting had alerted the militia, which came to cover Tom's escape. After the Indians left, he went back and retrieved the mutilated corpse of his father. Tom Quick vowed to avenge his father's death by killing 100 Delaware Indians. In family papers, his oath was recorded: "The blood of the whole Indian race is not sufficient to atone for the blood of my father."

Over the next forty years, Tom made hunting down and killing Delawares his profession and obsession. Setting about his mission of vengeance with grim precision, he equipped himself with "Long Tom," a Pennsylvania rifle with a fifty-eight-inch barrel that he could aim with deadly accuracy at long range. Nobody knows the name of the first Delaware man or woman he killed or just how much money he claimed for the grisly proof of his handiwork that he bore to Pennsylvania authorities, but the scalping bounty remained forty dollars until the end of the French and Indian War in 1763. The same year, when the uprising led by the Ottawa chief, Pontiac, swept the Pennsylvania frontier, Governor John Penn (grandson of the first Quaker proprietor), increased the scalp bounty. Any Indian male above age ten who was captured alive fetched a $150 bounty; scalped, he was worth only $134; a female over ten, only $30.

At a time when many Americans were coming to hate Native Americans absolutely and generally, Tom Quick became celebrated as Pennsylvania's foremost Indian killer. One story circulated that during Pontiac's Rebellion he even ambushed women and children. He would sometimes lure Delawares to his campfire for a hot supper and a warm night's rest and then kill them in their sleep. He invited unsuspecting braves to hunt with him, then pushed them off cliffs. He set up elaborate little massacres that sometimes bothered even his calloused neighbors. After butchering one Indian's entire family, he was asked why he hadn't spared the baby. "Because," he said, "nits make lice."

Scouring the mountains of Pennsylvania, New Jersey, and New York for his quarry, Tom Quick soon became quarry himself after Delaware councils began to notice that entire parties were not returning from hunting trips. He was captured five times but always managed to escape, taking more Indian scalps as he went. One Indian prophet cast this divination, "The missing braves have fallen victim to the rifle of Tom Quick, who haunts the forest of the Delaware like an evil spirit."

Three of Mushwink's young warriors volunteered to track down Quick and bring back his scalp. When they finally found him after a year's search, Quick detected their ambush and set one of his own, shooting two braves as they glided by in a canoe. The third man was allowed to escape so that he would take back word of the humiliation. In the warriors' canoe Tom found his father's Meerschaum pipe, engraved "TQ 1724."

Tom Quick and Long Tom eventually triggered an uproar in official Philadelphia as aggrieved Quaker merchants demanded an end to his depredations. After the French had finally surrendered in 1763, Philadelphia firms had been granted trading rights with Indians throughout Pennsylvania and the Ohio Valley. Now the tribesmen were to exchange their pelts for guns and powder, hatchets and knives, clothing and trade goods made in England instead of France. But such commercial considerations did not sway Tom Quick from his revenge.

Late in 1764, he found himself at Christopher Decker's tavern on Neversink Mountain near present-day Reading, Pennsylvania. There, one evening shortly before the end of Pontiac's Rebellion, a Delaware Indian came up and offered to drink with him. Maybe Tom Quick recognized the man in the dim, guttering candlelight of the tavern; probably he did not, for it had been nearly ten years since his father's murder. In any case, Quick refused. The Indian, very drunk, persisted.

"You hate Delawares," he said in English. "I hate you."

Quick still refused.

"You kill Delawares. I kill your father."

"Prove it."

Staggering to him, the Indian pulled out the silver sleeve buttons cut from Tom's father's coat. "See?"

Quick jumped up and grabbed a musket off the tavern wall. "March," he ordered, shoving Mushwink ahead of him out the door. "You will never kill another white man." Moments later, there was a shot.

Mushwink's murder deep inside Pennsylvania in peacetime finally brought about Tom Quick's arrest. It was not so much the loss of Mushwink—who had probably been as drunk when he scalped Tom's father as he was when Tom shot him—as the fact that it occurred after the peace treaty, to the detriment of business as usual. So long as Tom Quick preyed on them, the Indians were understandably reluctant to come out to trade. A Berks County justice of the peace issued a warrant, and a platoon of militia arrested Quick, who was bound, tied to a sled, and driven south to stand trial for murder.

But Tom Quick had many friends. At Milford, Daniel Van Gordon learned of Tom's destination and dashed back to Decker's tavern to tip off the townspeople. When the prison cavalcade halted at the tavern, where Quick had killed Mushwink, the whole town turned out, feigning a celebration to honor the militia for capturing the feared Indian killer. Decker played his fiddle, women danced with the militiamen, and barmaids distributed free hot toddy—and meanwhile someone cut Tom Quick's ropes and helped him from the sled. Dashing for the river, Quick plunged through the ice and swam to Pinckney's Island, where a 100-man posse somehow failed to find him. In several weeks Quick resumed his quiet miller's life at Milford, with only occasional outings to hunt Delawares far away. No further attempts were made to arrest him.

As the years passed, the opportunities to kill an Indian close to home became increasingly rare. For Tom Quick, the biggest problem was that as a result of a series of treaties with the British colonial authorities in the late 1760s, the Delaware nation had withdrawn west of the Ohio River. He nevertheless continued to pursue the Delawares, ranging as far as 400 miles from home, until the Revolution intervened.

Tom Quick's name does not appear on any Revolutionary War muster roll. His services, if he did in fact offer them to the Revolutionary army, might have proved an embarrassment, since the Delawares were the first northern tribe to sign a separate peace treaty with the Continental Congress. It was their mistaken understanding that at the war's end they would become the fourteenth state. In the developing campaign against the Iroquois nations, only the Delawares were spared.

Tom Quick's personal war with the Delawares undoubtedly contributed to the deteriorating relationship between settlers in the remote frontier valleys and the tribes that sided with the British. His unappeased appetite for revenge fueled the ferocious cycle of reprisal and counterreprisal that ultimately destroyed the entire Iroquois Confederacy. Much as he may have wanted to, Tom Quick did not choose—or perhaps was not allowed—to play a part in the final eradication of Native American power in New York and Pennsylvania. That is a story that grows out of, and belongs with, his.

By the summer of 1778, the American Revolution had settled into a long stalemate; for the first time, George Washington could turn to dealing with the Indian problem on the frontiers. His relations with the Indians had never been good, and war exacerbated them. The Iroquois had aligned themselves with their old allies, the British. Loyalists from the Mohawk Valley in New York escaped to Fort Niagara and persuaded the Iroquois tribes of the Mohawks, the Cayugas, and the Senecas to rally to the standard of George III. With Loyalist rangers under Major John Butler and his son, Walter, they raided frontier villages for hundreds of miles, pillaging, burning, and scalping. Early in June, a force out of Niagara destroyed the settlements in the Wyoming Valley near present-day Wilkes-Barre, Pennsylvania. John Butler reported taking 227 scalps and only five prisoners.

The Wyoming Massacre shocked and terrified the frontier and spawned numerous atrocity stories. For example, the half-breed Seneca called Queen Esther, it was said, had arranged fifteen victims in a ring and, circling and singing a dirge, she had tomahawked them one by one.

Led by Mushwink's son, a band of renegade Delawares fighting with the British struck farther east and succeeded in capturing Tom Quick and his seventeen-year-old niece, Maggie, while the pair were canoeing. Two of the Delawares were appointed to march them off to certain torture and death. But one night, as their two captors were bending over a fire, cooking the day's catch of trout, Quick got loose and sprang, killing both men with their own hatchets. It was the last time anyone tried to bring Tom Quick to account.

When more joint Loyalist-Indian expeditions raided German Flats on the Mohawk River (below Utica) in September 1778 and struck Cherry Valley, only fifty miles west of Albany, Washington decided that November to detach enough Continentals in the spring to destroy the Iroquois homelands of the Finger Lakes and the Genesee Valley of western New York. He chose Major John Sullivan of New Hampshire and gave him terse, carefully formulated orders. "The immediate objects are the total destruction and devastation of their settlements ... [The Indian country] may not be merely overrun, but destroyed." Tom Quick would have approved.

Sullivan was to lead a three-pronged attack, assembling his main force of 2,500 Continentals at Easton, Pennsylvania. General James Clinton of New York was to start from Albany with 1,500 Continentals and proceed to the headwaters of the Susquehanna River at Otsego Lake and descend the river to meet Sullivan at Tioga. A third column was to set out from Fort Pitt—the former Fort Duquesne—with 600 regulars under Colonel Daniel Brodhead. In all, Washington had detached 4,600 Continentals, nearly one-third of his regulars. Sullivan was also to take artillery: The Iroquois, in all of America's century-long wars with European colonists, had never faced cannon. Washington stipulated that Sullivan's men were to attack with bayonet and war whoop, "with as much impetuosity, shouting, and noise as possible."

Three months of delays for supplies and road building for 1,200 pack horses, 100 officers' mounts, and 700 cattle for "beef on the hoof" brought Sullivan's main force to Tioga by August 11, 1779. The Seneca stronghold with "Queen Esther's Palace" was deserted. Loyalist John Butler had been alerted by deserters about Sullivan's expedition, but the British commander at Quebec, the Swiss-born General Frederick Haldimand, shrugged off the report: "It is impossible the Rebels can be in such force as has been represented by the deserters." But green-uniformed Loyalist rangers roused the Indians to prepare to defend their homeland.

Meanwhile, General Clinton had assembled his 1,500 men at Canajoharie, forty miles west of Albany on the Mohawk, with 200 bateaux, or flat-bottomed boats. He cut a twenty-five mile road over a high ridge and downhill to Lake Otsego. Hauling his boats by wagon to the lake's northern tip and paddling them to present-day Cooperstown, he camped and waited for Sullivan. He was chagrined to find out how low the Susquehanna River was as it flowed out of the lake. Ingeniously, he ordered a temporary dam built. Six weeks later, on August 9, when a courier brought word from Sullivan to begin moving south, Clinton breached the dam, and the bateaux floated thirty miles in one day. En route, the New York troops burned deserted Indian villages. At Onondaga, a Loyalist settlement, they torched a Christian church and some log houses with stone chimneys and glass windows. When they rendezvoused with Sullivan, a military band sent along by Washington "played beautifully" as artillery fired a salute.

The delays now proved fortuitous. The Indians' ripe crops awaited as the troops attacked Chemung two days later. Fields full of corn, beans, squashes, and pumpkins either fed the New York troops or were destroyed. The Indians fled, sniping from the woods while the soldiers gorged. One soldier wrote that he ate ten ears of corn, a quart of beans, and seven squashes. The troops marched off with pumpkins impaled on their bayonets.

On August 27, 1779, Sullivan's 4,000-man combined expeditionary force moved north with nine fieldpieces, including four 6-pounders, four 3-pounders, and a cohorn (a small easily portable mortar that was also called a "grasshopper"). The packhorses hauled solid shot and canister shot (the latter was timed to explode in the air and shower the enemy with small projectiles).

Many of Sullivan's officers blamed the artillery for slowing down the march. Major Jeremiah Fogg recorded in his diary, "The transportation … appears to the army in general as impractical, and absurd as an attempt to level the Allegheny Mountains."

But when Sullivan's army struggled up the narrow, steep Chemung Valley defile and approached the Indian village of Newtown on August 29, the artillery proved welcome. Sullivan had brought along several Oneida Indian scouts. One of them climbed a tree on a 700-foot hill and made out painted Indians crouching behind a log breastwork camouflaged with green branches. The Loyalist-Iroquois position was well chosen. In all, a thousand Indians under Chief Joseph Brant, as well as 250 of Butler's Rangers and fifteen British redcoats, awaited Sullivan's advance.

Sullivan halted his column, sending a strong force to attack the hilltop detachment from the rear. He placed his artillery and opened fire on the breastwork with solid shot, spraying the defenders with canisters loaded with grapeshot and iron spikes. The terrified Iroquois endured the cannonade for half an hour, but the shells bursting behind them convinced them that the enemy had outflanked them. They ran, the Loyalists with them. On the hilltop, the Native Americans and Continentals seesawed in hand-to-hand combat until Brant signaled them to flee. Only three of Sullivan's men were killed and thirty-six wounded; twelve Indian men and one woman died. The men were all scalped. One Continental officer skinned two Indians from the hips down to make two pairs of leggings, one for himself, one for his major.

While casualties on both sides were light at the Battle of Newtown, the artillery barrage was decisive. The terrified Iroquois never again put up a fight. Sullivan's army was unopposed as it burned a swath from Elmira—where the men cut down eighteen-foot stalks of corn—to the St. Lawrence River and southwest into the Genesee country. Detachments raided and burned Indian settlements in the Mohawk Valley, on the west side of Seneca Lake, and on both sides of Cayuga Lake. Typically, in a principal Indian riverside village southwest of present-day Genesco, the army collected an immense amount of corn, packed it into more than 100 well-appointed, "very large and elegant" houses, and then burned them all. At Aurora they girdled and destroyed 1,500 peach trees. In all, Sullivan's army of 4,000 (Brodhead's column had turned back for want of shoes) destroyed forty villages and an estimated 160,000 bushels of corn, plus immeasurable quantities of other vegetables and fruits.

Marching back to Elmira, the army celebrated its 500-mile expedition to the roar of a triumphant fireworks and an ox roast, with a bull and a barrel of rum for each brigade. A few days later, back at Tioga, they put on war paint. Led by an Oneida sachem, they joined in a war dance, each step ending with a whoop. Finally demolishing their forts, they returned to the Wyoming Valley. They had lost only forty men and had virtually eliminated the Iroquois Confederacy, its survivors crowding into Fort Niagara and, as Washington had hoped, consuming precious British supplies all winter.

Tom Quick survived the Revolution, and at some point notched his ninety-ninth Delaware. His life ended as had thousands of Indians'—felled by the white man's disease smallpox. In 1796, at age sixty-two, Tom Quick lay dying in his substantial stone home in Milford, his family gathered around him. A daughter later recorded his dying wish: that a final, 100th Delaware be brought close enough for him to fire Long Tom, its stock all but worn away. But there were no Delawares left for 300 miles. Tom Quick died disappointed.

Nearly a century later, in August 1889, near the site of the scalping of Tom Quick's father, a crowd gathered for the dedication of a handsome, eleven-foot monument. It was

> erected to the memory of Tom Quick, the Indian slayer ... the Avenger of the Delaware ... and of his father Thomas Quick Sr.—the latter the first white settler and the former the first white child born on the site of the present Borough of Milford.

There was no list of the victims of this serial killer. Nobody knows the name of the first person he killed or of the ninety-ninth—only his boyhood friend, his betrayer Mushwink, earned a place in the family records.

The monument in Centre Square was dedicated in an oration by a young hometown politician, Gifford Pinchot, recently graduated from Yale and later to become the famed conservationist governor of Pennsylvania, and by William Bross, lieutenant governor of Illinois. A descendant of Tom Quick, Bross had published *Legend of the Delaware: An Historical Sketch of Tom Quick*, a local best seller. About 2,000 people packed the town for a day of speeches and celebrations. The next morning the *New York Times* carried its own paeans of praise, under the headline "In Honor of Tom Quick."

QUESTIONS FOR THOUGHT AND DISCUSSION

1. How did Tom Quick's experience in colonial Pennsylvania contrast to that of Teedyuscung?

2. What event transformed Quick into the most notorious Indian killer of his day?

3. Do you think Quick was mentally stable?

4. What does the raising of a monument to Quick nearly 100 years after his death say about attitudes toward Native Americans in the late nineteenth century? Would such a monument be celebrated by the American media today?

SUGGESTED READINGS

Calloway, Colin G. *The American Revolution in Indian Country: Crisis and Diversity in Native American Communities.* Cambridge, Eng.: Cambridge UP, 1995.

Downes, Randolph C. *Council Fires on the Upper Ohio.* Pittsburgh: U of Pittsburgh P, 1940.

Flick, Alexander C. "The Sullivan-Clinton Campaign of 1779." *New York Historical Association Proceedings,* 15(1934), 185–216.

Randall, Willard Sterne. "Tom Quick's Revenge." *MHQ: Quarterly Magazine of Military History.* Summer, 1992, pp. 70–75.

_____. *A Little Revenge: Benjamin Franklin and His Son.* Boston: Little, 1984.

_____. "Penn's Dream Dissolves." *In The Founding City.* Ed. by David R. Boldt and W. S. Randall. Philadelphia: Chilton/Inquirer, 1976.

Stanley, George F. "The Six Nations and the American Revolution." *Ontario History,* 56(1964), 217–232.

Steele, Ian K. *Warpaths: Invasions of North America.* New York: Oxford UP, 1994.

Wallace, Anthony F. C. *Teedyuscung: King of the Delawares.* Philadelphia: U of Pennsylvania P, 1949.

5

Benjamin Franklin

Life in the England of the late seventeenth century was hard. Young Josiah Franklin, whose family name meant "free man," could not expect to follow the family trade of five centuries—blacksmithing. The family freehold had been sold to the lord of the manor; a new blacksmith worked the forge. Apprenticed to an older brother in Banbury, Josiah learned to be a wool dyer, eventually setting up his own shop, marrying, and fathering three children. He could barely sustain himself despite endless fifteen-hour days. His trade, seasonal at best, was stifled by trade laws. There was no turning to another trade unless he undertook another unpaid, seven-year apprenticeship. Then, in 1683, Banbury officials suppressed Dissenter meetings. Disgusted, the Nonconformist wool dyer and his wife decided to take the drastic step men and women all over England were taking. They would emigrate, build a new life in a new England.

TO BE BORN on the Sabbath was considered by Puritan Boston the sign of a great sin. By popular superstition, it was believed that a child born on the Sabbath had been conceived on Sunday. Even marital relations on the Sabbath were against God's law. If the birth date of Constable Josiah Franklin's new son became public, the infant, Josiah's fifteenth, would be considered a child of the Devil. There was nothing to do but keep the circumstances of Benjamin Franklin's birth on January 6, 1706, a family secret.

If suspicion was to be averted, little Benjamin must be baptized at once, on the day he was born. He must be cleansed of his sin in the freezing waters of Christian baptism. When his mother, Abiah, finished intricately winding Benjamin in swaddling clothes, Josiah bundled the baby under his heavy cape and herded his other children across the icy paving stones into unheated Old South Church. After the three-hour service, the congregation crowded to the rear to bear witness as the pastor cracked the ice in the baptismal font. Murmuring the words intended to save the baby's soul, if not his shivering body, he splashed him thoroughly with icy water. Then Josiah, now a prosperous tallow chandler, led a hymn of joy. His tenth son would be his offering of thanksgiving to God, go to Harvard, and become a minister of the Puritan church.

When Josiah Franklin and his first wife, Anne, had come to Boston, he had been shocked to learn that brightly colored fabrics were forbidden by Boston's religious laws. He had to find another trade. Surveying the town, he saw no overhanging storefront sign offering soap or candles. As he no doubt noticed at a Puritan meeting on a warm day, few people bathed frequently. Families saved their fat and boiled tallow once a year, using most of it to make candles to read the Bible. As a tallow chandler, his hard, smelly work began with gathering fat from markets amid clouds of flies, hauling it home in a wheelbarrow, and rendering it in wooden vats. The Franklin house was filled with a perpetual rancid stench.

After giving birth to seven children in eleven years, Anne Franklin died. Widower Josiah took little time finding a new wife, dark-haired Abiah Folger from Nantucket, who was visiting her sister when Josiah met her in church. They married shortly after Anne Franklin's death. They had ten children.

Benjamin's first images of life were from the hearth of the small rented house on Milk Street in the oldest and poorest part of Boston, where Abiah nursed all her brood. "My mother had an excellent constitution," Benjamin wrote in his autobiography. "She suckled all her ten children." There was scarcely a time Abiah did not have a baby at breast as she spun, wove cloth, sewed, cooked, cleaned, kept her husband's accounts, sang psalms, and taught the children their prayers.

After the drowning of Benjamin's sixteen-month-old brother in an unattended tub of soapsuds, Josiah bought a larger house in Boston's commercial district and set up his tallow business in a separate building. He was prospering and was elected to a series of minor town offices. Despite the fact that Josiah prayed over, preached at, beat, berated, neglected, pampered, and menaced his children, the Franklin family still enjoyed what the youngest, Jane, remembered as a good, although Spartan life. "It was indeed a lowly dwelling we were brought up in but we were fed plentifully, made comfortable with fire and clothing, had seldom any contention among us."

Benjamin's father had progressed through the Puritan church ranks until he had been appointed a tithingman to enforce church discipline over one quarter of the families in Boston. When he was not checking on the conduct of apprentice boys and servant girls, he would march down the aisle on the Sabbath to poke with his staff of office anyone nodding off or whispering. The Franklin family attended two church services on Sundays, lectures on Thursday afternoons, conducted family prayers morning and evening, and said grace over meals. Josiah's children did all they could to avoid his wrath. Benjamin's childhood was an unremitting struggle, under so much restraint that it finally made all but inevitable his self-imposed exile from his family and it forever soured him on religion. Once he left his father's house, he never again joined a church and rarely attended one.

At eight, Benjamin trudged off to the Boston Grammar School. He studied Latin and Greek until he could translate Aesop's Fables into Latin verse. By the end of the year, he had overtaken pupils who had started a year before him and he had moved to the head of his class. Then Josiah took him out of school: he had decided his son shouldn't be a clergyman but should learn a useful trade.

Whenever he could now, Benjamin began to slip down to the docks. His father placed him in an inexpensive school, where he failed mathematics. He lost interest in school, became aggressive and began to settle arguments with his fists. He longed to run away to sea but, realizing he was too young, taught himself to swim expertly, rigged a kite and used the wind to tow him, naked, across a pond.

By 1718, Benjamin, twelve, was the only son left at home. It didn't occur to Josiah or other fathers of his generation to ask the boy what he wanted to do. It was a matter of money. Josiah's nephew had just opened a cutlery shop. There would always be dull blades. But the cutler wanted his uncle Josiah to pay the usual apprenticeship fee and Josiah refused. He took Benjamin to his older brother, James, a printer. The boy would be his apprentice and bound servant for the next nine years. Benjamin recounted the feeling of being imprisoned to his own son years later: "I was to serve as an apprentice till I was twenty-one years of age." His brother quickly made it clear that Benjamin would receive no special favors. If he complained, he would be beaten. After a few sound beatings, Benjamin was convinced.

Between 1719 and 1723, through four years of humiliation at the hands of his brother, James, who could not admit that Benjamin was better read, a better thinker, and a better writer than himself, Benjamin, a teenage boy, remained indomitably proud, always looking to increase his wealth of knowledge and to flaunt it. Denied formal education, he taught himself. Because Boston's only public library had burned, he talked his way into the Reverend Cotton Mather's great personal library. Another friend, a bookseller's apprentice, slipped him new books at night on condition he return them unharmed the next morning before opening time. To steal hours for reading he skipped church.

An ambitious student of writing, Benjamin quickly learned the printer's trade, then mastered the art of satire, the form of writing he always preferred. He used it in his "Silence Dogood" letters, written stealthily on Sundays when other Boston fifteen-year-old boys were in church, slipping the letters under the door of his brother's shop before it opened Mondays. Masterful parodies of popular London writings, the letters, fourteen of them, created a stir in Boston, making his brother's paper, the *New England Courant*, controversial. Benjamin was cockier than ever, especially after it was finally revealed that it was he, posing as a young bride, who had written the saucy critiques of the Puritan way of life. His brother saw profit in Benjamin's ready pen. When a lighthousekeeper and his family drowned, Benjamin wrote a ballad. The *Courant* was snapped up. When Blackbeard the pirate died, more purple quatrains flowed. Benjamin showed off his verses to his parents but his father ridiculed his "performances," telling him "versemakers are generally beggars."

But Benjamin's writing skill finally won his freedom. When the *Courant* chided officials of the Massachusetts General Court for acting slowly against marauding pirates, the Court jailed James. It was left to a boy of seventeen to publish the paper alone. This Benjamin Franklin did, filling it with his own writings. When the authorities finally released James, it was with a court order to cease publication altogether. Clever James interpreted this to mean that the paper could continue as long as it was published by someone else. Benjamin could become the publisher in name only. To legitimize the ruse, he signed a release on the back of Benjamin's articles of apprenticeship.

Benjamin realized that James could never show the papers in court unless he wanted to be arrested for contempt. He had his passport out of Boston. With the help of a friend, he sold some books, stole aboard a ship and lay hidden for three days while his family frantically searched for him. He told the captain he had gotten a girl pregnant and was trying to run away. Sailing to New York, and then walking across New Jersey, he returned to Boston only once every ten years.

Seventeen-year-old Ben Franklin had only a Dutch dollar and a copper shilling in his pocket when he arrived in Philadelphia, but was certain he would make his fortune. Instead, he began seven years of hard luck that tempered the way he dealt with people for the rest of his life.   .

Bright, fast-talking, and likable, he had no trouble finding a job with a printer. He rented a furnished room in the home of Widow Read—a room down the hall from the landlady's daughter, a plump, blue-eyed girl named Debby—and lost no time making new friends and ambitious plans. As soon as possible, he would leave the printer who had just employed him and set up his own shop.

In May 1724, less than seven months after his arrival, the tall, brash young man returned to Boston to make peace with his family—and borrow the money to sail to England to buy his own printing equipment. His father turned him down. Back in Philadelphia with little money left, Benjamin found an even better solution. He had been introduced to the Pennsylvania governor, Sir William Keith. They had talked history over drinks for hours. The governor glad-handedly promised to appoint the eighteen-year-old boy the official provincial printer, even give him letters of introduction and credit, if only Ben would sail 3,000 miles to London to buy his own press. Elated, Ben prepared to leave as soon as he could save the money for his passage.

There was one other item of business: for a year, he had been courting the plain, homespun, all-but-illiterate Debby Read: "I had great respect and affection for her, and had some reason to believe she had the same for me." Ben and Debby talked about marriage but Mrs. Read, who controlled her daughter's dowry, did not want the youngsters "to go too far" when Ben was about to leave for an indefinite time. Apparently, Mrs. Read also thought Debby could do better than this itinerant young printer's devil.

Undeterred, the two youngsters exchanged promises and Ben sailed off for England. He discovered too late that the governor, a notorious bankrupt, had no credit to offer and, in his cups, had forgotten to send along the preferred letters to London. It was Benjamin Franklin's first bitter lesson in dealing with a British official. Stranded, a "poor ignorant boy" in the largest, most expensive city in Europe, Ben took two jobs concurrently in leading printing houses, and immediately tried to break a publishing tradition. Printers usually were strapped because they bought beer for each other all day long, beginning with a breakfast eye opener. Ben refused to buy drinks when his turn came. He substituted warm gruel for beer, pocketed the silver he saved, and preached the virtues of gruel to his fellow printers. Few cared to argue the point with the powerful youth after watching him haul two heavy trays of lead type upstairs and down: most men labored under one.

Making the best of his plight, Ben became the sporting companion of a young Philadelphia poet, James Ralph, who had deserted his wife to come to London. They roared around together drinking, whoring, and going to plays and parties. Ben often magnanimously paid for his friend's adventures and, as usual, wanted full value for his hard-earned money. When Ralph went out of town, Ben expected the favors of the poet's mistress. He was taken aback when he was refused.

He had mixed luck in other affairs. He managed to publish an outrageous pamphlet on metaphysics that he later attempted to buy back and destroy. He tried but failed to arrange an interview with Sir Isaac Newton and settled instead for the new secretary of the Royal Society. They chatted about the curiosities of the New World, and Ben managed to sell him an asbestos purse for a handsome profit. Yet with little prospect of accumulating enough money to buy a printing press, Ben floundered in London. He never once wrote to Debby.

For awhile, he played with the idea of opening a swimming school on the Thames and staying in London. A number of noblemen had watched him swim the three miles in the rough current from Chelsea to Blackfriars and wanted him to teach their sons. After two years in London, he returned to Philadelphia, taking a job with a merchant and becoming, in his own words, "expert in selling." When the merchant died, the nervy young man asked for his old job back from printer Samuel Keimer—and got it. Franklin left Keimer again and went into a partnership with a young friend. The partnership, too, split up. At age twenty-two, Franklin was the sole owner of a successful printing business and publisher of the *Pennsylvania Gazette*.

Franklin improved every business venture he put his hand to. For example, when he became postmaster of Philadelphia (in part to get free mailing privileges for his newspaper), it produced only £150 income a year. By the time the British fired him forty years later, he had become deputy postmaster general for North America and was clearing £1,500 a year after turning £3,000 over to the Crown.

Established in business, he decided to settle down. He was tired of

> that hard-to-be-governed passion of youth (that) hurried me frequently into intrigues with low women that fell in my way which were attended with some expense and great inconvenience, besides a continual risk to my health by a distemper which of all things I dreaded, though by great good luck I escaped it.

Whatever the exact truth of Franklin's deepest secret, on September 1, 1730, a little more than a year after he became publisher of the *Pennsylvania Gazette*, he "took to wife," as he later put it, Deborah Read. There could be no public ceremony. Legally, Deborah was still married, even if, as the rumors said, her first husband, John Rogers, was a bigamist with a wife and child in London and even if he had already, as the scuttlebutt had it, been killed in a barroom brawl in the West Indies. She had no legal proof of either rumor. All she knew was that she could not marry again under Pennsylvania law without being branded a felon, liable to thirty-nine lashes at the public whipping post and imprisonment for life at hard labor. Formal marriage was out of the question so long as Rogers' death could not be proven, and, in any event, Franklin would have had to assume Rogers' debts to make the contract binding. So the couple lived at common-law for all of their forty-four years together.

The arrangement and the business thrived. Franklin made himself known throughout the city in many ways. He set up a reading group, called first the "Leathern Apron Club" and then the Junto, whose members debated literature and science. He bought books for the subscription library that was the forerunner of the city's first public library. He also made himself humbly conspicuous, pushing a wheelbarrow filled with newspapers for sale through the street, a task usually performed by an apprentice.

His specialized skills as a printer enabled him to take on a large press run of Pennsylvania currency with such skill that he was named Clerk to the Pennsylvania Assembly. All of the province's printing and advertising flowed to the little shop by the Jersey Market on High Street. Franklin supervised the printing while Deborah sold soap made by the Franklins of Boston, printing and writing materials, legal forms, books, quills, ink parchment, sealing wax, spectacles, and soon, a new Franklin production, *Poor Richard's Almanac*. Franklin had, for that time, the rare gift of the gambler's instinct combined with shrewdness in business that led to his lifelong ability to parlay one asset or accomplishment into the next. One early manifestation of this instinct was his introduction of an almanac on an already-crowded market in 1732. Besides the Bible, almanacs, with their combination of weather forecasts and folksy sayings, were one book found in almost every colonial American home. Most almanacs, though, were poorly printed and poorly written. Franklin combined his printing and writing talents to produce a sensation that soon was selling 10,000 copies a year and did more than anything else to make Poor Richard's creator a rich man.

The secret of its success wasn't originality. The title was a more or less straightforward steal from "Poor Robin," a personality created by Benjamin's brother, James. What Franklin did was take the thoughts of others and polish them into homilies, parodies, aphorisms, and epigrams that usually had a practical point, sometimes a risque slant, and always possessed a memorable quality.

Here's a sampling:

He that lies down with dogs shall rise up with fleas.
To lengthen thy life, lessen thy meals.
Marry your son when you will, but your daughter when you can.
He that falls in love with himself will have no rivals.
It is easier to suppress the first desire than to satisfy all that follow it.
Work as if you were to live 100 years, pray as if you were to die tomorrow.

It is hard to imagine that any expressions of the pioneer American virtues could have been more timely. Europeans with little money were flocking through Philadelphia to settle the lands to the west, and Poor Richard's homespun philosophy went with them.

He was also perpetually pursuing plans for self-improvement, a drive for "moral perfection" as he put it. The scheme, well publicized (by him) in later life, included keeping a list of items of his personal conduct needing improvement and then grading himself weekly. The thirteen headings, together with a latter-day evaluation of how he did, included:

"Temperance. Eat not to dullness, drink not to elevation." Franklin evolved from a vegetarian in his teens into a trencherman who preferred old Madeira and kept five kinds of French wine in his cellar. Yet he was never seen drunk. He never took snuff or smoked tobacco.

"Silence. Speak not but what may benefit others or yourself. Avoid trifling conversation." Garrulous among friends, Franklin kept silent in public except to ask or answer questions. He often gave the appearance of being asleep.

"Order. Let all of your things have their places. Let each part of your business have its time." This was Franklin's inevitable failure. He was too busy most of his life to organize his time and papers. His records as minister to France were such a mess he made John Adams nearly apoplectic with rage. Fortunately, Franklin had a superb memory that compensated somewhat for this failing.

"Resolution. Resolve to perform what you ought. Perform without fail what you resolve." As a young man, he paid more heed to this item than as an elder statesman who had learned the advantages of necessary changes of position and direction.

In three categories—frugality, industry, and justice—Franklin would rate himself higher than others would. Under "cleanliness," he would earn high marks from the French secret police, who, while investigating him at one point searched his apartment and marveled at the cleanliness of his linen underthings. But in two areas of self-perfection, Franklin failed badly. Under "Sincerity: use no hurtful deceit," he'd have to admit his love of the written hoax and the spoken evasion had won out, especially in his masterfully deceptive diplomacy. When it came to "Justice: wrong none by doing injuries or omitting the benefits that are your duty," he was, for starters, grossly unfair in words and deeds to his brother James, whom he libeled regularly and often throughout his life.

Under the heading "chastity," Franklin was most vulnerable to attack. His common-law relationship with Deborah and his fathering of an illegitimate son made him the target of political mudslinging. After taking Deborah "to wife," however, there's little convincing evidence that he ever philandered other than once. In London in 1767, artist Charles Wilson Peale, arriving unannounced from Philadelphia, made a quick sketch after peeping through the cracked door of the sixty-one-year-old Franklin's apartment. He drew a couple in amorous encounter. The features of both lovers are indistinct, however. It may or may not have been Franklin and his landlady's daughter, pretty Polly Stevenson, who was with Franklin much of her life and was with him at his death.

Franklin also tried to order the lives of his family, again with mixed success. His wife, Deborah, who endured a great deal from him and apparently loved him greatly, needed little prodding. In the early years together, she made all his clothes in addition to keeping his house and his shop. Yet, by his lights, she strayed occasionally, as Franklin later attested, particularly in regard to frugality.

> My breakfast was for a long time bread and milk (no tea) and I ate it out of a twopenny earthen porringer with a pewter spoon. But mark how luxury will enter families, and make a progress, in spite of principles. Being called one morning to breakfast, I found it in a china bowl with a spoon of silver. They had been bought for me without my knowledge by my wife and had cost her the enormous sum of three and twenty shillings, for

which she had no other excuse or apology to make but that she thought *her* husband deserv'd a silver spoon and china bowl as well as any of his neighbors.

Deborah bore Franklin two more children, a son, Francis Folger, and a daughter, Sally. Frankie was Benjamin's favorite. The child's death at four of smallpox was one of the great blows of Franklin's life. Years earlier, Benjamin and his brother James had attacked the first inoculations in Boston in James' newspaper as an unwise experiment. When an epidemic swept Philadelphia in November 1736, Franklin hesitated until the boy could recover from a fever. In the meantime, the child died. He blamed himself for the child's death. To save others his grief, Franklin editorialized in favor of inoculation in his *Gazette*, but nearly half a century later, he still broke down and cried when he talked of his little Frankie.

Benjamin Franklin's first political excursion came when he successfully organized militia to counter French privateering raids up the Delaware River in 1747. For years the city had trembled with fear periodically due to its exposure to enemy attacks since the controlling Quaker pacifists refused to violate their religious scruples by appropriating funds for defense. When Franklin organized a volunteer militia association, more than 1,000 men immediately flocked to his standard. Secretly, the Quakers were pleased: their business and properties, not to mention their lives, were protected at no financial or moral cost to them. The ruling Penn family, however, was annoyed, mainly since they saw Franklin as a potential threat.

In the late 1740s, Franklin stayed out of local politics, drawing from both the Proprietary Party loyal to the Penns and the Anti-Proprietary Party for contributions to the numerous public charities he espoused, including the founding of Pennsylvania Hospital and the Academy of Philadelphia. But more and more after 1750, the prosperous middle-aged printer-postmaster-philanthropist, by now obviously one of the leading figures in the colony, was drawn into the melee of Pennsylvania politics. In 1751, he became an assemblyman. As a French and Indian invasion again threatened in 1754, Franklin became the military leader of the province. After bloody Indian raids at present-day Easton and Bethlehem, he supervised construction of forts along the frontier. Although he wore common buckskin and slept in cold cabins with the other citizen-soldiers, he heard himself called "General Franklin" by the German immigrants those forts were protecting.

For two reasons Pennsylvania couldn't adequately defend itself. The Quakers had blocked the appropriation of funds for arms and the Penns had refused to allow their huge land holdings to be taxed equitably. The first impediment was removed when many Quakers chose to abandon provincial politics rather than renounce their religious beliefs in the face of angry outcries over the slaughter in the frontier settlements. The second obstacle—money from the Penns—would prove greater. In 1757, the Assembly voted to send Franklin to London to prevail personally on the Penns. That failing, he was to lobby before Parliament to convert the province into a crown colony and bring it under royal protection.

The esteem given a colonial agent in London in that era was even less than that accorded a Washington lobbyist today. This held true especially since the Penns were forewarned and organized their powerful friends against him. Yet Franklin had a new form of influence. Since April 1756, Franklin had been a member of the prestigious Royal Society, a tribute to his pioneering experiments in electricity, which had been going on, at this time, for more than a decade. He had begun these experiments at age forty-two after he had sold his printing business enterprises for a modest fortune. This afforded him time to devote himself, and his time, to things that interested him. Steadily, he drifted into the still primitive domain of science.

When Franklin's Junto had, a few years earlier, turned its attention to scientific reading and discussion, the idea of leather-aproned artisans dabbling in science was considered something of a scientific curiosity in itself. To egg them on, an English Quaker merchant named Peter Collinson, who was the bookbuying agent for their private club, the Library Company, sent the library a large glass tube, over three feet long and as thick as a man's wrist, with instructions for making sparks. Collinson's gift of glass served to focus Franklin's interest. "I never was before engaged in any study that so totally engrossed my attention and my time as this has lately done," Franklin wrote Collinson on March 28, 1747. "I have during some months past had little leisure for anything else."

Franklin spent five years of tedious and repetitive trial and error, working with the crudest of tools: glass tubes, tubes of resin, a gun barrel and a cork, iron shot, wax, and glass plates. He reported each step in letters to Collinson, who published Franklin's results in a series of five articles in the *Proceedings of the Royal Society*. He was the first to grasp the principle that electricity flows in a current like a fluid, never destroyed, "the fire only circulating." He coined the terms *positive, negative, plus, minus, armature, battery, brush, charge, condense,* and *conductor* as he went along. His theories and statements on electricity made in those first supercharged months of experimentation still stand, with few changes, more than two centuries later.

Franklin himself did not initially appreciate what he had done. After three years, Franklin halted his experiments, and disappointed, he wrote Collinson, "that we have hitherto been able to discover nothing in the way of use to mankind." By this time, fortunately, he'd sent off to England his theories on thunderstorms and electricity. "The electric current is attracted by points," he wrote Collinson on July 29, 1750. "We do not know whether this property is in lightning. But since [it] agrees in all particulars wherein we can already compare them, is it not probable they agree likewise in this? Let the experiment be made."

Franklin was well aware of the dangers electricity posed. Six of his friends had been knocked senseless during one electrical experiment in his house, and he himself had been knocked out twice and badly bruised by electrical charges. In an attempt to make use of electricity's lethal potential, he had even used the current to kill and cook a turkey for a picnic. It wasn't until a muggy June day in 1752 that Franklin finally got around to testing his own hypothesis in a thunderstorm in an open field (now called Franklin Square) used to graze sheep near his house. With his tall, twenty-two-year-old son William, Franklin put on a loose coat and took an odd-looking kite made of a large thin silk kerchief with a sixteen-inch wire atop it. At the other end, an insulating tail of silk ribbon was connected to the twine leader by a small housekey. They hurried through the pelting rain to a shepherd's shed at the edge of the common. While Benjamin stood inside the shed, William raced across the field to get the cumbersome kite aloft. The first pass was a flop; no bolt of lightning darted down the wire, and the kite collapsed. Again, William streaked across the field. The kite soared and whirled. Thunder roared. This time, the puzzled Franklin didn't tap the key with his knuckle, but watched amazed as the silken strands on the ribbon separately stood out straight. Carefully, Franklin touched the key. Electric current coursed through his arm. Luckily, the electricity had come from the dense clouds; it was not lightning as such. Had lightning danced down the wire, Franklin and his son would have been incinerated. When the loose-knit international fraternity of amateur scientists learned of his feat from the Royal Society's journal, he became world-famous.

Living with Franklin in those days was risky. He was the archetypal mad scientist, cramming his house with odd-looking paraphernalia. The house was wired with lightning rods and wires that ran down hallways and walls. The wires were connected to bells that made a thunderstorm worse by ringing, ringing, ringing whenever the current passed down the wires through the house. He made other, more immediately useful inventions, however, such as bifocals, a copying machine, the Franklin stove, and the first catheter. He made them all public, along with his lightning rods, and never patented them. He was not interested in monetary profit from his scientific inventions.

His new pre-eminence was bringing him dividends of another sort: the correspondence and, later, the friendship of the leaders of the government of his time, most of them amateur dabblers in science themselves. Franklin was able to make even more effective use of his new intellectual credentials. The entree it gave him in England, where his reputation as a scientist and philosopher preceded him, made him a sensation during his first sojourn as Pennsylvania's agent from 1757 to 1762. He received one honor after another: a reception at Cambridge University with "particular regard shown by the chancellor and vice-chancellor," a triumphal trip through Scotland and Ireland. Edinburgh made him a burgher and guild brother of the city. St. Andrews University made him a doctor of law, and Oxford conferred an honorary doctorate. Franklin parlayed his scientific fame into political influence.

The full reasons why Franklin came home are not clear. He had, apparently, toyed with the idea of settling permanently in England. He told his closest friend he couldn't stay because his wife couldn't make the voyage. He wrote to her, "I gave ... two reasons why I could not think of removing hither. One my affection to Pennsylvania, and long-established friendships and other connections there; the other (being) your invincible aversion to crossing the seas." It was not to be an auspicious homecoming. During Franklin's absence, his constituents had routinely returned him each year to his seat in the Pennsylvania Assembly. On returning to Philadephia, he found growing opposition to his anti-Penn feud. Quaker leaders, usually divided, joined forces to unseat him, dredging up a long-ago slur he had made against the Germans (whom Franklin had called "Palatine boors") to turn the German settlers against him. Franklin was drubbed by 1,000 votes, a large margin at the time.

Franklin had lived well in London, hiring a coach and giving lavish dinners for his friends. He had witnessed the zenith of British imperial conquest, the victory over France and the resplendent coronation of young George III. There was little to compare to this in provincial Philadelphia, yet he tried to console himself by ordering construction of a handsome, three-story house with courtyard and arches. He wasn't to stay in Philadelphia long enough to see it finished, however. Soon after his trouncing in the Assembly, his party, openly voting for a change to royal government, sent him back to London as colonial agent. Governor John Penn wrote to relatives in London that Franklin had been like a sorcerer, manipulating members in secret caucuses to accomplish this. Again, Deborah stayed behind. In the last eighteen years of her life, she was with her husband only once.

Franklin returned to an England preoccupied with more important matters than Pennsylvania's government. The long war with France had mired England in debt. The new government insisted that America, which, after all, had been freed by British arms from the French menace, pay its fair share of the debt. In February 1764, a few weeks before Franklin landed, George Grenville proposed a Stamp Act in the House of Commons. The measure touched off a year of riots in America, and struck a match to the long fuse of revolution. Because he'd recommended two of the three American stamp tax commissioners and several collectors, Franklin was suspected in Pennsylvania of advocating the unpopular measure in the first place. In fact, he did think it was a good idea at first. For nine days, his family and friends in Philadelphia had to barricade themselves with guns inside the house on Race Street until the mob's ardor cooled. Franklin got the message that Americans didn't like the Stamp Act, shifted his ground, and, more than anyone else, organized pressure in England for the Stamp Act's repeal.

As British merchants and manufacturers protested that thousands of workers faced unemployment if American trade continued to decline, Franklin was called to the bar before the House of Commons to testify on behalf of America. Night and day for three weeks he'd been lobbying intensively. He hired a man to hand out cartoons at the entrance of Commons and wrote a series of articles for his friend Strahan's *London Chronicle*. Now, as the unofficial ambassador of America, he'd been called to answer carefully planted questions. For four exhausting hours, Franklin coolly fielded some 170 questions. During those hours, he gave England's rulers a rare view of the mind of America, a mental picture that would linger for decades. It can be argued that had Parliament paid closer attention, England might have kept her American colonies. At the bottom line of Franklin's performance was the key to the quarrel: "Is there a power on earth that can force (the Americans) to erase the resolutions (of the Stamp Act Congress)?" "No power, how great soever," Franklin replied, "can force men to change their opinions."

When Franklin returned to England in 1764, he presented Pennsylvania's petition for royal rule to the King's Privy Council, where consideration of it was postponed indefinitely. Instead of accepting this defeat, Franklin dug in for a long fight, making himself part of the political landscape of London, using his status as the most celebrated American in Europe to the private advantage of himself and his friends.

With his son, William, the Whartons of Philadelphia, Sir William Johnson (the Indian commissioner for the northern colonies), and many leading English politicians, he formed the Grand Ohio Company to seek a royal charter for a vast new wilderness province. The scheme nearly succeeded, but unrest in New England turned English leaders sour to anything that might benefit Americans. When

Bostonians polluted their harbor with 10,000 pounds of East India tea, Franklin had to set aside his personal speculations.

He also undertook a step that quickly ended his career as a British official. The city of Boston had been a tinderbox since 1768 when two regiments of tough British troops were unloaded on Long Wharf. Few Bostonians knew that two Americans were responsible for the good fortune of having the troops visited upon their city. As postmaster for the colonies, Franklin became aware of correspondence from Massachusetts Governor Thomas Hutchinson and Hutchinson's brother-in-law, Andrew Oliver, the Massachusetts chief justice, to a former British official. The letters indicated that Hutchinson and Oliver had urged the British to punish the Boston patriots. In his role as agent to Massachusetts, Franklin secretly forwarded the purloined letters to Sam Adams and other radical Bostonians. But Sam Adams couldn't keep a secret. Soon, all America and England knew of the correspondence.

At first, Franklin kept silent about his involvement. But then the son of the addressee accused one of William Franklin's friends of having purloined the letters. The two fought one indecisive duel and had scheduled a rematch when Franklin finally decided to step forward. He admitted his misdeed in the *London Advertiser*. Immediately his enemies seized this chance to haul him before the Privy Council. In effect, Franklin was placed under arrest. In the darkest scene of his life, Franklin appeared at the Cockpit, the grand hall where the Privy Council of the House of Lords met. On January 29, 1774, before a packed gallery, he was treated to a merciless hour-long lambasting by British Solicitor General Alexander Wedderburn. With mocking, slashing rhetorical questions, Wedderburn declared that "no gentleman's letters would now be safe" from the postmaster general. "Franklin will henceforth esteem it a libel to be called a man of letters," he chided.

Throughout the sarcastic tirade, Franklin stood silent, but there was no concealing his deep humiliation. When the grilling was over, he left without uttering a word in his defense. The next day, as expected, he received a letter firing him from the post office. Franklin refused to follow the advice of family and friends to come home. He refused to give up his personal crusade for American causes, although he was savagely attacked in the British press as "this old snake," "the grand incendiary," "this living emblem of iniquity in grey hairs," "Old Traitor," and "Old Doubleface."

"My situation here is thought by many to be a little hazardous," he wrote home with considerable understatement, "for that, if by some accident, the troops and people of [New England] should come to blows, I should probably be taken up [arrested]; the ministerial people affecting everywhere to represent me as the cause of all the misunderstandings." In this crisis, Franklin suffered another blow: the news that his wife, despairing of ever seeing him again, had died on December 19, 1774.

Finally, Franklin decided to sail for home. He arrived in Philadelphia on May 5, 1775, this time to a tumultuous welcome. He was elected to the Second Continental Congress as a special delegate from Pennsylvania. With him he had brought his handsome grandson, Temple, the sixteen-year-old offspring of William, who now formally acknowledged him. The three Franklin men met in Philadelphia and began one of the most painful dialogues any family ever endured. Benjamin and William, now the royal governor of New Jersey, met at the Trevose farm of Joseph

Galloway. They argued over drinks of port late into a night and again the next day over Benjamin's decision to rebel against arbitrary English power and William's determination to remain loyal to his oath of office to the King. Something about the debate was unnatural—the old, wise man arguing for rebellion, and the younger man for order, stability, and reconciliation. But their points of view were as irreconcilable as those of England and America.

Plunging back into the work of Congress, Franklin served on ten key committees. He was the first American to understand that most of the important work of government is done in small committee meetings, not in open debate in the public eye. In addition to chairing the post office committee and becoming postmaster general, he supervised construction of defenses and obtained munitions for American forces as far away as Charleston and Cambridge. He remodeled Pennsylvania's cumbersome revolutionary government into a close-knit, autocratic Committee of Safety. This mode was quickly emulated by other states and later adopted in the French Revolution by the Jacobins. "My time," the sixty-nine-year-old congressman wrote his close friend, chemist Joseph Priestley in England, "was never more fully employed. In the morning at six I am at the Committee of Safety ... which holds till near nine, when I am at the Congress, and that sits till after four in the afternoon." In the full sessions of the Congress, Franklin rarely spoke, sitting with eyes closed most of the time.

It soon became apparent to Congress that America could not withstand the inevitable British onslaught without foreign aid. Franklin became America's first emissary and a sort of secretary of state. He was, initially, a wandering troubleshooter, going first to Canada. On July 4, 1776, as Franklin led the Pennsylvania delegation in voting for independence from England, a British armada sailed into New York harbor. Its admiral, Lord Howe, was authorized to offer the hand of peace on England's terms and, failing that, the fist of punishment. Franklin and Howe knew and respected each other. They had talked of reconciliation in London during chess matches in Howe's sister's house. They parlayed again on Staten Island.

One of Franklin's fellow emissaries, John Adams, would later complain about a lot of Franklin's habits but one stood out in his memory. At a tavern in Perth Amboy, they could find only a single room in a crowded tavern. An advocate of fresh air at night, Franklin opened the window. Adams, like most people of that age, believed night air bore disease and slammed it shut. Franklin objected that he would suffocate. He launched into a long dissertation on his theory of fresh air baths. But before Franklin could finish, Adams gave in, opened the window and fell asleep.

The next day, the British emissaries offered the Americans the olive branch— on the condition that the Americans recant their declaration of independence. The British also refused to recognize Congress. Concluding that further talks were pointless, the American emissaries returned to Philadelphia.

Congress appointed Franklin to a supersecret committee with "the sole purpose of correspondence with our friends in Great Britain, Ireland, and other parts of the world." Most of them were Franklin's contacts and old friends. Now Franklin took a fateful step: twice he had fought France, and he'd grown up, like most Americans, fearing and hating the French, yet now he felt that America had to turn to them for help against the British. Franklin dashed off letters to old friends there, asking them to feel out the mood of the French government. Finally, a long letter came back indicating that Franklin would be received sympathetically if he came to France. As the British unleashed their New York military offensive, Congress unanimously, and secretly, voted to send Franklin as minister to France.

Franklin said what he was sure were last goodbyes to his daughter Sally. He then took his grandson, Temple, whose father already had been packed off to a Connecticut prison as a Loyalist, and another grandson, six-year-old Benjamin Franklin Bache, aboard the sloop *Reprisal* and set sail for France. The ship outran British cruisers twice, as Franklin most assuredly would have been hanged for treason had he been intercepted. The fast little ship made the rough winter passage in six weeks, arriving in Nantes on December 3, 1776, where Franklin was treated to a hero's welcome. Aboard ship, Franklin had suffered one of his recurring outbreaks of what was probably acute psoriasis, making it impossible for him to wear his customary wig. Instead, he donned a fur hat he'd bought in Canada. The sight he presented with a fur hat, wispy gray hair, spectacles, and plain brown suit charmed the French. It was to be their lasting image of the American. Franklin would remain for years their symbol of the new republican man. "Everything in him announces the simplicity and innocence of primitive morals," exuded one French philosopher.

On December 28, 1776, two days after George Washington's surprise victory at Trenton (but weeks before the French knew about it), Franklin met for the first time with Vergennes, the French foreign minister. Franklin extended the lure of a commercial treaty, avoiding asking outright for a military alliance. Eight days later, he wrote to ask officially for much more—eight fully equipped and manned ships-of-the-line. Knowing such a grant would draw France into the war, he added that by "the united force of France, Spain [France's ally], and America, she [England] will lose all her possessions in the West Indies, much the greatest part of that commerce which has rendered her so opulent, and be reduced to that state of weakness and humiliation which she has, by her perfidy, her insolence, and her cruelty, so justly merited."

Franklin helped things along by waging his own war of nerves on the French, opening a correspondence with his British connections that he made to appear like serious peace negotiations. On January 6, 1778, this maneuver led to a two-hour talk with British master spy Paul Wentworth, a meeting that did not escape the notice of the French. On February 5, 1778, Franklin was summoned to the French foreign ministry at Versailles to sign the formal alliance. Edward Bancroft, an aide, observed that Franklin was dressed in an old suit of Manchester velvet he dimly recalled seeing somewhere years before. Then Bancroft realized that it was the same suit Franklin had worn during his humiliation by the Privy Council at the Cockpit. When he asked Franklin why he was wearing such an out-of-style outfit, Franklin smiled and said, "To give it a little revenge."

It would take three years of delays and fighting before joint Franco-American forces scored a decisive victory at Yorktown. That victory, coinciding with French naval victories in the Caribbean and collapse of the pro-war British cabinet, made England eager for peace. The negotiations, which took almost two more years, were

The Historical Society of Pennsylvania

The oldest American revolutionary, Benjamin Franklin was famous in Europe as the man who dared the lightning and invented useful devices like the bifocals.

to prove Dr. Franklin's greatest diplomatic achievement. Franklin made astonishing demands: full and immediate independence, withdrawal of all troops, a western boundary along the Mississippi, a north border along the Great Lakes and above Maine, and fishing rights on the Grand Banks. Boldly, Franklin was bidding for twice the lands that the thirteen colonies had occupied at the outset of the war.

The final round of negotiations, occurring after a time-out for another change of government in London, lasted six days and nights. The British were adamant about Loyalist compensation (England was thronging with 30,000 vociferous refugees) and equally insistent that the Americans be barred from the prized fishing grounds off Newfoundland. Bitterly, Franklin refused to give in on the Loyalists. The most he would allow was a recommendation that Congress reimburse their losses. (He knew, of course, that Congress years ago had turned treatment of the Loyalists over to the individual states, so that such a recommendation was worthless.) John Adams had joined Franklin by now, and he skillfully led the British to give New England fishermen the "liberty" to fish off Newfoundland instead of the "right" they had earlier claimed. The shading of these two words appeased the British negotiators, anxious above all for an end to the fighting that once again had bankrupted England. Without protest, they signed away the rights to all the land between Canada and the Gulf of Mexico, between the Atlantic and the Mississippi. Franklin had won one-fifth of the continent, the rich land from the Appalachians to the Mississippi so long coveted by frontiersmen, without ever seriously arguing the point.

Returning to Philadelphia in 1785 at age seventy-nine, Franklin was quickly elected president of Pennsylvania, an office he filled three years until the pain of gout and bladder stones made it difficult for him to carry on his duties of office. Carried to sessions of the Constitutional Convention during the blistering summer of 1787 in a sedan chair borne by prisoners, Franklin, as usual, left the brunt of the debating to others until the very end. On the last day, too ill to attend, he sent along a note to be read aloud. A fellow Pennsylvanian, turning toward George Washington, read from the paper:

> Mr. President, I confess that there are several parts of this constitution which I do not at present approve. But I am not sure I shall never approve them ... for having lived long, I have experienced many instances of being obliged by better information ... to change opinions even on important subjects.

In January 1788, Franklin suffered a severe fall on the stone steps in his garden. Walking became difficult. His kidney stone became excruciatingly painful, forcing him to take laudanum (a mixture of opium and honey), which gave relief but exhausted him. He revised his will, leaving only a small bequest to his Loyalist son William (see sketch on pages 59–73). The last year of his life, he never left his bedroom, but he could still write letters to the newspapers.

One was on the slave trade. Franklin, president of the Pennsylvania Society for Promoting the Abolition of Slavery, had for thirty years owned house slaves but he had grown sensitive to the anomaly of slavery in a revolutionary society proclaiming human rights. In the 1780s, he began to correspond with such antislavery reformers as Granville Sharp of London and Anthony Benezet of Philadelphia. In one of his last letters to the press, he now attacked slavery as an outrage against humanity:

> Can sweetening our tea with sugar be a circumstance of such absolute necessity? Can the petty pleasure thence arising to the taste compensate for so much misery produced among our fellow creatures and such a constant butchery of the human species by this pestilential, detestable traffic in the bodies and souls of men?

In November 1789, he signed the abolition society's public appeal for funds to provide relief for freed slaves, secure jobs for them, and provide schooling for their children. On February 12, 1790, in his last public act, he signed the society's petition to the First Congress to restore "liberty to those unhappy men who alone in this land of freedom are degraded into perpetual bondage."

On Saturday evening, April 17, 1790, Benjamin Franklin died at 84 after two years of intense suffering. With death, as with most things, Franklin held few illusions. Years before, already old, he had written to an old friend: "Let us sit till the evening of life is spent; the last hours were always the most joyous. When we can stay no longer, 'tis time enough then to bid each other good night, separate, and go quietly to bed."

QUESTIONS FOR THOUGHT AND DISCUSSION

1. What made Benjamin Franklin succeed as a businessman? Why was he not content to remain a successful printer?

2. Was Franklin a true genius, or would you account for his scientific inventions and social innovations by his being in the right place at the right time?

3. How significant was the role Franklin played in the American Revolution? Would you describe him as a great patriot?

SUGGESTED READINGS

Lopez, Claude-Anne. *Mon Cher Papa: Franklin and the Ladies of Paris.* New Haven: Yale Press, 1966.

Lopez, Claude-Anne and Eugenia W. Herbert. *The Private Franklin.* New York: Norton, 1975.

Randall, Willard Sterne. *A Little Revenge: Benjamin Franklin and His Son.* Boston: Little, 1984.

Shoenbrun, David. *Triumph in Paris: The Exploits of Benjamin Franklin.* New York: Harper, 1976.

Tourtellot, A. B. *Benjamin Franklin: The Shaping of Genius.* Vol. 1: The Boston Years. New York: Doubleday, 1977.

Van Doren, Carl C. *Benjamin Franklin.* New York, 1938.

Wright, Esmond. *Franklin of Philadelphia.* Cambridge, Mass.: Belknap, 1985.

6

William Franklin

In a typically succinct piece of New England crackerbarrel wisdom, John Adams once said that his father had worked the soil so that his son could study law so that his son could be a poet. No clearer example of this American evolution can be found than the Franklin family. From wool-dyer-turned-soap-chandler Josiah, to printer-turned-statesman Benjamin, the Franklin family continued to evolve. Benjamin's son grew up a tradesman's son with gentlemanly pretensions. He rode his own horse by age ten, learned French, limned poems in Philadelphia's genteel provincial society, and yearned to go to London. There he became one of a handful of American-born English barristers and the first royal official appointed by King George III. Such a family was bound to have its share of tensions— enough to pull it apart when the American Revolution came.

FOR THE FOURTH icy January day since they had left the fortified town of Bethlehem, the Pennsylvania militiamen slogged northwest along the Lehigh River. Hunched under sodden wool coats, they bent into the burning cold wind, their muskets hanging heavily in the hard, slanting rain. Aware that the natives were spying them out, they scanned the thick rocky cover to the left, bushes, boulders, and trees to the right. As they trudged along the narrow wagon road, their boots crunched through ice-crusted puddles. They covered no more than a mile an hour, occasionally looking up for signals from the officer at the head of the column.

Captain William Franklin, the only seasoned officer on the march, rode the lead horse. His scarlet grenadier's uniform was a conspicuous target for Native-American snipers. He had deployed his 172-man force with an eye to avoiding the fatal mistakes made by General Edward Braddock. Braddock's campaign to Fort Duquesne had recently ended in disaster with half the British troops killed in battle and 400 settlers dying in subsequent raids. Here, twenty-two cavalrymen were strung out behind Franklin to give the appearance of a much larger force. Behind them, Indian fashion, marched the Pennsylvania militia in single file, ready to take cover quickly. A small contingent of scouts shielded the main body against ambush, probing thickets and ravines and occupying hills as the column approached.

Bringing up the rear were heavy Conestoga wagons pulled by six-horse teams. Halfway back in the column, clad in a great blue coat, rode Benjamin Franklin, colonel of the militia and father of Captain Franklin.

The two men leading the grim little column personified the changes sweeping war-torn America as 1756 began. Benjamin Franklin, at age fifty, had already lived through two wars between English and French colonial empires. Half his age, William Franklin, Benjamin's illegitimate son, had already been hardened by years of military service on the frontier and by long canoe trips into the wilderness. He had felt at home on horseback since he was ten. The father's wealth was self-made as printer, storekeeper, and provincial politician; the son was self-assured, assimilating all his father's hard-bought knowledge, wealth, and position. William was determined to find new ways to shape the world his generation would inherit. The two men were unusually close, together vehemently attacking any enemy, political or military, who threatened either of them. It was with this same vehemence that they would later oppose each other when William refused to join his father in the revolutionary movement and went to prison for his loyalty to the British government.

William Franklin remained close to his famous father for twenty-five years before the Revolution eventually made them enemies. However, his important contributions to his father's successes—political, military, and scientific—have been all but forgotten. After they became enemies, Benjamin all but expunged his son from his famous autobiography. Only a few telltale reminders of how close they had once been remained unedited. Franklin's famous memoir began, "Dear Son." And when he wrote thirty years later about their dangerous fort-building expedition on the Pennsylvania frontier, Benjamin acknowledged that William had been "of great use to me."

Until his dying day, William Franklin was apparently unsure of the date of his birth, although he always referred to Deborah Read Franklin as his mother. Benjamin Franklin remained silent on the subject of who William's mother was, even to his own family, for twenty years. In 1750, he told his own mother that William was nineteen—when William had already been away from his Philadelphia home for four years, including two years spent as an army officer. It was not a likely story, but Benjamin was clearly ashamed to tell his parents the full truth.

There was nothing luxurious about William's early childhood as he grew up above the Franklin printing shop and general store. Benjamin had an almost spiritual attachment to meager meals served plainly. Deborah helped long hours in the shop, ran their house, took care of William, made all their clothes, and destroyed her eyesight by hand-sewing bindings on books and pamphlets at night by candlelight. It was six years after Benjamin took Deborah as his common-law wife before she bore Benjamin another son, Francis. However, Francis died of smallpox at the age of four.

Growing up in Philadelphia in William's boyhood meant following the seasons: kite flying in the spring, swimming and fishing in the summer, and skating and sledding in the long winters. He also took part in activities frowned on in the Quaker city: amateur theatricals in a warehouse and horse racing on Race Street. But long periods of boredom intervened, and ships arriving with goods from as far away as India made William restless. They came up the Delaware laden with prizes from King George's War. Their crews carried sacks of gold to spend freely in the shops and taverns. It was only a matter of time before William did as his father had and tried to run away to sea.

Like so many fathers, Franklin was too busy during the boy's adolescence to notice subtle changes in him. When he was not in his print shop or at the State House copying debates, he was traveling on Post Office business or attending meetings of the numerous societies he founded to improve city life. His conversations must have been sprinkled with bits of wisdom that rarely probed a boy's problems. If there were problems in the rented house on Race Street they had recently moved to, Benjamin Franklin was unaware of them. At fifteen, William ran away. Franklin hurried from ship to ship, looking for him. In his memoirs Franklin recalled:

> My only son, left my house unknown to us all and got on board a privateer, from whence I fetched him. No one imagined it was hard usage at home that made him do this. Everyone that knows me thinks I am too indulgent a parent as well as master. When boys see prizes brought in and quantities of money shared among the men and their gay living, it fills their heads with notions that half distract them and put them quite out of conceit with trades and the dull ways of getting money by working.

Until then, Benjamin had devoted little thought to his son's future. His son had been tutored in math, had cast his father's meteorological charts for *Poor Richard's Almanac*, read proof, kept the books for his business, and helped supervise the apprentices. His father had talked, briefly, about founding a college in Philadelphia, but that would happen too late for William. Continuing his education did not seem to be an option for William as it had been for his friends. Thus, William's formal education was over. If the young man wanted adventure, Benjamin reasoned, let him join the troops enlisting for the latest British expedition against French Canada. The privations of military life would surely make him eager for the comforts of a tradesman's life.

To Franklin's surprise, William did not hurry back. He thrived on the dangers of frontier war. He learned drill and discipline, tactics, weaponry, and fortifications. In August 1746, after French-led Indians attacked and burned Saratoga, New York, and surrounded Albany, William, wearing a red ensign's uniform, rode north with a company of German-born laborer-volunteers called "pioneers." The Pennsylvania troops found themselves surrounded by a large and determined force. William's regiment was slowly decimated by wounds, disease, and desertion. When they sent hunting parties from their crude stockade, sixteen men in one patrol were killed in an ambush. Men who went out to fish were tomahawked. Yet William didn't complain and he didn't hurry home. The youngest of the Pennsylvania officers, he was promoted to the highest provincial rank: captain. He was praised in official dispatches for his conspicuous bravery on patrols. But even when his son was promoted, Benjamin did not mention it in his newspaper, the *Pennsylvania Gazette*.

Captain Franklin's dreams of a military career did not die naturally: they were killed by lack of money. To become a career officer in the British military establishment, one had to buy a commission from the colonel of a regiment when a post became vacant. When the war ended, there were more officers available than regular army commissions. Although William had gained personal distinction and cultivated prominent connections during his military career, his father showed no interest in laying out the large amount of cash needed to buy a commission.

Unwilling to return to his father's shop, William, who had learned of a major expedition into Indian country being organized by Philadelphia merchants, was scouted by Pennsylvania Indian agent Conrad Weiser. Appointed official courier to the Pennsylvania Land Office, William attended the Treaty of Lancaster of 1748. At this meeting, fifty-five Indian leaders offered Philadelphia merchants the exclusive franchise for fur trading. When Weiser, leader of the first Pennsylvania trade mission to the Ohio Valley, left Lancaster to plant the first British flag west of the Alleghenies, he asked Captain Franklin to go along as Land Office agent. As the first English officer to carry the Union Jack across the mountains, William sensed the great promise of the West and his own place in it.

Young Franklin returned from his 1,000 mile trek by horse and canoe something of a celebrity, but his father was unimpressed:

> Will is now nineteen years of age, a tall proper youth, and much of a beau. He acquired a habit of idleness on the expedition, but begins of late to apply himself to business, and I hope will become an industrious man. He imagined his father had got enough for him, but I have assured him that I intend to spend what little I have, myself, if it please God that I live long enough.

In William's years away in the army, he missed his father's first experiments with electricity, but he quickly made himself invaluable as his father's laboratory assistant. When the elder Franklin traveled, he left instructions that electricity from thunderstorms passing overhead should be gathered in great glass bottles. Once Benjamin was ready to test his lightning rods, William scaled the roofs to install them. When Benjamin was ready for his climactic experiment to draw lightning from the clouds with the aid of a kite and a key, it was William who designed and built the kite. He raced across a cow pasture three times in an electrical storm to get the kite aloft while Benjamin stood sheltered in a shepherd's shed nearby.

The Franklins' kite-and-key experiment proved that lightning was electricity, but from what direction the current came was a more difficult question. Benjamin assumed that it came down from electrical storms, but in July 1753, William was able to demonstrate that the opposite was true. Benjamin was in Boston on postal inspections one night when a heavy dark cloud passed over their workshop during a downpour. Lightning flashed through a three-story house nearby, blasting out bricks, boring holes in the woodwork, melting lead sashweights, and singeing roofing shingles. William, clambering over the roof and prying into every corner of the house, took notes and made drawings in a long, excited letter proving to his father that the lightning had passed upward. Nearly ten years later, when Oxford University awarded Benjamin an honorary doctorate, university overseers voted William an honorary master's degree for his contributions.

As Benjamin Franklin devoted more time to politics, he gave William a share in this work as well. Elected to the Pennsylvania Assembly in 1751, he turned his paid post of Assembly Clerk over to his son. When he became Deputy Postmaster General of North America, he appointed William Postmaster of Philadelphia and comptroller of the North American postal system, a job that required skill in accounting, tact in collecting money, and patience in making detailed reports.

At age twenty, William decided to pursue a legal career. He went to work as a clerk in the law office of Joseph Galloway, a member of the town's elite group. Benjamin had a low opinion of lawyers. "God works wonders now and then. Behold, a lawyer, an honest man," wrote Poor Richard. Yet Franklin promised his son that, when he had completed the customary three-year term of clerkship in the office of a leading lawyer, he would send him to England to study at London's ancient law school, the Inns of Court.

The personable young William, on good terms with all factions of Philadelphia society, contributed to the success of Benjamin's efforts. Yet each year, he was less attracted to his father's artisan friends and more closely linked to his father's rivals. Joining a circle of aristocratic young friends, William danced with the daughters and wives of the Penn political faction as a founding member of the Philadelphia Dancing Assembly. And when French and Indian attacks came in 1755, he organized the best-equipped, best-trained horsemen into a cavalry unit, helping his father raise the rest of the 500-man militia.

With four-fifths of Pennsylvania controlled by the French, the Franklins led a relief expedition to fortify the frontier towns from Lancaster northeast to Bethlehem, Easton, and the Pocono mountains on the New York border. The Franklin plan called for building standardized frontier forts fifty feet square. These forts were armed with small swivel guns taken from ships in Philadelphia harbor and defended by sharpshooters firing from platforms and twin blockhouses. Indians rarely attacked a fortified place and a log fort, though rickety, was safe against an enemy who had no artillery. Forts were to be built every ten miles along seventy miles of mountains to shelter frontier families. Ranger companies, organized and trained by Captain Franklin, were to patrol constantly between the forts to guard against surprise attacks. It was William, acting as his father's aide-de-camp, who did all the training and wrote out all the orders, drawing on his British Army training. In seven weeks, building a fort every five days, the Franklins, never closer in all their twenty-five years of collaboration, spiked the French and Indian winter offensive.

The dashing veteran of the French wars met seventeen-year-old Elizabeth Graeme at the Assembly balls in the late winter of 1756. Elizabeth was the daughter of Dr. Thomas Graeme, a member of the Governor's Council and one of Benjamin's political rivals. It did not please Benjamin that his son was dancing every week with the daughter of a political enemy. When Benjamin founded the Pennsylvania hospital and, as president, hired its first staff, he did not hire Graeme. Graeme never forgave him. Opposition from both armed camps did not deter William from courting Betsy and, one year later, proposing marriage to her. Their engagement came at a time when Benjamin was determined to break the Penn family's control of Pennsylvania.

After Benjamin was appointed the Assembly's agent to Parliament, he had his son appointed the clerk of the mission. William wanted to know why he should leave the promise of a marriage that assured not only his happiness but his success. To win over his son, Benjamin offered to pay the young man's expenses to study law at the Middle Temple, thus assuring he would be admitted to the London bar and become a leading American lawyer. He also wrote a new will, making William his heir and executor as well as leaving him a legacy equal to five years of his current income, a house, a town lot, his father's extensive library, and all his scientific apparatus. These tempting opportunities proved too much for William. When he proposed a secret marriage, Betsy, apparently afraid to infuriate her father, declined. They postponed their wedding until he returned. After he reached London, their letters grew shorter and fewer. Soon, William stopped writing Betsy altogether.

During his first year in London, William crammed massive doses of law. By the end of the autumn term of 1758, he was ready to stand before the Masters of the Bench at Middle Temple Hall for a grueling oral examination. On November 10, after proceeding with his classmates down the aisle of Westminster Abbey, William Franklin, bastard son of a provincial printer, was called to the English bar. That evening, at the Middle Temple, William Franklin, Esquire, took his turn at the dark little table made from a hatch cover of Sir Francis Drake's flagship, *Golden Hind*, and signed the call book. Then he was invited up to the Bench. He had become an English gentleman.

England's foremost publisher, William Strahan, described William as "one of the prettiest young gentlemen I ever knew." William went to work in the law office of the influential barrister, Richard Jackson, who introduced him to influential friends. He accompanied Jackson to fashionable Tunbridge Wells spa with his good friends, Dr. Johnson, Mrs. Thrale, and the actor David Garrick. William, Benjamin, and "Omniscient" Jackson, as he was known, collaborated on *An Historical Review of the Government and Constitution of Pennsylvania*, an incendiary anti-Penn book that verged on libel and sedition. In private, Benjamin gave William much of the credit: "Billy afforded great assistance and furnished most of the materials," he wrote. Benjamin was clearly pleased by the effort. He shipped five hundred copies back to Philadelphia for sale in his bookstore. William packed several dozen copies of the book into their carriage to give to influential politicians as they toured England and Scotland together in the summer of 1759. Benjamin called this tour "six weeks of the densest happiness I have ever met with in any part of my life."

But for William, now twenty-nine, living and working at such close quarters was beginning to gall. He wanted a career and a private life of his own. He sought both in London. He gave up the idea of marrying Betsy Graeme and joined wholeheartedly in the society of Northumberland House. Next to a direct royal summons to the Court of St. James, an invitation there was a sure sign of Court favor and of a young man's chances to rise in the new imperial society and find a substantial post in the expanding colonial service. It must have been at one of the Friday evening parties there that he met a golden-skinned, languidly gracious beauty named Elizabeth Downes, daughter of a Barbados sugar planter. By the spring of 1761, a new king, George III, waited to be crowned and all England seemed to angle for his favors. William and Elizabeth became fixtures in London society, dancing at balls, strolling in St. James Park, and frequently attending the theatre in Covent Garden.

So high was William's star rising that he was invited to the coronation of George III. William marched in the royal procession into Westminster Hall and to an assigned seat while Benjamin had to stand outside. Three weeks afterward, a new prime minister, the Earl of Bute, began a shakeup of royal posts. On August 20, 1762, Lord Bute informed the Board of Trade that the King "was pleased to appoint William Franklin, Esq. to be Governor of Nova Caesarea, or New Jersey." For the rest of William's life, it was his glory that he was the first royal governor appointéd by the new King. But at this hour of his son's greatest triumph, Benjamin Franklin left England without him. Four days before he was sworn in as governor, William married Elizabeth Downes. Benjamin was absent for this event in his son's life as well.

On the icy morning of February 25, 1763, a gay cavalcade of sleigh-riding aristocrats rode out to welcome William and Elizabeth Franklin into the eastern capital of Perth Amboy, one of the Province of New Jersey's two government centers. Indeed, as the townspeople managed a swirling welcome, there was little to hint that Franklin, already a career politician, would remain in the Jerseys any longer than it had taken his predecessors to find more lucrative posts elsewhere in His Majesty's service. If he planned to base his career on his first experience administering a colony, there were challenges enough in governing the 70,000 farmers and townspeople. Sixty years of royal rule had done little more than unite the two Jerseys on paper. There was no governor's residence, no government buildings, no acceptable boundary line, few good roads and bridges, no thriving seaport, and only one incipient college at Princeton. Worse still, from Governor Franklin's standpoint, each winter and summer the governor was obliged to curry favor among penny-pinching legislators to have his salary renewed, hopefully at no decrease, for it was cynically assumed he would find some device for enhancing his meager allowance.

If he succeeded in keeping the delicate peace among liberal western Quakers, conservative eastern gentry, and thousands of riot-prone Scotch-Irish squatters in the north, and if he somehow followed the time-lapsed, unsympathetic, yet dreadfully precise instructions of the remote Commissioners of Trade in London, he could expect, in a reasonable number of years, advancement out of the colony. At first it appeared young Franklin faced the additional handicap of his shadowy birth. "It is no less amazing than true," wrote irate Pennsylvania proprietor John Penn to his friend, William Alexander in New Jersey, "if any gentleman had been appointed it would have been a difference ... I make no doubt but the people of New Jersey will make some remonstrance upon this indignity put upon them."

If the legislators assembling in the western provincial capital of Burlington in May 1763 objected to the bar sinister on the new governor's coat-of-arms, they had a strange way of showing it. They increased his salary by a healthy £200 and voted him a housing allowance. Apparently many were pleased with his good sense in passing up the proffered invitation to reside in the eastern capital of Perth Amboy to dwell in the nearly completed Proprietary Palace, a symbol of faction between poor rural voters and land-rich proprietors.

Instead, he chose the bustling river town of Burlington, seat of Quaker dominance only seventeen miles upriver from Philadelphia. He began buying area real estate. He built a handsome three-story brick house of his own. He could sit on the columned porch, look out over the broad lawn to the sycamore-lined Delaware River and ponder the persistent problems that plagued every governor in the colony's colonial history: insufficient currency, almost no foreign exchange, simmering feuds over land titles and no way to pay official salaries without, from his viewpoint, grovelling before the Assembly. From his veranda, he could see a possible solution to this last problem. In the Delaware River were unclaimed islands with rich farmland. It occurred to him that this land might be annexed by the Crown, rented back to farmers, and the income thus realized earmarked to pay official salaries. He communicated this scheme to London at once.

While there was no guarantee that the Assembly would abide such a barefaced grab for its power over the pursestrings, it was nevertheless ominous for Franklin that the Commissioners of Trade in London ignored the request and left Franklin's administration at the mercy of the Assembly. Without support from London on this key issue, it would be virtually impossible for him to untangle the colony's fiscal problems, which multiplied as the era of post-French and Indian War economic decline set in.

While New Jersey had minor casualties at the hands of marauding Indians along its exposed northwest frontier, it had gained great dividends in the war. Great Britain poured in troops who freely spent hard-earned money. Parliament paid subsidies to the Jerseymen that were applied, in an early example of revenue-sharing, to eliminate provincial taxes. The hungry war machine exchanged hard coin-of-the-realm for hemp, black oak, and pine for shipbuilding; wheat, corn, and cotton; barrel hoops and staves; and anything that could assist in the worldwide struggle.

In a temporary lapse of mercantilism and the royal prerogative, the British allowed the Assembly to issue paper money, which debt-ridden colonists shrewdly sent to creditors in England to retire long-standing accounts. But the boom swung back at war's end, the artificial prosperity deflated, and the second-smallest populace of any colony in America woke up saddled with a £300,000 debt, the highest in America. While the American colonial debt averaged eighteen shillings, in New Jersey it amounted to £15 for every male between the ages of eighteen and sixty, rivalling the £18 burden of England! As the depression deepened, Parliament seized the moment to reassert its right to regulate colonial currency. In February 1764 they outlawed paper money as legal tender. Parliament also claimed the absolute power of taxation, serving notice of its intent to impose a stamp tax—similar to England's—on all newspapers and legal instruments to help defray the cost of maintaining a 10,000-man garrison in America. Jerseymen groaned at the news.

Governor Franklin, as part of an unprecedented legislative package of thirty-five bills, proposed and won London's approval of trade-nourishing bounties on hemp, flax, and silk, apparently was no less surprised than most Americans.

One trained observer, Woodbridge printer James Parker (erstwhile partner of Benjamin Franklin), denounced the stamp tax in a letter to Attorney-General Cortlandt Skinner:

> There is such a general scarcity of cash that nothing we have will command it and real estates of every kind are falling at least one-half in value. Debtors that were a year or two ago responsible for £1000 can not now raise a fourth part of the sum .... There is an entire stop to all sales by the sheriffs for want of buyers, and men of the best estates amongst us can scarce raise money enough to defray the necessary expenses of their families .... Under the insupportable distress we are now called upon for many thousands of pounds sterling to be paid by a stamp duty.

Parker, secretary of the British postal service in America, issued the first revolutionary newspaper, the *Constitutional Courant*, on September 21, 1765. The paper, which was distributed on the streets of New York City and along country roads by post riders, was quickly suppressed.

Again setting the pattern for other colonies, New Jersey's lawyers met in Perth Amboy on September 19, 1765, and agreed to conduct no business requiring the obnoxious stamps. This meant no business at all. Five months later, when they met again, many were suffering hardships from their protest. All were under pressure from the presence of 800 Sons of Liberty. The lawyers voted to suspend business until April 1, 1776, when, if the law was not repealed, they would break it and resume practice without using stamps, giving in to the wishes of the radicals.

All over New Jersey, there were protests. When the stamps arrived off New York on the *Royal Charlotte*, Franklin, on the advice of a member of his advisory Council, William Alexander, refused to let them be landed, saying there was no safe place on the entire coast. The stamp commissioner, William Coxe was refused the rental of a house unless he could guarantee it would not be pulled to pieces by the mob. He resigned before the law took effect, forfeiting a £3,000 bond. To make sure he did not reconsider, the New Brunswick Sons of Liberty followed him all the way to Philadelphia, coercing him to take an oath not to handle the stamps.

Pleading that he had no clear instructions from London, Governor Franklin exhibited uncommon diplomacy during the crisis. Since there was no collector for stamps and no armed place in New Jersey to protect them, he arranged to have a British troop contingent on alert in New York, and had the stamps transferred to HMS *Sardoine*, anchored in the harbor off Perth Amboy. When the captain asserted that he had to put the ship into drydock and strip it of its guns for the winter, Governor Franklin stalled, appealing to Lieutenant Governor Cadwallader Colden of New York for permission to store the stamps at Fort George. That would be impossible, Colden replied, because the fort was filled with troops and supplies. There simply was no room! Turning to the Royal Navy again, he convinced the *Sardoine's* captain to take the stamps wherever he planned to keep his ship's stores for the winter, reasoning shrewdly that the citizens of one colony would not attack the stamps of another.

Despite Governor Franklin's efforts at discouraging the Assembly, the legislators met at Sproul's Tavern in Perth Amboy after he had dissolved the House and voted to send delegates to a continental Stamp Congress in New York. When New

Frick Art Reference Library

Benjamin Franklin's son, William, was a British royal governor and Loyalist leader. His father disinherited him.

Jersey Speaker Robert Ogden refused to sign the resulting petition to the King, he was burned in effigy all over New Jersey and felt obliged to resign promptly from public life.

At this time, Benjamin Franklin's long involvement in Philadelphia politics bore bitter fruit. The Proprietary Party, accusing the Franklins of fostering the Stamp Act—and William in particular of trying to block the New Jersey delegates from attending the New York Congress—publicly libeled him. Forced to issue broadsides throughout the city, William hurried to the Franklin home in

Philadelphia, where his mother Deborah and his sister Sarah had armed and barricaded themselves along with friends against the menacing mobs.

By now, William Franklin, thoroughly shaken, appealed to the public press. His absolute denial of any involvement in the Stamp Act swung the mob's wrath away from him. Fortunately, word reached Philadelphia of his father's brilliant defense of American rights before the House of Commons. Young Franklin, somewhat aged by the affair, admitted he had feared his house would be "pulled down about my ears and all my effects destroyed." When news of repeal reached Burlington, the governor and his lady joined the public celebration, firing off two small cannons on his lawn and joining in eighteen toasts, to everyone's obvious relief.

Young Franklin was sympathetic to the Whig-American cause. He referred to "the people" while other Crown officials deplored "the mob." He openly refused to support the hated Customs Service as the stamp crisis was followed by the Townshend crisis, and a burgeoning smuggling industry developed in Cape May, Delaware Bay, and Little Egg Harbor Inlet. Jerseymen were startled to find they had a governor who was not afraid to compromise to uphold the Crown's prerogative. He often had to bully the Assembly. While he seems to have despaired of wringing a higher salary and living allowance from the legislators and dropped his plans for a suitable official residence in the face of widespread economic dislocation, he pushed vigorously for badly needed reforms. His welfare plan to feed and clothe destitute Sussex and Monmouth County farmers, his support of the Anglican Church's retired clergy, his espousal of a second college in the colony (Rutgers), his campaign for more and better roads and bridges built with the proceeds of public lotteries, and most of all, his successful eleven-year battle for a loan office to issue paper money to alleviate the cash shortage and to self-liquidate government operational expenses, all were visionary pieces of liberal legislation years ahead of their time. And while each excited the wrath of various factions, they combined to free him to pursue a grander scheme.

When the British, by the Proclamation of 1763, took over the huge wedge of real estate bordered by the Ohio and Mississippi Rivers and the Appalachian Mountain chain, the land was reserved as an Indian reservation under Crown protection. But part of the plan was to drive off thousands of squatters and subsequently to sell the land and provide a large source of quit-rents to reduce the national debt and defray costs of the royal military establishment.

The Franklins, father and son, along with leading Quaker merchants in Philadelphia and Indian agents in New York, grasped the possibility of creating new provinces, one of which was to be called Vandalia (much of present-day Indiana and Illinois). Long before promoting the development of this colony, Governor Franklin had explored the territory with Conrad Weiser.

It was crucial to keep friendly relations with the Indians inhabiting the lands. The Franklins surreptitiously pursued this end with pen and sword, leading the unpopular protest against the Paxton Boys' massacre of Christianized Conestoga Indians in Lancaster County, Pennsylvania in 1764, and the similar killing of peaceful Indians in northwestern New Jersey. Their plan was bold and it cost the elder Franklin his Assembly seat in the bitter 1764 election. This stand permanently antagonized frontier Jerseymen against William Franklin when he insisted on hanging the white murderers of Native Americans.

Meanwhile, Governor Franklin expanded his real estate holdings, buying up valuable lands in New York and New Jersey. Acquiring 575 acres of choice river-front in Burlington county, he turned his country estate, Franklin Park, into a showcase scientific farm, where he conducted experiments in husbandry, tilling, and breeding that he evidently intended to practice on a grander scale farther west. It is apparent from his outspoken stands before the Assembly that he was sure his great scheme would ultimately succeed. He accused them of neglecting the public welfare by ignoring his programs of public works and crop bounties. He obviously hoped to be royal governor of a new western province.

After a decade of push and tug, Governor Franklin and the Assembly finally parted company in 1773 over the theft of the tax returns of East Jersey from a trunk in the home of Treasurer Stephen Skinner. Although Franklin had the Samuel Ford gang hunted down and two of its members confessed the theft of £7,854 from the Treasurer's house, the Assembly insisted that the wealthy Perth Amboy aristocrat had been negligent. Refusing to investigate further, they demanded restitution from Skinner and his resignation. Franklin, angrily protesting this incursion on the royal prerogative, doggedly held on for five months until Skinner finally resigned. This public furor masked a deeper malaise, however, brought on by the increasing frequency of mob violence centering in Essex County. Many of its residents were transplanted New Englanders with radical views who for nearly thirty years had intermittently rioted against the East Jersey proprietors, mobbed crown officials, and managed to keep their leaders out of jail.

Governor Franklin saw the storm clouds gathering. By now the Vandalia charter seemed a distant dream, as officials in London went out of their way to destroy the Franklins. The younger Franklin, tarred as a radical along with his father, came under suspicion and was passed over for promotion to the governorship of Barbados, birthplace of his ailing wife. Late in 1773, Governor Franklin, angered that his father's politics had damaged him and irritated that his father thought him so subservient, took a bold step. Placing Franklin Park and his Burlington mansion on the market, he moved the seat of government to Perth Amboy, where he could be near his few close friends on the Council in the growing crisis.

His move to the magnificent Proprietary House, with its marble floors, rich paneling, and stables for twelve carriage horses, seems to have severed him from Whig affections as much as his loyalty to the Perth Amboy aristocracy. This finally brought him within the orbit of the very Tories who had once spurned this bastard but now sought the comfort and protection of his official presence. By now his enemies were many, powerful and determined to bring him down.

Governor Franklin was sickened by the growing dissension. Soon after hearing of his father's disgrace before the Privy Council, William urged him to come home. They had drifted apart ideologically over the years. The son, the younger Franklin, remained the more moderate. The father, the elder Franklin, had decided by 1774 that:

> Parliament has no right to make any law whatever binding on the Colonies.... I know your sentiments differ from mine on these subjects. You are a thorough government

man, which I do not wonder at, nor do I aim at converting you. I only wish you to act uprightly and steadily, avoiding that duplicity which … adds contempt to indignation. If you can promote the prosperity of your people and leave them happier than you found them, whatever your political principles are, your memory will be honored.

While it was evident that the two Franklins had parted politically, the son feared for the safety of his father. Writing to him December 24, 1774, he pleaded with him to come home:

If there was any prospect of your being able to bring the people in power to your way of thinking, or of those of your way of thinking being brought into power, I should not think so much of your stay. But as you have had pretty strong proofs that neither can be reasonably expected and that you are looked upon with an evil eye in that Country, you had certainly better return.

By September 1774, as the First Continental Congress assembled at Philadelphia to protest the closing of the Boston port after the Tea Party, Governor Franklin and his good friend Joseph Galloway, Speaker of the Pennsylvania Assembly, had decided that what would make their people happiest would be peace. If Benjamin Franklin had abandoned hope for reconciliation, the younger men must make the effort. Galloway modified the plan of union the elder Franklin had advanced in Albany twenty years earlier. He argued passionately in the Continental Congress for a continental legislature co-equal with Parliament and presided over by a Supreme Executive appointed by the King. The plan was tabled by Congress by a narrow six to five vote. This followed a last-ditch attack by the New England democrats who bitterly opposed an Anglo-American commonwealth. However, it was praised in New York and London after the plan was forwarded to England.

As the determined Sons of Liberty enforced nonimportation in New Jersey and as protest and recruitment flourished, events swept past Governor Franklin, leaving this erstwhile Whig moderate a dogged conservative in their wake. In January, 1775 even before the bloodletting at Lexington-Concord, he gravely addressed the New Jersey Assembly:

It is not for me to decide on the particular merits of the dispute between Great Britain and her colonies, nor do I mean to censure those who conceive themselves aggrieved for aiming at a redress of the grievances. It is a duty they owe themselves, their country, and their posterity. All that I could wish to guard you against is the giving any countenance or encouragement to that destructive mode of proceeding…. You have now pointed out to you, gentlemen, two roads, one evidently leading to peace, happiness, and a restoration of the public tranquility—the other inevitably conducting you to anarchy, misery and all the horrors of a civil war.

This sober appeal served to suspend New Jersey in the eye of the hurricane for many months until news thundered south over the old Post Road that farmers and redcoats had clashed bloodily outside Boston. Everywhere, instantly, militia met, marched and drilled. Citizens associated, swore oaths, and enforced them. They seized and disarmed recalcitrant Tories, purging them from their ranks.

In a bitter falling-out, Governor Franklin purged Lord Stirling from his Council for accepting a militia command. Stirling, raiding British mails, intercepted Franklin's "secret and confidential" official correspondence to London, and with the approval of Congress ordered a guard placed on the governor's palace at Perth Amboy at 2 A.M. on January 8, 1776.

In this climate, Governor Franklin prevailed on the Assembly to instruct its delegates to Congress against independence and instead to petition legally, through him, to the King for redress of grievances. The Assembly agreed. Alarmed, Congress sent three delegates to Burlington to argue against a separate peace. The Assembly wavered and fell into line—"not wanting to appear singular." An angry Governor Franklin refused to forward their petition.

Upon receiving a special message of King and Parliament offering limited grounds for negotiation, Governor Franklin, now the last hope of reconciliation, summoned the Assembly to meet on June 10. The rebel New Jersey Provincial Congress, in urgent session, decided that this was in direct contempt of a Continental Congress resolution "that it is necessary that every kind of government under the Crown should be suppressed." The Provincial Congress ruled that the governor had "acted in direct contempt and violation of the resolve of the Continental Congress" and ordered his arrest.

For months, the courageous Franklin had stayed on in the face of personal danger, long after other royal officials had fled. His gallant stand, which he justified by saying he would not give Congress the excuse of creating a government because he had left none, masked his fear. In a letter to Lord Dartmouth in September 1775 he wrote, "It would mortify me extremely to be seized upon and led like a bear through the country to some place of confinement in New England."

Only a month after he was taken in June 1776 from his ailing wife—who would flee to New York and die there without seeing him again—the great British fleet arrived off Perth Amboy and the Governor's father came to negotiate with the British peace commissioners. There is room to speculate what a difference the presence of both Franklins would have made at the parley.

By then, however, he had been tried by a court he refused to recognize, insulted by its president, the Reverend John Witherspoon, president of the College of New Jersey, because of his "exalted birth," and guarded so closely he sometimes could not "answer nature's call." Then he was led off, as he had dreaded, to Connecticut and a succession of ever-worsening prisons. Two years later he was released after 250 days in solitary confinement in Litchfield Jail without clean clothing, furniture, books, pen, or paper and nearly starved: "considerably reduced in flesh."

Before the long civil war ended, Governor Franklin stood accused of authorizing, as president of the Board of Associated Loyalists, the brutal retaliatory hanging of a rebel officer. In the ensuing furor, he was never allowed to testify and was bundled off to Britain, ostensibly to plead the Loyalist cause.

But the most bitter hour had already passed, as his wife lay dying and the Continental Congress refused him a pass to see her one last time. Certainly it would only have taken a word from his father to see that his only son received mercy should he ever need it. But the father would never forgive the son. He would do all he could to chastise all Loyalists at the signing of the Treaty of Paris ending the war in 1783. He would go to *his* grave denouncing William in his will. It seems ironic that William Franklin, who had much more to forgive, would try to heal the open wounds in his shattered family. He went to *his* grave in exile in London in 1813, writing of their dream of so long ago, of the new land in the West he and his father had envisioned.

QUESTIONS FOR THOUGHT AND DISCUSSION

1. In what ways did William Franklin build on the career of his more famous father?

2. How did William Franklin secure the position of royal governor of New Jersey? Why was this not an easy time to serve as a crown-appointed governor?

3. In what ways did William Franklin's experience and personal lifestyle lead him toward greater sympathy with the British point of view when the Revolution neared? Can you understand his Loyalist sentiments?

4. Why do you think Benjamin Franklin could never forgive his son for his loyalty to England? Was the elder Franklin wrong in failing to reconcile with William?

SUGGESTED READINGS

Fennelly, Catherine. "William Franklin of New Jersey." *William and Mary Quarterly*, 3d ser., (1949): 362–382.

Randall, Willard Sterne. *A Little Revenge: Benjamin Franklin and His Son*. Boston: Little, 1984.

_____. *The Proprietary House at Amboy*. Trenton, N.J.: Whitechapel, 1975.

_____. "William Franklin: The Making of a Conservative." In East, Robert A. and Jacob Judd. *The Loyalist Americans: A Focus on Greater New York*. Tarrytown, N.Y.: Sleepy Hollow Restorations, 1975.

Wright, Esmond. *Franklin of Philadelphia*. Cambridge, Mass.: Belknap, 1985.

7

Tadeusz Kosciuszko

The American Revolution has traditionally been portrayed as an all-English war with a French accent on the American side, a war of the WASPs (White Anglo-Saxon Protestants), a war in which English American colonists were trying to break away from the English mother country, as well as a civil war between Englishmen for and against American independence from England. In fact, more and more modern research shows that it was a struggle in which at least twenty different non-English ethnic groups fought, in which very few Englishmen actually took part, and in which many of the Americans were not of English origins. Careful analysis of the long struggle for American independence shows that minority groups contributed significantly to the American side.

A HISTORY OF the Revolution based on evidence would present a rich ethnic tapestry, not an all-white, all-WASP mythology. Among other things, it would have much less of an English accent. Revolutionary politics and the ranks of revolutionary soldiers included Czechs, Poles, Hungarians, Greeks, Danes, Swedes, Italians, Bohemians, Dutch, Germans, Scots, Irish, Scots-Irish, Swiss, French, African Americans, Native Americans, Protestants, Catholics, and Jews. The British Army was preponderantly made up of Irish, Scottish, and German mercenaries. In fact, more Germans fought on the English side than Englishmen. British Major General James Robertson, who had served in the American colonies for a quarter century, reported that half the rebels were Irish. This estimate accords with the testimony of Joseph Galloway, a Loyalist Pennsylvanian, before the English Parliament. A modern Irish historian has concluded that thirty-eight percent of the soldiers were Irish.

Yet Galloway and Robertson may not have been differentiating between Irish Catholics and Protestant Scots-Irish like Charles Thomson. His ancestors had settled in Ireland temporarily and re-migrated to America in the first half of the eighteenth century after enduring frequent crop failures and increasingly repressive English laws and taxes. Thousands of Scots-Irish came to America in the 1770s when the linen-weaving industry collapsed in Ulster. By 1776, an estimated 300,000 Scots-Irish had come to the mainland English colonies of America. Many Scots-Irish, like

Patrick Henry, who became the first governor of Virginia, and Charles Thomson, who served as Secretary of all the Continental Congresses, took active roles in the earliest protests against the British. Others, like John Rutledge, took part in the Continental Congress's debate over independence. Still others, like Henry Knox, Washington's chief of artillery, fought all through the eight-year-long war.

The Scots-Irish were only slightly more numerous than German immigrants. By 1776, at least 225,000 Germans of at least 250 different Protestant sects migrated to America in the wake of European religious wars. Many of them left behind the constant warfare of Europe only to march off to the war for America, some with clergymen like Frederick Muhlenberg. Other Germans came not to settle but to fight beside the Americans. Most notable was Baron von Steuben, a Prussian professional soldier who drilled the American troops at Valley Forge into a tightly disciplined, highly maneuverable army. Steuben stayed in the new United States after the Revolution. So did 12,562 of the 29,875 German mercenaries brought mostly against their wills, who were rented out by their feudal overlords to fight on the British side.

Ethnic Americans took part in virtually every military engagement. Polish American sailors in the crew of the American ship, the *Bon Homme Richard*, fought under a famous Scottish-American captain, John Paul Jones, lobbing grenades into the powder magazine of the British man-of-war *Serapis* until it exploded and sank. Thirteen-year-old Italian-American Pascal de Angelis fought under Benedict Arnold in the naval Battle of Valcour Island on Lake Champlain that saved the new United States from being cut in two by British armies and navies in 1776. Twenty Hungarian hussars came to America to fight under their Polish friend, Casimir Pulaski. Pulaski was a dashing cavalry officer who did stunt riding outside Washington's headquarters at Morristown to attract the commander-in-chief's attention. He commanded four cavalry regiments in the South until he was killed.

Two regiments of Italians recruited in their homeland fought under the French flag at Yorktown while their countryman, Filippo Mazzei (Thomas Jefferson's next door neighbor in Virginia), took a musket and marched off as a private in 1776. Then he went to Italy as Virginia's diplomatic agent to drum up financial and political support in Florence for the American cause by writing pamphlets and books. Joseph Vigo, an Italian who left his Piedmont home, came to New Orleans with a Spanish regiment and became a leading Mississippi Valley fur trader. When George Rogers Clark captured Vincennes and British troops recaptured it, Vigo found himself caught between the lines. He carefully observed British troop strengths and gun positions. Released because of his Spanish citizenship, Vigo supplied vital information to Clark in time for the American counterattack—as well as badly needed money and excellent credit that helped the Americans recapture Vincennes. By pledging his entire fortune to help the American cause, Vigo helped to extend American territory into the modern-day Midwest. Greek knights journeyed to America and fought as volunteers under the French Marquis de Lafayette in Virginia; at least half a dozen Greek-American patriots suffered the horrors of imprisonment on the disease-ridden British prison ship, the *Jersey*.

North and South, African Americans fought on both sides, both sides offering them freedom if they survived. An estimated 7,500 blacks fought under

Washington, and more than double that number fought on the British side. Throughout the war, Jewish Americans fought, suffered, and often gave all they had to keep the Revolution and its armies and navies alive. Many revolutionary leaders had no income as they served in Congress, relying on the generosity of patriots. James Madison wrote, "When any member of the revolutionary Congress was in need, all that was necessary was to call [Haym] Solomon." Bernard and Michael Gratz equipped the 150 Virginians who made the original surprise attack on the Old Northwest. Moses Levy as partner of Robert Morris built and crewed privateering warships that captured and destroyed British shipping. The Jews of Charleston, South Carolina, marched off in the Jews Company to defend their city against invading British and German forces. Colonel Mordicai Sheftall acted as Commissary General for the southern Continental army and was held prisoner on a British prison ship with his sixteen-year-old son for two years in horrible conditions and with very little food. Jacob Pinto of New Haven, Connecticut, a member of the town's revolutionary committee, and his brother, Benjamin, fought in the 7th Regiment of the elite Continental Line.

A leading Jewish-American revolutionary was David Salisbury Franks. Only days after the fighting had started at Lexington in 1775, a crowd gathered in Montreal, Canada, where King George III's bust had been smeared with a coat of black paint. Young David Franks, who was to become Benedict Arnold's aide-de-camp, admitted his handiwork and was dragged off to jail. When Arnold led an American invasion of Canada later that year, Franks did everything he could to organize French Canadians to fight on the American side. When the Americans retreated south, he went with them and enlisted in a Massachusetts regiment. Arnold's treason meant a court martial for Major Franks, who cleared his name and, at war's end, was honored by being asked by Congress to carry the signed treaty of peace to Paris.

One of the many unsung ethnic heroes of the Revolution was Tadeusz Kosciuszko, the impoverished son of Polish gentry who fled his homeland after he tried to elope with the daughter of a nobleman who then ordered his arrest. Tadeusz studied at the French royal military academy, Ecole Militaire, in Paris, and the royal artillery and engineering school at Mezieres, and specialized in river and harbor defenses. Kos, as the American officers called him (Washington misspelled his name eleven different ways), came to Philadelphia in 1776 as a volunteer military engineer. He quickly showed he had a genius for river fortifications and was thoroughly grounded in European warfare. The Continental Congress commissioned him as colonel of engineers for the Northern Department. But before he could ride north, Benjamin Franklin, in charge of defending Pennsylvania, commandeered Kosciuszko's talents. Together, they planned the elaborate network that was to impede the expected British attack on the American capital. More than 5,000 men— one in five Philadelphians—joined the gigantic defense-building effort that began in the summer of 1776 and lasted until the British attack came in October, 1777.

On the New Jersey shore opposite present-day Philadelphia International Airport, Kosciuszko laid out two forts on the marshy banks of the Delaware River. Fort Billings, the first parcel of federal land, was purchased by Congress on July 5, 1776. Kosciuszko created a large, 180-foot square redoubt with strong points at the corners, parapets for riflemen, and walls pierced for eighteen heavy guns. On the land side, he laid out earthen breastworks and a deep ditch, or fosse, filled with felled trees. The branches of the trees were sharpened to impede infantry attack.

The main purpose of Fort Billings was to protect the downstream end of *chevaux de frise*. These barricades were French river defenses submerged to pierce the hulls of ships passing over them and hold the ships while the fort's guns poured cannon fire into them. Floated to the assembly area at Gloucester, New Jersey, were 239 extremely tough hemlock timbers, fifteen to twenty inches thick. Pine timbers were lashed to the bottoms and sides of these to form giant cribs sixty feet long. Damaging iron-tipped prongs, some of them seventy feet long, were attached and braced with iron straps and angles. The cribs were floated out into the channel, each loaded with thirty tons of rock rafted down the Schuylkill River on barges from the quarries of Conshohocken, Pennsylvania. They were then sunk by removing plugs from their sides and bottoms. Submerged six or seven feet below the waterline, the iron-tipped spikes spread out into a deadly, sixty-foot-wide fan. In all, there were seventy uncharted *chevaux de frise*, spread over eight miles of river between the guns of Fort Billings and Fort Mercer, the second fort built by Kosciuszko.

Fort Mercer, at Red Bank above present-day Woodbury, New Jersey, showed Kosciuszko's dual genius as engineer and artilleryman. Its guns could fire down from a forty-foot high bluff to link up with gunfire from Fort Mifflin, across the mile-wide Delaware, both guarding the approaches to the *chevaux de frise*. Any British ship that slowed down to pick its way through the underwater trap came under heavy fire from Fort Mercer. Because of its elevation, it was high above the reach of British naval guns. It was also virtually impervious to amphibious assault by British ground forces because of its formidable landward defenses.

To the north of the fort, a dirt road ran due west from Deptford and Haddonfield, New Jersey. The road was flanked by heavy woods to the south and swamps to the north. Kosciuszko ordered orchards cut down to make a clear field of fire and had deep trenches dug around the fort's walls, which ran from north to south 350 yards. Then he laid out long, low breastworks for 200 yards to protect infantry along the river bluff. A moat filled with the standard abatis of sharpened trees and protected by breastworks made up the outerworks. It was to be manned by sharpshooters to slow down attack on the main fort, a solid-looking earth-and-log redoubt with walls fifteen feet high and twelve feet thick.

General Washington, headquartered farther upriver at Whitemarsh, sent two French officers from his staff, his aide, Marquis de Lafayette, and his chief engineer, Chevalier Mauduit du Plessis, to inspect Kosciuszko's work at Fort Mercer in early October 1777. They found the fort lightly garrisoned by two companies of Rhode Island Continentals, black troops (three fourths of them slaves who had been promised their freedom in exchange for military service), and black freemen under the command of a tough former Quaker, Colonel Christopher Greene. The black troops, Lafayette reported to Washington, were waiting grimly behind eighteen heavy guns. At du Plessis' suggestion, Colonel Greene built another embankment between the inner and outer works on the north side to conceal a hidden artillery battery. Here, on the New Jersey shore, a decisive battle was about to take place pitting forces that were almost exclusively non-English against each other.

Culver Pictures

Among the twenty nationalities fighting in the Revolution, few men contributed more to the fight against the British than Polish engineer Tadeusz Kosciuszko.

The British attack came soon enough. On October 11, a combined land-sea attack by 2,000 British regulars encircled Fort Billings downriver. Only six cannon had arrived: they all faced the river and were quite useless against the land attack. During the night, the 350-man garrison of New Jersey militia spiked the cannon so they would blow up if the British tried to use them. The bakehouse, barracks, and stockade were all blown up, and the garrison retreated toward Fort Mercer. Before they could reinforce it, British ships opened fire on Fort Mercer. The British, in turn, came under fire from Pennsylvania Navy galleys anchored at the foot of the bluffs under Fort Mercer's guns. While the Pennsylvania vessels, small, open boats propelled by oars and sails, would be no match for the British men-of-war in a naval battle, they managed to deter an amphibious landing.

The brunt of the British attack came from the land side. The assault was entrusted to Hessian mercenaries led by thirty-seven-year-old Count Karl Emil von Donop, an able field commander still smarting from his defeat by Washington at Princeton the winter before. Some 3,400 Hessians marched from their base at present-day Camden to Deptford, where they rested for the night. There, they were observed by an American named Jonas Cattell, a fleet-footed courier who ran nine miles from Deptford to Fort Mercer that night to warn the garrison. Until then, the attack had been expected from the water. All that night, the African-American soldiers from Rhode Island sweated as they hauled the big guns around to the land side to set their trap. Posting sharpshooters inside the outer breastworks, Colonel Greene placed two heavy guns, double-loaded with grape-sized shot and canisters of shrapnel, inside the tree-branch-and-brush-camouflaged inner embankment.

Drums beating and bugles blaring, the Hessians paraded down the lane at noon the next day. They fanned out to form a cordon that extended from swamps to a flat plain south of the fort. Swinging down from his brown stallion, von Donop handed the reins to an aide and told him to carry this message to Greene: "The King of England orders his rebellious subjects to lay down their arms and they are warned that if they stand the battle, no quarters [mercy] whatsoever will be given." Greene shouted back his reply: "We'll see King George damned first! We want no quarter and we'll give none."

Hessian axemen attacked from north and south under a galling fire from the walls of the fort. They hacked through the sharpened abatis as grenadiers bayoneted their way through the thin line of African-American skirmishers in the south ditch. Then hundreds of screaming Hessians charged the walls. A few made it to the top before they were riddled with point-blank fire. On the north side, at the first Hessian volley the black Americans, as planned, fired once and then dropped back. Charging and huzzahing wildly, the Hessians poured over the outer breastworks and into the inner defenses, racing toward the high north wall.

Then, yanking away tree branches, the hidden American gun crews fired. Count von Donop, leading the charge, was shot in the hip, chest, and face at such close range that the cannon's cotton wadding was imbedded in his face. Blinded, he fell along with scores of his German veterans and fifteen other officers. From the river, the Pennsylvania Navy gunboats, many of their crewmen also free blacks from Philadelphia, opened a crossfire against Hessians attempting to scale the west wall. More German grenadiers were mowed down.

Inside fifteen minutes, the Battle of Fort Mercer was over. The surviving Hessians ran back to the woods and jettisoned their cannon in a creek. They paused long enough to fashion stretchers with their muskets for wounded officers before fleeing back to Woodbury. They left 414 dead and dying on the field, in the ditches, and sprawled all over the fort. Count von Donop died slowly and painfully in a house nearby, nursed for nine days by Chevalier Mauduit. Numerically, it was the greatest American victory of the Revolution. Only twenty-four revolutionaries were killed or wounded, nineteen of them when a carelessly swabbed cannon exploded while being loaded.

That night the furious British Navy command tried to maneuver its sixty-four-gun flagship, HMS *Augusta,* and its eighteen-gun escorting sloop-of-war, *Merlin,* through the upper *chevaux de frise* to avenge the defeat. Both ran aground. At dawn, the black Americans inside Fort Mercer discovered the ships' plight and poured in more than 100 cannonballs, many of them heated in a special furnace. Both British men-of-war were set afire. The powder magazine of the *Augusta* exploded with such force that windows shattered twenty miles upriver at Washington's headquarters. The *Merlin* was so badly damaged it had to be scuttled. It would take the British forty more days before they could clear out the river. They settled down, stunned, in Philadelphia, and never attempted, all that crucial winter of 1777–78, to crush Washington's army starving in the nearby hills of Valley Forge.

But by late October, the British had more bad news. Kosciuszko had gone north and had helped to lay another trap at a place called Saratoga, New York. For weeks, the American army had been slowly retreating in the face of a British invasion from Canada. Sent to strengthen the American fortifications at Fort Ticonderoga on the southern tip of Lake Champlain, Kosciuszko had been ignored when he urged the placement of artillery on the highest hill overlooking the fort. The British, promptly seizing this high ground, had forced the Americans to withdraw precipitously. By early September 1777, Kosciuszko, at the side of General Benedict Arnold and under the command of General Horatio Gates, was seeking the perfect place to lure the British into battle on American terms. Kosciuszko chose hilly ground around Saratoga, on the west bank of the Hudson River.

Stretching off to the west were high bluffs and steep forest-covered hillsides dropping off into deep ravines. If proper fortifications were built here, the British could not get around the Americans to the west or past them down the Hudson River for their plan to link up with a British Army supposedly marching north. The narrow pass at Saratoga would be a perfect place to build strong works and make an all-out stand. The British would have to try to outflank the Americans by attempting to circle to the west of the American line, but in the thick, hilly forests, their artillery and dragoons, indeed all their advanced European battle tactics, would be useless. They would be forced to fight American-style in the woods or, if they mounted a frontal attack, they could be beaten piecemeal.

Kosciuszko took paper from his portfolio and pencilled in redoubts, earthworks, bivouacs, and company streets. Arnold placed the troops, interspersing battle-seasoned Continental units among inexperienced New York and New England militia. Making free use of artillery taken from captured British forts in the lake country, Kosciuszko heavily fortified the American right wing overlooking the river. He placed more cannon to protect abatis, strengthening earthworks and redoubts that he stretched fully a mile west to block any British flanking attack. By the time the British arrived, the American defensive position was virtually impregnable.

Despite a series of attacks and artillery barrages over the next month, Kosciuszko's defenses held until a deadly American counterattack on Hessian redoubts, led by Arnold, convinced the weary British they should withdraw. Pursued and battered, the British surrendered. The first great American victory of the Revolutionary War persuaded the French government that the Americans would fight on and could actually win. The war would drag on for five more years until Franco-American combined forces won a second decisive victory at Yorktown,

Virginia. Kosciuszko's timely help in introducing state-of-the-art European warfare to a raw American army had helped to prevent the rout of the American colonists by the best soldiers of their age, the British redcoats, in the critical early stages of the war.

He served out the rest of the war performing equally important engineering feats almost routinely. He fortified the bend of the Hudson River with a series of overlapping-fire fortresses at West Point. He then kept the beleaguered Southern Army alive in the field by perfecting pontoon transport across the South's many deep, narrow rivers, always keeping the Americans a few steps ahead of an exhausted, exasperated British enemy in a new kind of guerrilla warfare. At the head of freed-black American soldiers, he fought and was wounded in the last battle of the war, outside Charleston. He returned to Europe, eventually to form a Polish Legion under Napoleon and then lead his own country's revolution. With a final departing flourish Kosciuszko wrote the cavalry handbook used for half a century at West Point. And then he freed the slave he had been given as a token of appreciation for building the impregnable American fortress that became the United States Military Academy.

Why has this complex mosaic of the American Revolution remained so long unknown while a WASP myth has endured? Perhaps Charles Thomson could explain. Thomson came to America a destitute orphan, became the protegé of Benjamin Franklin, leader of Philadelphia's radical Sons of Liberty, and a wealthy merchant. He served as Secretary of Congress from 1774 to 1789 but was then excluded from the new federal government.

Thomson declined to write a history of the congresses he had served despite the importunings of many of the Founding Fathers. One of the reasons they thought he might write a history was that Thomson had been gathering vast numbers of state documents and private papers from members for all those years, suggesting that he was going to use them to write a history of the United States.

But finally he wrote Benjamin Rush, saying, "No, I ought not. Let the world admire the supposed wisdom and valor of our great men. Perhaps they may adopt the qualities that have been ascribed to them, and thus good may be done. I shall not undeceive future generations."

QUESTIONS FOR THOUGHT AND DISCUSSION

1. How does Tadeusz Kosciuszko's active support for the American cause in the Revolutionary War reflect a larger truth about who fought on the rebel side?

2. Why do you think Kosciuszko and others such as Baron von Steuben, Joseph Vigo, and Casimir Pulaski were willing to come to America to help Americans win their independence?

3. In what way did Kosciuszko's efforts have a significant effect on pulling France into the war in support of the American cause against the British?

SUGGESTED READINGS

Davis, Burke. *Black Heroes of the American Revolution*. New York: Odyssey/Harcourt, 1976.

Harling, Frederick and Martin Kaufman. *The Ethnic Contribution to the American Revolution*. Westfield, Mass.: Historical Journal of Western Massachusetts, 1976.

Marchione, Margherita. *Philip Mazzei and the Constitutional Society of 1784*. Rutherford, N.J.: Fairleigh Dickinson UP, 1984.

Pascosolido, Carl and Pamela Gleason. *The Proud Italians*. Seabrook, N.H.: Latium, 1991.

Quarles, Benjamin. *The Negro in the American Revolution*. Chapel Hill: Institute of Early American History and Culture, 1961.

Sammartino, Peter, ed. *Seven Italians Involved in the Creation of America*. Washington D.C.: National Italian American Foundation, 1984.

8

George Washington

By the time of his death at the close of the eighteenth century, George Washington was already enshrined as a monument more than a man in the eyes of Americans and admirers in Europe. During much of the Revolutionary War, the French as well as the British had considered Benedict Arnold a far more important military leader than Washington. A French history of the war published at the time of Arnold's treason accorded him one and a half of its first two volumes and relegated Washington to footnotes as a logician. But by 1785, two years after the Treaty of Paris officially recognized the independence of the United States, Washington was already achieving mythical status.

When Thomas Jefferson, the American minister in Paris, was given the task by the Virginia Assembly of having a suitable full-size Washington statue sculpted, he turned to Houdon, who cast Washington in a Roman toga. Washington often saw himself as the Roman senator Cincinnatus, who set aside his plow to take up his sword, but Jefferson prevailed on Houdon to recast him in a general's uniform. The statue still stands in the Virginia capitol building in Richmond.

Yet Washington's aloof habits and purposeful reserve as he tried to imbue first the military command and then the Presidency with dignity and respect masked the fact that, behind the myth, he was quite human: raging, swearing, loving, hating, mistrusting, touchy in the extreme under any form of criticism, as prejudiced on the subject of Native Americans as any man of his time, and only reluctantly and belatedly coming to the conclusion that all men were created equal.

AS A BOY, nothing seemed to prepare George Washington for greatness. Born at Wakefield, a small farmhouse on Pope's Creek in Westmoreland County, Virginia, he was the fourth of nine children of Augustine Washington. Augustine, or Gus as everyone called him, was a towering, third-generation tobacco planter, partner in an iron furnace, and county justice. Augustine Washington had three children by the time his first wife died. Soon he married Mary Ball. George was her first and favorite child.

George Washington's boyhood was filled with children, chickens, dogs, pigs, calves, and horses. From 10,000 acres, much of it uncleared wilderness, his father, a member of the cash-poor, land-rich gentry, harvested a modest existence. When George was three, his father moved the family to Prince William County, the future site of Mount Vernon. Three years later, the family moved to Ferry Farm near the new settlement of Fredericksburg on the Rappahannock. By now, his father owned some fifty slaves and had carved a niche in upper-middle rank Virginia society. He sent George's two older brothers to the school he had attended in northern England, and George seemed destined to go there, too.

On Easter 1743, George Washington's world suddenly changed. George was away from Ferry Farm visiting relatives when word came that his father was dying. His older stepbrother, Lawrence, rushed home to manage family affairs. Fourteen years George's senior, Lawrence, as a captain during King George's War, had been adjutant of the American Regiment in the malaria-stricken British sieges of Cartagena, Colombia, and other Spanish ports in the Caribbean. An English-educated officer, Lawrence married Nancy Fairfax, daughter of Colonel William Fairfax, one of the wealthiest landowners in Virginia. Colonel Fairfax was agent for his uncle, Lord Fairfax, who owned over five million acres. The marriage gave the Washingtons entree into the highest social and political ranks of Virginia. Impressive Lawrence and impressionable George became devoted to each other. At eleven George moved to Lawrence's home at Mount Vernon. For four more years he studied with a series of private tutors at Mount Vernon.

The death of George's father cut short his formal education after four years in a small Fredericksburg school. Three of his notebooks survive. They show that he learned some elementary Latin, a good deal of mathematics, and read a little English literature. Unlike many of his class, he did not go on to the College of William and Mary in the provincial capital of Williamsburg. His lack of formal education later prompted John Adams to comment "that Washington was not a scholar," adding acidly that "he was too illiterate, unlearned, and unread for his station and reputation."

Washington's teenage years were a time of dancing and hearty meals, of hunting for deer, duck, and bear, of wagering on horse and foot races and cockfights, of boxing and billiards, and of engaging in wrestling matches that the powerful young Washington usually won. But what would he do if he didn't go to college? Pursue a naval career, Lawrence counseled. George's mother would hear none of it. Her husband was dead now; she would never give her consent for her oldest son to leave her and go to sea.

In Virginia drawing rooms in the 1740s, gentlemen talked incessantly of fortunes to be made by staking out unclaimed lands west of the Blue Mountains in the Shenandoah Valley. Migrating Native Americans had agreed to bypass the lush valley. Lord Fairfax, the English proprietor of the Valley, had come from England to settle the lands. The opportunity for a young surveyor was unsurpassed. George was ready. At sixteen, he set off on a thirty-three-day horseback expedition through the forests and mountains. They slept on the ground, in tents, and in vermin-infested taverns. They encountered Indian war parties and George, fascinated, spent two days and nights talking with the young warriors. As a surveyor, George matured rapidly. He quickly learned his secret to success, to scout the best lands along the frontier, buy them with earnings from one of the few cash-paying colonial occupations, and then rent them out for a handsome profit.

Stiff, awkward, and tongue-tied with girls, at Lawrence's plantation at Mount Vernon (named after the British admiral who had commanded the Caribbean expedition) George learned to play billiards and cards; he especially enjoyed fox hunting and taking long daily walks. So shy was he around young women, however, that he wrote dreadful doggerel about his plight:

Ah! woe's me, that I should love and conceal,
Long have I wish'd, but never dare reveal,
Even though severely
Loves Pains I feel.

It was about this time that he met eighteen-year-old Sally Fairfax, his neighbor's bride. George was infatuated with her graceful bearing, her wit, and her beauty. Their relationship may never have gotten beyond flirtation, but they had strong feelings for each other and corresponded for years.

At sixteen, George helped run the surveying lines Jefferson's father used to map the northern boundary of Virginia. When George was seventeen, he was appointed Culpeper County surveyor. In one month, he earned the equivalent of $3,500 today. At eighteen, he bought 1,459 acres of choice wilderness land. However, at nineteen Washington had to set aside his surveyor's tools. Lawrence Washington was slowly dying of tuberculosis. In an attempt to regain his health, Lawrence had to leave behind his wife, Nancy, and their newborn baby while he sailed to Barbados with young George as his nurse.

That was the only time George left mainland America. It was a memorable trip. First, he was "grievously seasick" from the ocean voyage. Next he contracted a near-fatal dose of smallpox that left his face and body permanently pitted with scars. Then came the first of six attacks of malaria. Lawrence went on to Bermuda and later came home to die. George reluctantly left Barbados' pleasant society, its theater, and the love poems he wrote to Sally Fairfax but never mailed to go home to Virginia to recuperate.

Lawrence's death left Mount Vernon abandoned, and cast George, now nineteen, back onto Ferry Farm, the small plantation his father had left him. He now ambitiously pursued the adjutant's post his half-brother's death left vacant. George buttonholed influential friends in the House of Burgesses and on the royal governor's council. He half-succeeded. Governor Robert Dinwiddie split the colony into four districts. At the age of twenty, with no military experience, Washington was placed in charge of the southern district, given the rank of militia major, pay of a meager $2,500 a year in today's money, and the honor he so craved.

To prove himself, Major Washington volunteered for a risky mission. France and Britain were vying for control of the rich Ohio Valley. Pushing down from Canada, French forces were wooing Native Americans and building forts on land England also claimed. Washington set off in icy weather, traveling through more than 1,000 miles of frozen wilderness in less than two months, to carry a warning to the French on Lake Erie and to spy on their forces. His ability to stay calm and sober while French officers drank and boasted, his tact in dealing with native leaders, and his narrow escapes from death created a stir in Virginia when he returned with warnings of French mobilization for war. After five days' rest and a new assignment from Governor Robert Dinwiddie, Washington left to raise men to race to claim the forks of the Ohio, Monongahela, and Allegheny rivers before the French could build a fort there. At twenty-two, he was commissioned a lieutenant colonel and given command of a force of militia. Promised 3,000 men, he could only raise 150. George Washington got his first taste of combat during a brief skirmish near Laurel Mountain where his small force clashed with a French party, killing ten including the French commander, and taking twenty prisoners. He earned promotion to full colonel but he probably triggered the seven-year-long French and Indian War.

When the French reinforced and counterattacked, young Washington had to take refuge in a hastily built stockade he called Fort Necessity. Washington was to learn many lessons from that day, July 3, 1754. He built his stockade on low ground that filled with water in a slashing all-day downpour. French and Indians raked it with deadly crossfire from dense surrounding forests. After his men broke into the rum supply, Colonel Washington finally had to surrender. It was a bitter defeat but Washington became famous; even King George II heard his name. To his brother he boasted, "We obtained a most signal victory," adding "I heard the bullets whistle and, believe me, there is something charming in the sound."

After a petulant spat with Virginia's colonial Governor Dinwiddie over his pay and rank, Washington resigned his provincial post. But it wasn't long before he was back in uniform. This time he was an aide-de-camp to the newly arrived British General Edward Braddock, commander of a mixed force of 2,000 British Regulars and American militia sent by London to drive out the French. During Braddock's ill-fated campaign against Fort Duquesne, Washington came to scorn the British officer class and regular troops, nearly one-half of whom were killed and scalped, and to respect guerrilla warfare tactics used by the Indians. "The English soldiers behaved with more cowardice than it is possible to conceive," Washington wrote to his brother. "The Virginia troops showed a good deal of bravery and were near all killed. The dastardly behavior of those they call Regulars exposed all others that were inclined to do their duty to almost certain death." Washington himself had two horses killed under him and his clothing torn by bullets as he commanded the rear guard and buried Braddock.

As commander-in-chief of Virginia militia in the next four years of border warfare, Washington became the best-known American soldier, although he felt neglected much of the time and tried unsuccessfully to win transfer to a more active command elsewhere. During this time he became seriously ill of dysentery and came home, he thought, to die. A Virginia hero, he still had to cope with a mother who pestered him as if he were still a little boy and there was no war: "I am sorry it is not in my power to provide you either a Dutch man (servant) or the butter as you desire," he wrote her from camp, "for we are quite out of that part of the country where either are to be had." When he was offered the highest commission in Virginia at age twenty-three, she wanted him to refuse it and stay safely at home. In 1758, after inheriting Mount Vernon, the distinguished young soldier—now owner of more than 5,000 prime acres and a handsome mansion—met the wealthy young widow Martha Dandridge Custis. His marriage to her made him the stepfather of two small children, Jackie and Patsy Custis, and a rich man. He also won an election to the Virginia House of Burgesses on his third attempt.

In the next fifteen years before he returned to soldiering, Washington built Mount Vernon into one of the colony's most successful plantations. He speculated in numerous land companies and staked out 34,000 acres of Western land. His father had left him ten slaves; by the time of the Revolution he owned 135. Historian Marcus Cunliffe, calling Washington "a man of his time and place," adds that "he did only what he and his neighbors would have thought proper."

He turned to manufacturing nearly everything his plantation needed. Washington fumed at the excessive prices and poor quality of goods shipped from England. The last straw may have come in 1768. When the family carriage broke down, Washington sent what amounted to a lavish sum to London with instructions for a new one "in the newest taste ... to be made of the best seasoned wood and by a celebrated workman." The gleaming, elegant coach that arrived lasted only two months. The wood wasn't seasoned and quickly fell apart.

Washington helped organize the first Virginia boycott of British goods. He developed the knack for summing up the American position in a few words: as he delivered George Mason's Plan of Association, the economic embargo against new British customs duties, he told fellow Burgesses, "They should not have their hands in our pockets."

When nervous colonial leaders converged on Philadelphia at the opening of the Continental Congress in 1774, Washington left little doubt where he stood— he was the only delegate in uniform. In its risky, radical deliberations, when Congressmen had prices on their heads, Washington sat coolly on a dozen committees, giving advice on military preparations. When war was made inevitable by events in Boston, all eyes turned to the tall gentleman in powdered wig and Virginia colonel's light blue uniform to be their commander-in-chief. Yet Washington insisted he had not sought the post. His inner turmoil was reflected in this letter to his wife at Mount Vernon:

> You will believe me, my dear Patsy, when I assure you, in the most solemn manner that, so far from seeking this appointment, I have used every endeavor in my power to avoid it, not only from my unwillingness to part with you and the family, but from a consciousness of its being too great a trust for my capacity.

Washington brought all the lessons of his Indian-fighting days to bear in his new command. Instead of committing his raw recruits to open combat with a superior enemy force, he encircled the British garrison at Boston with a network of trenches and besieged it. When the surrounding hills were frozen solid and British officers lulled to sleep by the winter winds, Washington ordered his men to make portable fortifications of hay bales, cornstalks, and bundles of sticks. Then, in the middle of the night under a full moon, an army of carts hauled the strange barricades to Dorchester Heights. When the British awoke the next morning, heavy artillery hauled all the way from Fort Ticonderoga in northern New York pointed down at them. They were forced to abandon the city.

Yet Washington sometimes learned painfully slowly. In a series of pitched battles on Long Island and in New York in 1776, he allowed his forces to be hopelessly outmaneuvered by fast-marching, well-disciplined troops. Beaten back steadily across New York and New Jersey, Washington resorted to a desperate surprise attack in the hope of shattering British morale. Early in December 1776, with British brigades hot on his heels, Washington retreated across the Delaware River to Bucks County, Pennsylvania, seizing every boat and ferry along eighty miles of riverfront. In those last months of the crucial year 1776, a change came over Washington. He complained bitterly when Congress refused to allow him to burn down New York City as the British Army approached. When it caught fire mysteriously, he was delighted to report to his brother Samuel: "Providence, or some good honest fellow, has done more for us than we were disposed to do ourselves, as near one fourth of the city is supposed to be consumed [by fire]."

On Christmas Day, 1776, as Hessian mercenaries recovered from overdoses of alcoholic beverages in Trenton, New Jersey, Washington struck. Forty-foot-long Durham boats, used in peacetime to shuttle iron products from foundries on the Delaware River to Philadelphia, first were loaded with soldiers and then with

National Portrait Gallery, Washington, D.C.

Portrayed here with his lavishly attired wife Martha, two grandchildren, and an elegantly uniformed slave, George Washington usually dressed in Republican black and insisted his family do likewise.

artillery. They were rowed through ice packs by Marblehead, Massachusetts, fishermen under Colonel John Glover. As was his custom, Washington stayed ashore until the boats made their crossing. Then, with his aides and two horses (his white charger and a brown sorrel he used in combat), he crossed separately on a ferry. As the Hessians slept off their Christmas party, Washington's men infiltrated the streets of Trenton, slipping into houses to warm and dry their gunpowder while General Henry Knox lined up cannon at the ends of the streets. The Hessians stumbled outside at dawn and were cut down in a bloody crossfire. Though small numbers were involved, it may have been Washington's most important victory.

Winter, more than British steel, was Washington's cruelest enemy. At Valley Forge in 1777–78, half his force of 11,000 men died or deserted, and some of his most trusted officers plotted to replace him. At Jockey Hollow in northwestern New Jersey in the winter of 1779–80, the harshest winter of the century buried 1,200 log huts holding twelve men each under twenty-eight snowfalls in a three month period. As long as his men had to live and suffer outdoors, Washington refused to take refuge in a heated house. Each winter, wrapped in his blue revolutionary's cape, he shivered in a white linen tent until the last private had a cabin to protect him.

Washington also suffered ill health alongside his men after years of living on a limited diet. His teeth had caused him pain and embarrassment since his first extraction at age twenty-two after the Fort Necessity fiasco. By the 1770s he was retaining Boston goldsmith Paul Revere to supply him porcelain dentures. In early June, 1781, British agents intercepted a secret message sent to New York by Washington. "A day or two ago," Washington was writing through the lines to his dentist, "I applied to you for a pair of pincers to fasten the wire of my teeth. I now wish you would send me one of your scrapers, as my teeth stand in need of cleaning." Washington frequently posed for portraits with his mouth packed with cotton wadding to fill out the contours of his face. Later, an oral surgeon, who supplied Washington with several sets of spring-operated "seahorse" dentures made from the tooth of a hippopotamus, told Washington that his dentures invariably turned black because "either [you are] soaking them in port wine" or "drinking it."

Morale became a worsening problem as the war ground to a stalemate in 1780. Mutiny and desertions increased and Washington reacted harshly. Deserters were ordered "shot on sight." A forty-foot high gallows was built in camp as a reminder to wavering patriots. When 300 New Jersey troops mutinied, Washington had them draw lots to decide which three would be executed. Twelve others were chosen to form a firing squad. Two died before Washington reprieved the third.

The years of frustration began to wear Washington down: "One year rolls over another, and without some change, we are hastening to our ruin," he wrote in June, 1780. Change came. Five thousand French troops under Rochambeau at Newport, Rhode Island, were reinforced by a French fleet that bottled up the British in Chesapeake Bay. Washington, his Continentals, and the white-uniformed French quick-stepped southward swiftly. The years of drilling in camp and of maneuvering in the field had given them ample time for practice. Now his army strode confidently to box the British into Yorktown. Washington personally touched the match that fired the first siege cannon. On October 17, 1781, the British surrendered.

Redcoated, redfaced troops marched out with arms shouldered, flags furled, and bands playing "The World Turned Upside Down." The fighting was over.

Yet as peace talks in Paris dragged on for nearly two more years, Washington grew ever suspicious of the British, writing to James McHenry on August 15, 1782, "'Tis plain their only aim is to gain time, that they may become more formidable at sea, form new alliances if possible—or disunite us. Be their object what it may, we, if wise, should push our preparations [for renewed fighting] with vigor; for nothing will hasten peace more than to be in a condition for war." The prolonged impasse and Congress's inability to pay his officers almost wrecked Washington's army. As mutiny loomed at his Newburgh, New York headquarters, only Washington's clever appeal to emotion saved the Revolution. Taking out a letter to read, Washington stumbled and hesitated as he groped in his pocket for glasses his closest friends had never seen the proud general wear. "Gentlemen, you must pardon me. I have grown gray in your service and now find myself growing blind." The only sound in the room was the weeping of his comrades.

When peace finally came in 1783, Washington assembled his officers at Fraunces Tavern in New York City to say goodbye before he returned to Mount Vernon:

> With a heart full of love, and gratitude, I now take leave of you. I most devoutly wish that your later days may be as prosperous and happy as your former ones have been glorious and honorable.

Washington went on: "I shall feel obliged if each of you will come and take me by the hand." One by one, the generals filed up quietly and embraced Washington. And when they were done, he left, boarded a barge, and sailed away.

In November 1783, two months after the formal peace treaty was signed, Washington gave up his virtually dictatorial power, resigning his commission to Congress at Annapolis, Maryland, and returning to the neglected fields of Mount Vernon. It would be nearly four years before he returned tentatively to public life, when he was elected a Virginia delegate to the Constitutional Convention in Philadelphia in 1787. Unanimously chosen its president, his presence signaled the unmistakable fact that he favored a strong federal government. After the convention, he refused to discuss the new Constitution, insisting on remaining neutral until it was ratified. He was always aware of his enormous influence.

Washington was the obvious and unanimous choice as first President in 1789 and carried every state, all sixty-nine electors. He proved to be a cautious, pragmatic President, more Chief Magistrate than Chief Executive. He delegated little real power to his hand-picked Cabinet. As he had as a general, he solicited the opinions of his department heads, then made all the important decisions himself, but then he backed up his Cabinet officers. He believed it was his role to invent the Presidency, its style, its traditions. He believed in simple, formal appearance, preferring to be called not "your Excellency" or "your high-mightiness," as some proposed, but simply, "Mr. President." The dignity of the office was paramount, and when he went out even for a carriage ride, it was in a six-horse-drawn state carriage. Yet he rejected living in an opulent mansion in downtown Philadelphia, choosing instead a more modest stone house in suburban Germantown.

His most important decision may have been to limit his own tenure to two terms. Term limits were not specified in the Constitution. He had intended only one term but returned for a second when it became clear that the government could collapse from infighting between his Secretary of State Thomas Jefferson, Treasury Secretary Alexander Hamilton, and the political parties forming around them. But he imposed a two term limit on himself, establishing a tradition that held until 1940 and is now part of the Constitution. Among other important precedents he set was to ignore seniority and to search widely for new, younger appointees to the Supreme Court.

As President, the former general was an off-again, on-again man of peace. He made peace immediately with the Spanish in Florida by signing the Treaty of New York in 1789. In 1791, as commander-in-chief, he sent forces under General Arthur St. Clair to subdue Native Americans who were resisting white settlement in the Northwest Territory. When St. Clair was defeated, Washington sent one of his most rapacious Revolutionary War generals, "Mad Anthony" Wayne, who crushed the natives at the Battle of Fallen Timbers. He also called out a large militia force when western Pennsylvania farmers, protesting Hamilton's imposition of an excise tax, staged the short-lived Whiskey Rebellion. Personally inspecting the troops, he harshly denounced the rebels, yet when the uprising collapsed without bloodshed, he pardoned the two ringleaders who had been condemned to death.

As Washington aged, he longed for Mount Vernon. His health had suffered. He had a tumor removed from his hip his first year in office and nearly died of pneumonia the second. He was surprised by increasing criticism of his policies during his second term, and he did not take criticism well. While his government kept a strict official neutrality in the European war of the 1790s, the bulk of American trade was still with the British. Ironically, the man who had led the rebellion against the British now followed Hamilton's advice and sided more and more with the British against his old ally, the French. Washington was alarmed by the French Revolution as it devolved into terror. For five years, his dear friend Lafayette was held in jail while thousands of French aristocrats were guillotined. Washington repeatedly sent his own money to help Lafayette's wife and children and arranged to have them spared from the guillotine.

When Washington had come to power in 1789, Americans were singing "God save great Washington" to the tune of "God save our gracious King" (today "My Country 'tis of thee"). But by 1793, a Philadelphia newspaper called him "a man in his political dotage," a "supercilious tyrant" who was "debauching the nation." While most Americans still were more respectful, criticism intensified with Jay's Treaty. He was called a "political hypocrite." More and more, Washington supported the policies of Hamilton (who saw cities, banks, and a stock market and industry in America's future) over the agrarian views of Jefferson. At a 1793 Cabinet meeting, he called the Republican journalist Philip Freneau a "rascal" who should be silenced. The clash led to Jefferson's resignation as Secretary of State. Washington raged at the Democratic-Republican Societies that supported Jefferson and eventually became the basis of a second political party. He took their criticism personally. He considered the Democratic-Republicans irresponsible and evil. His increasing hostility to changing political views around him prompted Jefferson to write, "I think he feels those things more than any other person." An indignant Washington gave up on winning back support of the new Democratic-

Republicans. "You could as soon scrub the blackamoor white," he wrote, "as to change the principles of a professed Democrat."

Yet Washington remained the most popular man in America and could have won re-election to a third term had he not refused it. Nevertheless, he did not consider himself indispensable. Just after his sixty-fifth birthday, he left the temporary capital of Philadelphia and rode south to Mount Vernon for the last time. There, he happily took over managing his farms. He spent long days in the saddle, offering hospitality to hundreds of visitors and writing hundreds of letters now that he felt free to speak his mind.

When the threat of war with Napoleonic France loomed in 1798, his successor, President Adams, called Washington back into command to raise an army. Washington was miffed that Adams appointed him without consulting him, yet he agreed to go off to war again "with as much reluctance," he wrote, as he would go "to the tomb of my ancestors." Fortunately, no war developed, and Washington was free to go on happily with his seemingly endless routines at Mount Vernon.

Then, on December 13, 1799, as the eighteenth century drew to a close, George Washington caught a cold. He had a chill and strep throat. The doctor was called; he bled him and then called in two consultants, who bled him again and again. Washington grew weaker. He refused the advice of the younger doctor, who warned against the bleedings and urged a tracheotomy. But Washington deferred to the senior men. At ten the next night, he died, a victim of his belief in authority as much as eighteenth century medicine that proved more deadly than all the bullets and all the plots aimed at him during nearly half a century as America's most admired leader. In his will, he granted freedom to his slaves at the death of Martha, his wife of forty years, and he provided annuities for their support when she was gone.

QUESTIONS FOR THOUGHT AND DISCUSSION

1. In what ways was George Washington's background quite unlike that of most other colonial Americans? In what ways was it similar?

2. Why was Washington chosen as the country's first president? Was his election a wise choice?

3. Why was Washington's decision not to run for a third term as president so significant?

4. Should Washington be remembered as a hero, or simply as an important figure in the founding of the United States? Explain.

SUGGESTED READINGS

Cunliffe, Marcus. *George Washington: Man and Monument*. Boston: Little, 1960.

Ferling, John E. *The First of Men: A Life of George Washington*. Knoxville: U of Tennessee P, 1988.

Knollenberg, Bernhard. *George Washington: The Virginia Period, 1732–75.* Durham, N.C.: Duke UP, 1964.

Longmore, Paul K. *The Invention of George Washington.* Berkeley: U of California P, 1988.

Randall, Willard Sterne. *George Washington: A Life.* New York: Holt, 1997.

Smith, Richard Norton. *Patriarch: George Washington and the New American Nation.* Boston: Houghton, 1993.

Wall, Charles Cecil. *George Washington: Citizen Soldier.* Charlottesville: U of Virginia P, 1980.

9

Margaret
Shippen Arnold

Under the English legal doctrine enunciated in 1765 by Sir William Blackstone in his Commentaries on the Laws of England, *married women had few legal rights. What rights they had were bound up in their husbands, who alone had a legal existence. They could not hold property (even if it was inherited from their parents), could not enter into contracts so long as their husbands lived (without their express written approval), could not keep any money they earned, and could not vote or hold office. They were better off single or widowed. Even widowed, however, they could only hold property until their first-born son came of age, when it was transferred to him. Blackstone's conservative views, first articulated at Oxford University in his Vinerian Lectures of 1758, were widely adopted in colonial America and became the legal gospel of the new republic, where his three-volume set was a bestseller.*

If married women had few rights, they had all the disabilities of the matrimonial state, especially in wartime, when they had no right to dissent from their husbands' political decisions. Yet women made vast contributions to the revolutionary cause. They melted down the great lead equestrian statue of King George III in New York City into some 42,000 bullets in workshops in Litchfield, Connecticut. They traveled with the army, cooking, serving, and washing in the camps and winter quarters. They made the uniforms and the bandages and ran the farms, the newspapers, and the stores.

But, in the long civil war called the American Revolution, if they were opposed to the revolutionary cause, like Loyalists Grace Growden Galloway, Elizabeth Graeme, or Margaret Shippen Arnold, they were evicted from their father's houses, stripped of their inheritances, and could be banished from their homelands. Chained to their husbands' destinies, their successes, or failures, the women of revolutionary America could look forward either to sharing in the final victory with their husbands or to being expelled, reviled, and exiled forever.

ALL HER LIFE, Peggy Shippen was surrounded by the turmoil of an age of wars and revolution. She was born with the British Empire in 1760, only weeks before the French surrendered all of Canada. Before her third birthday, British America had grown by conquest from a strip of small coastal colonies to nearly half of North America. The town of Philadelphia, where her father, Judge Edward Shippen, held a lucrative array of colonial offices, was the largest seaport in America. A center for trade and its regulation, Philadelphia was a natural target for protests when resistance to British revenue measures flared in the 1760s. By the age of five, she had seen riots in the streets outside her father's handsome brick town house.

The revolutionary movement grew throughout her childhood. At fifteen she listened at her parents' dinner table as their guests argued politics: George Washington, John Adams, Silas Deane, and Benedict Arnold were among the patriots who dined at the Shippens'; British officials and officers included General Thomas Gage and the intriguing John André. By the time Peggy was seventeen, the British army occupied Philadelphia and she was being linked romantically with André, the young British spymaster. After the Americans reoccupied the city, and before she was nineteen, Peggy married Military Governor Benedict Arnold and helped him to plot the boldest treason in American history—not only the surrender of West Point and its 3,000 men but the capture of Washington, Lafayette, and their combined staffs.

Delicately beautiful, brilliant, witty, a consummate actress, and astute businesswoman, Peggy Shippen was the highest-paid spy of the American Revolution. Understandably, the Shippen family destroyed any papers that could connect her to the treason of Benedict Arnold. As a result, for two centuries she has been considered Arnold's hapless and passive spouse, innocent though neurotic. But new evidence reveals that she actively engaged in the Arnold conspiracy at every step. She was a deeply committed Loyalist who helped persuade her husband to change sides. When he wavered in his resolve to defect, it was she who kept the plot alive and then shielded him, risking her life over and over. Ultimately expelled from the United States, she was handsomely rewarded by the British "for services rendered."

When Margaret Shippen was born on June 11, 1760, her father, who already had a son and three daughters, wrote his father that his wife "this morning made me a present of a fine baby which, though the worst sex, is yet entirely welcome." Judge Shippen was usually cheerful about his large family: the Shippens were one of colonial America's richest and most illustrious families. The first American Shippen—Peggy's great-great-grandfather, the first Edward—had immigrated to Boston in 1668 with a fortune from trade in the Middle East. He married a Quaker who was being persecuted by the Massachusetts Puritans. Both were granted sanctuary in Rhode Island by Governor Benedict Arnold, the traitor's great-grandfather. The couple resettled in Philadelphia on a two-mile-deep riverfront estate. Shippen later became Speaker of the Pennsylvania Assembly and the second mayor of Philadelphia.

Peggy's father, the fourth Edward in the line, was a conservative man who seemed constantly worried, usually about money or property. He followed his father's wishes and practiced law, also holding several remunerative colonial offices simultaneously—admiralty judge, prothonotary, and recorder of deeds. At first he was firmly on the British side in the long struggle that evolved into the Revolution. His tortured reactions to the almost constant tensions that accompanied years of riots, boycotts, and congresses in Philadelphia were the backdrop for his daughter Peggy's unusual childhood.

When Parliament passed the Stamp Act shortly before Peggy's fifth birthday in 1765, her father read aloud to her about "great riots and disturbances" in Boston. He considered the Stamp Act oppressive, but he opposed illegally destroying stamped paper. "What will be the consequences of such a step, I tremble to think. Poor America! It has seen its best days." By the time Peggy was eight and learning to read the leather-bound books in their library, her father's admiralty court had become the center of the storm over British taxation. When she was ten, his judgeship was abolished.

As the colonial crisis dragged on, Shippen lectured his favorite daughter on disobedience. Bad laws had to be repealed. Simply to ignore or resist them would open the door to anarchy. Despite his drawing-room bravery, however, Shippen refused to take a public stand, careful to avoid offending radicals or street mobs that might attack his property or harm his daughters. He burst into a rare fit of rage over Thomas Paine's book, *Common Sense*, which argued in favor of total separation from England. Shippen found *Common Sense* "artfully wrote, yet might be easily refuted. This idea of independence, though sometime ago abhorred, may possibly, by degrees, become so familiar as to be cherished." No doubt Peggy had to learn the arguments against independence by heart.

Judge Shippen seems to have taken over Peggy's education from her mother. He was disappointed in his only son, Neddy (the fifth Edward), who had shown himself early on to be inept at business and would eventually squander much of the family fortune. The judge decided to educate Peggy as if she were his son. Peggy curled up in a wingback across from her father to read Addison, Steele, Pope, and Defoe—all the latest British writers. Her mother saw to it that she was instructed in needlework, cooking, drawing, dancing, and music, but in none of her surviving letters is there any of the household trivia of her time.

Peggy had a distinctive literary style and wit and, like her father, she wrote with unusual clarity. A quiet, serious girl, she was too practical, and too interested in business and in making the most of time and money for frivolity. By age fifteen, as the Revolutionary War began, she was helping her father with his investments. Years later, she wrote to thank him for "the most useful and best education that America at that time afforded." At her father's elbow, she learned the finer points of bookkeeping, accounting, real estate and other investments, importing and trade, and banking and monetary transactions—and she basked in her father's approval.

Peggy had been also studying her sisters' manners and social behavior. It was at the fortnightly Dancing Assemblies at Freemasons Hall that young men who danced with her older sisters began to notice Peggy. She was tiny, blond, dainty of face and figure, with steady, wide-set blue-gray eyes, and a full mouth which she pursed as she listened intently.

Judge Shippen would invite partisans of all stripes to his brick mansion on Fourth Street in Philadelphia's Society Hill section to air their views at his dinner table. This was as far into the new politics as he would delve. In early September 1774, when

Peggy was fourteen, she and her family entertained some of the delegates to the First Continental Congress. Few, if any, foresaw a war of revolution against the mother country. Many expected to reconcile their complaints with Parliament peacefully. Of all the colonies, Pennsylvania was the most divided. The majority was made up of pacifist Quakers and members of more than 250 German pietist sects, and there was the strong Penn proprietary party that remained loyal to the British.

That steamy September, Philadelphians agonized over the course of the New England radicals' confrontation in British-occupied Boston. Post riders, delegates, militiamen, and redcoats came and went down the broad cobbled streets, making it increasingly difficult to remain neutral. Congressional delegate Silas Deane wrote to his wife that "this city is in the utmost confusion." Rumors of British invasion also were flying. During one panic, Pennsylvania militiamen drilled and marched past the Shippens' house even as the last redcoated British regiment in the middle colonies strode to the waterfront and boarded troop transports taking them north to reinforce Boston.

One young British officer who could have chosen to join them was Second Lieutenant John André of the 7th Foot, the Royal Welsh Fusiliers, who had arrived in Philadelphia just a few days earlier. Sent out from England to join his regiment, André was en route to Quebec. He had been a peacetime officer for five years and had never fought in battle. Instead he had pursued the life of a dilettante poet, playwright, and artist.

From the safety of England, André had taken the unrest in America lightly, but upon arrival he found Philadelphia in the grip of anti-British frenzy. It was not a safe place for a young, solitary British officer. Oddly, he decided to travel not aboard a British warship, but on foot alone north to Lake Champlain. He sailed on to Quebec on a schooner, wrapped in a bearskin robe in the company of a black woman, an Indian squaw in a blanket, "and the sailors round the stove." It was the first of John André's strange and romantic journeys through an America he would never understand.

As André meandered north, thirty-three year old shipowner and revolutionary Benedict Arnold, who had arrived in Philadelphia with the Connecticut delegation to the Congress, was accompanying his mentor, Silas Deane, to a series of political caucuses and dinners. A self-made man of means and long a leader of the radical Sons of Liberty in New Haven, Arnold was helping to plan the systematic suppression of antirevolutionary dissent. The purpose of the Congress was to protest British oppression, but Sons of Liberty, from a dozen colonies, were discussing the elimination of Loyalist opposition.

Yet Arnold and Deane had time for dinners in Philadelphia's best houses. And one Loyalist family, the Shippens, stood out for their hospitality. Deane and Arnold were invited to the Judge's dinner table, where Shippen introduced his daughters, including the youngest, the precocious Peggy. Although only fourteen, she was already one of the city's most popular debutantes. Flirtatious and quick-witted, she could talk confidently with men about politics and trade. Benedict Arnold met her for the first time at dinner that September.

Peggy heard Benedict Arnold's name frequently in the next few years as the Revolution turned to war and its leaders put on uniforms and fanned out to fight the British. Arnold's attack on Fort Ticonderoga, his heroic march to Quebec and daring assault on the walled city, his naval campaign on Lake Champlain, his wounding, and his quarrels over promotion often put his name in the Philadelphia newspapers. A few blocks from the Shippen house, a new ship in the Pennsylvania Navy was given Arnold's name, and that was in the papers, too.

News of the war often touched close to home. Peggy's oldest sister's fiancé, a rebel, was missing and presumed killed in the American rout on Long Island. Her brother, Neddy, eighteen, on the spur of the moment decided to join the British army in Trenton for the Christmas festivities. When Washington attacked, Neddy was captured. He was freed by the Shippen's erstwhile dinner guest, George Washington himself. All of Judge Shippen's careful neutrality was jeopardized. Stripping the youth of any further part in family business affairs, the Judge turned his son's duties over to Peggy.

When the Americans invaded Canada late in 1775, the British made a stand at Fort St. Jean on the Richelieu River, surrendering only after a long siege. One of the officers captured was twenty-five-year old Second Lieutenant André. Freed on parole, he was sent south with the baggage of his fellow officers to house arrest in Pennsylvania. In Philadelphia, while he attended to provisions for his fellow prisoners, André had time to explore "the little society of Third and Fourth Streets," the opulent town houses of Peggy's neighborhood. The romantic young officer was ushered into the Fourth Street home of Judge Shippen and introduced to fifteen-year-old Peggy Shippen. Before he left for an indefinite term in captivity on the Pennsylvania frontier, he played his flute, recited his poetry, and asked to sketch her.

One year later, André was exchanged for an American prisoner. Then, in the autumn of 1777, when Peggy was seventeen, the British Army drove the Americans out of Philadelphia and marched up Second Street, two blocks from the Shippens'. André had recently given the orders for a British regiment to fix bayonets, remove the flints from their muskets, and attack a sleepy American unit at nearby Paoli. The increasingly callous young André tersely described the massacre in his regimental journal, calling the Americans a "herd" as nearly 200 men were killed and a great number wounded. He noted they were "stabbed till it was thought prudent to desist."

An aide at British headquarters in Philadelphia, André decided to follow the example of his commanders and seek diversions from the toils of killing. He and his elegant friends reconnoitered in the best society they could find and André began calling on the Shippens. He was accompanied by his friends, Captain Andrew Snape Hamond of HMS *Roebuck* and Lord Francis Rawdon, who considered Peggy the most beautiful woman he had ever seen.

Even a conquering officer, however, could not hope to escort a Philadelphia debutante to the incessant round of military balls without a round of prior introductions. The first step was the morning visit to the drawing room of the intended partner. André, sketch pad under his arm, frequently came for obligatory cups of tea, and chaperoned talks about the latest books, balls, and plays. In the evenings, André and his assistant, New York Loyalist Captain Oliver DeLancey, were hard at work turning a former warehouse on South Street into a splendid theater. They painted a waterfall and wooded scenes on the curtain and a brook meandering through a darkly shaded forest toward a "distant champagne country." For five months an entranced Peggy joined the resplendent crowd of redcoated officers and their Tory ladies.

Peggy Shippen probably fell in love that winter for the first time with the charming major. But André flitted from one drawing room beauty to another, serious about none of them. Still, he liked to be with Peggy; he liked to sketch her, showing her as elusively elegant and poutish, sometimes turning away, and sometimes fixing him with an enigmatic smile. He enjoyed breakneck sleigh rides with her at his side, and her friends crowding in with them under heavy bearskin rugs.

But when Peggy stepped out for the evening, it was more often on the arm of Royal Navy Captain Hamond, who later said, "We were all in love with her." One of the season's highlights was a dinner dance aboard the *Roebuck*. Peggy was piped on board the ship, which was illuminated with lanterns for the occasion. She sat down at Hamond's right for a dinner served to 200 invited guests, and then danced until dawn.

By late April 1778, the British learned they were to withdraw to New York City to prepare for the arrival of the French—the revolutionaries' new ally. Philadelphia was too exposed. A new British commander was coming; General Howe was being recalled. John André volunteered to prepare a lavish farewell, a Meschianza, including a waterborne parade, a medieval tournament, a dress ball, and an enormous dinner party. No other effort of André's ever approached this opulent festival. He designed costumes for fourteen knights and their squires and "ladies selected from the foremost in youth, beauty, and fashion." For the ladies, he created Turkish harem costumes evoking images of the Crusades. He designed Peggy's entire wardrobe and sketched her in it. André's own glittering costume featured pink satin sashes, bows, and wide baggy pants. Peggy's father grumbled, but he shelled out enough gold to outfit three of his daughters. As Peggy rode home the next morning, a Quaker diarist wrote, "How insensible do these people appear while our land is so greatly desolated." Before André left a few weeks later, he gave Peggy a souvenir that showed how close they had become: a locket containing a ringlet of his hair. Though parted, they wrote each other secretly, through the lines, at great risk to Peggy, directing the letters through a third party.

In May 1778, as the British evacuated Philadelphia, the new American military governor of Philadelphia, Major General Benedict Arnold, the wounded hero of Quebec, Ticonderoga, and Saratoga, drove into the city in his coach-and-four with his liveried servants, aides, and orderlies. From their brick mansion, the Shippens could see the American light horse ride by. Arnold's duties as military governor included evenings filled with social activities. Once himself a poor orphan, General Benedict Arnold moved freely in Philadelphia's elite circles. Soon he, too, was keeping an afternoon round of tea sipping with the Shippens, the Robert Morrises, and other wealthy merchants. Arnold hosted many members of Congress at lavish dinners at his headquarters. He often encountered Peggy at these gatherings. As the summer progressed, she became known as the general's lady. Frequently, his carriage was seen parked in front of the Shippen house, where British officers had come to call only a few months before. At first, resentment that the American hero of Saratoga was courting the Loyalist belle of British officers' balls was confined to a little sniping in Congress. Arnold's insistence on inviting Loyalist women to revolutionary social events brought increasing criticism, yet Arnold seemed oblivious as he spent more and more time with eighteen-year-old Peggy.

In September 1778, Arnold declared himself a serious suitor in two letters, one to Peggy and one to her father. One of Peggy's relatives wrote that "there can be no doubt the imagination of Miss Shippen was excited and her heart captivated by the oft-repeated stories of his gallant deeds, his feats of brilliant courage, and traits of generosity and kindness." Peggy seemed especially touched that he paid for the education and upbringing of the four children of his friend, Dr. Joseph Warren, who had been killed at Bunker Hill. But Peggy had other reasons for falling in love with Benedict Arnold: he was still young, thirty-six, ruggedly built despite his wounded leg, animated, intelligent and witty, strongly handsome, and sometimes charming. It was obvious that a life with "the General," as she always called him, would not be dull.

Judge Shippen did not say yes, but he did not say no. He wrote to *his* father to seek advice. But the more Arnold was publicly criticized for his leniency to Loyalists and his quite open love of one, and the longer the Judge balked, the closer the two lovers drew together. Arnold had come to appreciate her "sweetness of disposition and goodness of heart, her sentiments as well as her sensibilities." He had faced few more implacable adversaries than Judge Shippen, who worried about his daughter marrying an invalid. Finally, however, relatives persuaded the Judge that Arnold was "a well-dispositioned man, and one that will use his best endeavors to make Peggy happy." The Judge also liked the fact that Arnold settled a £7,000 country estate named Mount Pleasant on her as a wedding present.

On the other hand, the judge didn't like what he was beginning to hear about Arnold's private business dealings. Months of attacks on Arnold by radical political opponents had made Peggy all the more determined to marry him. In the end, Judge Shippen seems to have consented to his daughter's engagement only when his continued refusal made Peggy, now thoroughly in love, hysterical to the point of fainting spells. The Shippens invited only family members to the wedding in their parlor. On April 8, 1779, Arnold's nineteen-month siege ended. He rode down Fourth Street with his sister, his three sons from a previous marriage, and an aide for the evening ceremony. In his dark blue American uniform, Benedict Arnold, thirty-eight, married eighteen-year-old Peggy Shippen. A young relative wrote that Peggy was "lovely, a beautiful bride" as she stood beside her "adoring general."

In May 1779, within one month of their wedding, the couple entered into a daring plot to make Arnold a British general who would lead the Loyalist forces and bring the long war to a speedy conclusion. All through their courtship, there had been a mounting furor in the press about Arnold's alleged profiteering as military governor. Until then, there had been no proof that he had done anything more than use his office to issue passes that helped Loyalist merchants. The merchants, in turn, cut him in for a percentage of their profits, and he once had diverted army wagons to haul contraband into Philadelphia for sale in stores. Both were common practices, but Arnold was often stiff-necked and arrogant in his dealings with Pennsylvania revolutionaries. When Pennsylvania brought formal charges against Arnold, George Washington refused to intervene and, far from supporting him, treated him with the same cold formality he reserved for all officers facing court-martial. Arnold had already endured years of censure and controversy, and Washington's aloofness coupled with a ferocious attack from Congress and in the newspapers evidently drove him over the edge. Peggy seems not only to have approved of his decision to defect to the British but to have helped him at every turn in a year and a half of on-again, off-again secret plotting that, at least once, she alone managed to keep alive.

Both the Arnolds apparently decided, after the year-long radical campaign against Benedict, that they did not want to live under the new revolutionary government that had made Arnold's enemies powerful enough to force his court-martial by the army. When Arnold's prosecutors produced no evidence to convict him and when Washington, whose generals were preoccupied, was unable to bring about a speedy court-martial to clear him, the proud hero could tolerate the public humiliation no longer. On May 5, 1779, he wrote a drastic letter to Washington: "If your Excellency thinks me criminal, for heaven's sake let me be immediately tried and, if found guilty, executed."

Apparently that same day, Arnold opened his secret correspondence with the British, using Peggy's friends and Philadelphia connections. A china and furniture dealer, Joseph Stansbury, who was helping Peggy decorate the Arnold house, acted as courier through the lines to Major André at British headquarters in New York City, where Stansbury often went on buying trips. Peggy already had been sending harmless messages to André with Stansbury. She now worked with Arnold to encode the messages, using a cipher written in invisible ink that could be read when rinsed with lemon juice or acid: a symbol in one corner indicated which to use.

On May 21, 1779, Peggy sat down with Arnold in a bedroom of their Market Street house and pored over the pages of the twenty-first edition of *Bailey's Dictionary*. (André had preferred Blackstone's three-volume *Commentaries on the Laws of England*, but they had rejected it as too cumbersome.) According to Stansbury, they used one of two copies of the compact dictionary: "I have paged for [them], beginning at A... Each side is numbered and contains 927 pages." The Arnolds added "1 to each number of the page, the column, and of the line, the first word of which is also used, too. Zoroaster will be 928.2 and not 927.1.1. Tide is 838.3.2 and not 837.2.1." It usually took ten days for Stansbury to slip through to André in New York and as long to return. Late at night he would send a servant to the Arnolds, and Peggy would carefully decode the message and encode Arnold's reply. Only rarely did the Loyalist Stansbury see the General; he almost always dealt with Peggy. André had instructed Stansbury to deal with "the Lady." In October 1779, when the British at first failed to meet Arnold's terms after six months of negotiations, Peggy wrote a cryptic letter in code to André and kept the negotiations alive until the two principles struck their bargains. This time she sent her note with a British prisoner who was being exchanged and sent back to New York. She had become far more than a go-between, as historians have tended to portray her; she was now an active co-conspirator:

> Mrs. Moore [Moore was one of Arnold's code names] requests the enclosed list of articles for her own use may be procured for her and the account of them and the former [orders] sent and she will pay for the whole with thanks.

The shopping list, evidently not the first, included cloth for napkins and for dresses, a pair of spurs, and some pink ribbon. André, who had feigned indifference in recent messages, became alarmed. He saw through Peggy's list. Although the negotiations with her husband had been fruitless so far, she was telling André that they were not hopeless. He put aside her shopping list and informed Sir Henry Clinton, the British commander-in-chief, that Arnold had finally stated his price: as Stansbury told André £20,000 if he succeeded, £10,000 if he failed. What

The Historical Society of Pennsylvania

Receiving more money than her husband, Benedict, for plotting to betray Washington, Peggy Shippen Arnold raised her son, Edward, to be an English officer.

Clinton wanted was detailed plans of West Point, the new American stronghold fifty miles up the Hudson from British lines. André sent the proposal back to Peggy, referring to Peggy's list as "trifling services from which I hope you would infer a zeal to be further employed."

It was late October 1779, before André received another coded note from Peggy:

> Mrs. Arnold presents her best respects to Captain André, is much obliged to him for his very polite and friendly offer of being serviceable to her.

To entice the British, the Arnolds sent much vital military and political intelligence through the lines in the seventeen months from May 1779 through September 1780. In June 1779 they tipped off the British commander that Washington would leave his base at Morristown, New Jersey, as soon as the first hay was harvested and move north to the Hudson for a summer campaign. This leak gave Clinton time to strike first up the Hudson before Washington could reinforce his forts there. The couple disclosed that Congress had decided to all but write off Charleston, South Carolina, the largest and most important town in the South, if the British once again attempted to take it. (They did and succeeded.)

The Arnolds also informed Clinton about American currency problems and about congressional refusal to give agents in Paris full power to negotiate a peace treaty with Britain. The Arnolds believed the French alliance was shaky, and that if it fell apart, the Americans would have to sue for peace. Arnold thought he could then be useful in bringing about a reconciliation between responsible Americans and the British. "I will cooperate with others when opportunity offers," he wrote, adding a postscript: "Madam Arnold presents her particular compliments."

Ironically, one of the Arnolds' early messages to the British led to the interruption of his court-martial in June 1779, soon after it finally began, when the British took his advice and attacked up the Hudson. As Washington and his army dashed north, Arnold lurked behind at headquarters, talking to other officers about Washington's plans for the season of war.

The Arnolds encoded top-secret information about American troop strengths, dispositions, and destinations. He was the first to warn the British of an American expedition "to destroy the Indian settlements" of Pennsylvania and New York. But his most devastating tips were dispatched on July 17, 1779: the latest troop strengths; expected turnout of militia; the state of the army; the location of its supply depots; the number of men and cannon on the punitive raid against the Mohawks; troop locations, strengths, and weaknesses in Rhode Island and in the South; the location and movements of American and French ships. Peggy Shippen Arnold met alone with Joseph Stansbury during these treacherous July 1779 negotiations as Benedict Arnold showed the British what he was willing to give in exchange for a red uniform and at least £10,000.

More months dragged by before Washington could spare general officers to convene Arnold's court-martial. Meanwhile, Arnold had resigned as military governor of Philadelphia. Not until December 1779, was he allowed to defend himself and although the generals recommended a formal reprimand, the Arnolds learned of his conviction in April 1780, only weeks after the birth of Edward, the Arnold's first child. He never forgave Washington for publicly censuring him in writing. But

Washington considered it only a minor affair and promptly offered Arnold another field command, this time as his number two general.

The Arnolds were determined to defect, and Arnold himself now put it in writing to André and Clinton that West Point would soon be his to command and his to betray to the British. But Washington insisted that Arnold join him with his troops. Peggy was at a dinner party at the home of Robert Morris when news reached Philadelphia that Arnold had been appointed to command the left wing of the Continental Army, not West Point. She fainted.

What Peggy did not learn for three weeks was that Arnold, pretending his old injuries had flared up, had finally persuaded a puzzled Washington to rewrite his orders, installing him as commandant of West Point, where he took command on August 4, 1780. He sent word to Peggy in Philadelphia to leave his sons by his first marriage in the care of his sister and to come by carriage with the baby and her two servants. Meanwhile, he went about weakening West Point defenses by deploying men so they could not defend it against a British attack and arranging the details of his defection with Major André, who had been promoted to chief of the British secret service inside New York City. Plans for a first meeting on the Hudson planned for September 11, 1780, miscarried and Arnold was almost killed by gunfire from a British gunboat.

After two months apart from her husband, Peggy at last arrived at West Point, and their days and nights took on the added excitement of plotting their defection. Peggy's weeks without Arnold, the longest she had ever been away from him, had been one of the loneliest periods of her life, filled with desperate anxiety. But the same day she rejoined him, they received a letter cutting short the time they could expect together. Washington was coming north from his New Jersey headquarters, he wrote Arnold secretly. Arnold was to provide an escort and meet him as he rode without his army to confer with the French in Hartford. Realizing how vulnerable Washington would be, Arnold sent off an urgent message to André: if the British moved quickly, their warships on the Hudson, helped by a few hundred dragoons, could capture Washington and his generals as he crossed the river with a few score troops. In a bold military coup, Arnold would seize Washington and negotiate an American surrender that would quickly end the war. If the plot succeeded, Arnold could expect a dukedom from a grateful King and Peggy would be a duchess.

Peggy's first and only Sunday as the mistress of West Point, September 18, 1780, was a tense affair. Arnold's staff filed into the wainscoted dining room of Beverley, the commandant's house, to take their seats with Arnold's weekend Loyalist house guests. It was an early dinner since Arnold was soon to go downriver with Washington's hand-picked escort. They were hardly seated when a courier arrived with two coded letters for Arnold from André, who was aboard the *Vulture*, a British ship twelve miles downriver. Trying not to betray his excitement, Arnold pocketed the letters. After dinner, he rode off with forty life guards to meet Washington. Circling back alone that night after his last meeting with Washington, Arnold waited for the British attack, but Clinton procrastinated and it did not come. He had learned, however, that Washington would be inspecting West Point on September 23; the British would have a second chance. Three more anxious days passed at Beverley. Shortly before dawn on September 21, Arnold kissed Peggy goodbye and slipped off to meet André. Late that night, an open boat bearing André, wrapped in a navy blue caped coat, thumped ashore two miles below Haverstraw. At last the two men met. For two hours, Arnold and André conferred in a darkened grove of fir trees. Arnold turned over papers to André and returned to West Point.

Peggy, still exhausted from her nine-day journey to West Point in an open carriage in the summer heat, had stayed with the baby in Beverley's master bedroom while Arnold was gone. The room was a sunny, quiet place with big open windows and a balustraded porch. Now, on Saturday, September 23, she stayed in the room late, planning to go downstairs later when Washington arrived. Arnold and his staff had just been served breakfast when a messenger, muddy and dripping, was shown in. He informed them that John André had been captured! The papers, in Arnold's handwriting, had been sent on to Washington. Arnold hurried upstairs to Peggy, locked the bedroom door, and whispered to her that André had been caught, and the plot had been discovered. Washington was expected any minute. Peggy must have reassured her husband that she and the baby would be safe; it is unlikely that Peggy tried to talk him out of fleeing for his life. She agreed to burn all of their papers and stall for time. Embracing her and taking a last look at Neddy, Arnold hurried out, ordering an aide to saddle a horse. At the river, Arnold jumped into his eight-oared barge, drew his pistols, and told his crewmen he would give them two gallons of rum if they got him down river. The boat lurched into the Hudson channel, Arnold in the stern. By the time Washington arrived a few minutes later, Arnold was on his way to the *Vulture* and the British lines.

Peggy's years of studying theatrics now saved her husband's life, although her performance could have cost hers. As Arnold was making his escape, she ran shrieking down the hallway in her dressing gown, her hair disheveled. Arnold's aides rushed up the stairs to find her screaming and struggling with two maids who were trying to get her back into her room. Peggy grabbed one young aide by the hand and cried, "Have you ordered my child to be killed?" Peggy fell to her knees, the aide later testified, "with prayers and entreaties to spare her innocent babe." Two more officers arrived "and we carried her to her bed, raving mad." The distraught twenty-year-old so distracted Arnold's staff that no one thought to pursue him until Washington arrived.

Peggy Shippen Arnold's world had been exploded by a plot she had encouraged, aided, and abetted. The sheer nervous tension of the day of discovery helped her to completely fool everyone around her. It would be the twentieth century before the opening of the British Head Quarters Papers proved what the eighteenth century refused to believe—that a young and innocent-appearing woman was capable of helping Benedict Arnold plot the conspiracy that nearly delivered victory to England in the American Revolution. When Peggy learned that Washington had arrived, she cried out again and told the young aides that "there was a hot iron on her head and no one but General Washington could take it off." The aides and a staff doctor summoned Washington, the commander in chief, but when Peggy saw him, she said, "No, that is not General Washington; that is the man who was going to assist ... in killing my child." Washington retreated from the room, certain Peggy Arnold was no conspirator. A few days later, he sent her and the baby under escort to her family in Philadelphia.

When news of Arnold's treason spread throughout America, Peggy was ordered expelled from Pennsylvania. The same officials whose hounding of Arnold had provoked him into treason now unwittingly aided her escape through British lines to join the traitor in New York City. She arrived at Two Broadway, the house Arnold had rented next door to British headquarters, in time to learn that John André had been hanged by Washington after a drumhead court-martial for espionage. She secluded herself in her bedroom for weeks, rarely appearing with Arnold at headquarters functions.

Paid £6,350, Arnold was commissioned a British brigadier general. He raised a regiment, the American Legion, made up exclusively of deserters from the American army—no British officer would serve under him—and led it on bloody raids through Virginia. Arnold's troops sacked the capital at Richmond, nearly capturing Thomas Jefferson, and his native Thames River valley of Connecticut.

Peggy spent the last year of the Revolution—her last year in her native country—a celebrity in New York. She was pregnant much of the time with her second child. Some of her old Philadelphia neighbors were also Loyalists living in British-occupied Manhattan. Her former Society Hill neighbors kept tabs on her and wrote back news to Philadelphia. Peggy was grieving for André, even if her marriage to Arnold was serene. Mrs. Samuel Shoemaker wrote in November 1780 that Peggy now "wants animation, sprightliness, and fire in her eyes." When she did appear in public, however, it was as the new favorite at British headquarters balls. Peggy "appeared a star of the first magnitude, and had every attention paid her," especially after she received a personal pension of £500 a year from the Queen.

After the British surrender at Yorktown, where American troops celebrated victory by burning Arnold in effigy, the Arnolds sailed for England in a 150-ship convoy. They arrived on January 22, 1782, and according to the London *Daily Advertiser*, took "a house in Portman Square and set up a carriage." She was, wrote one nobleman, "an amiable woman and, was her husband dead, would be much noticed." The Arnolds' warmest reception was at the Court of St. James, where they were introduced to the king and queen. Arnold, King George III, and the Prince of Wales took long walks together, deep in conversation. Queen Charlotte was especially taken with Peggy, and her courtiers, as one wrote, "pay much attention to her." The Queen doubled her pension to £1,000 a year and provided a £100 lifetime annuity for each of her children. Peggy was to raise five children and eventually received far more from the Crown than Arnold did. Her pensions guaranteed that she could bring up her children comfortably and that, based on their mother's prestige alone, they would be introduced into society as English gentry. All four of the Arnolds' sons became British officers; their daughter married a general.

Arnold never got another farthing. When peace came, he became a half-pay pensioner and had to strap family resources to build a ship and return to the life at sea that had once made him wealthy. As her husband sailed to Canada, Peggy, twenty-five years old, suddenly felt the loss of her American home and family. Life with Benedict Arnold was hard on Peggy's nerves, without him, harder. Arnold was gone for nearly a year and a half, during which Peggy ran their business affairs, collected and invested their pensions, and fought lawsuits. When he returned, she had to pack everything up again—this time, they were moving to Saint John, New Brunswick. Arnold had established a shipping business there, was buying up land, and had built a general store. Late in 1787, only six weeks after they arrived in Canada, Peggy gave birth again.

For the first time since she left Philadelphia, Peggy was able to make close friends. She lived in a big gambrel-roofed clapboard house elegantly decorated with furniture Arnold brought from England. There were blue damask-covered sofas, matching drapes, and a mahogany table that seated twelve on blue damask-covered Sheraton cabriolet chairs that Arnold designed himself. After pouring her guests tea, she served them dinner (she was considered an accomplished cook) on Wedgwood giltware. But the house was an opulent island in a sea of deprivation. The new city was crowded with impoverished Loyalist refugees, and few people could afford to pay Arnold for his imported goods. He made new enemies as he faced frequent decisions about whether to sue or to put men in debtors' prison. When his warehouse and store burned, there were whispers that he had torched them for the insurance. A former business partner was one of his accusers, and when Arnold confronted him, the man said, according to the court record, "It is not in my power to blacken your character, for it's as black as it can be." The insult directly resulted in the denial of Arnold's insurance claim—and in the first jury trial for slander in New Brunswick history. Arnold won, but instead of the 5,000£ he sought, the judges based the award on the value of his reputation and gave him only twenty shillings, an unbearable insult. At the same time, a mob sacked the Arnolds' home. Peggy and the children were safely away at the time. After five years in Canada, the Arnolds moved back to England.

Like many Loyalists, Peggy planned to return one day to live in the United States, where she kept her inheritance invested in Robert Morris's Bank of the United States. However, when she went to visit her ailing, aged mother, the arrival of the traitor's wife in Philadelphia, even as a convention was deliberating a new Constitution, stirred controversy. Her brother-in-law recorded that she was treated "with so much coldness and neglect that her feelings were continually wounded." Old friends said her visit placed them "in a painful position." Others whispered that "she should have shown more feeling by staying away." After a five-month visit, Peggy left her family forever, deeply saddened. She wrote back to her sister:

> How difficult it is to know what will contribute to our happiness .... I had hoped that by paying my beloved friends a last visit, I should insure to myself some portion of it, but I find it far otherwise.

By early 1792, Peggy was back in London, unpacking after the Arnolds' third transatlantic move in ten years. Benedict Arnold's final years were occupied with a long string of business misadventures and also with his obsessive defense of his reputation. He expanded his Caribbean operations, and in his last eight years sent or sailed thirteen different ships on trading voyages. Often offended publicly, he fought a duel with the Earl of Lauderdale, who had insulted him on the floor of the House of Lords. Peggy wrote to her father that the days before the duel were filled with "a great deal of pain." She "had not dared to discuss the duel with the silent general," fearing that she would "unman him and prevent him acting himself." The duel produced no casualties, but it "almost at last proved too much for me, and for some hours, my reason was to be despaired of."

As the Napoleonic Wars engulfed Europe, Arnold outfitted his own privateering ship to attack French shipping in the Caribbean. This time, he was gone eighteen months. They were agonizing months for Peggy, who learned that her husband had been captured by French revolutionaries and managed to escape only shortly before his scheduled execution. When Arnold returned and she once again became pregnant, Peggy's health began to decline. On December 5, 1795, she wrote to friends in Canada, "For my own part, I am determined to have no more little plagues, as it is so difficult to provide for them in this country." For years Peggy lived in dread that the Queen would die and her pensions would stop. This was a legitimate fear after her husband's captains defrauded them of some £50,000 and she had to sell her private investments to bail him out. In 1801, at age sixty, Benedict Arnold became dispirited and, after a four-month illness, died "without a groan." Peggy, oppressed by his creditors and stunned by his loss, lived for three more years, only long enough to pay off all his debts "down to the last teaspoon."

"Years of unhappiness have passed," she confided in a letter to her brother-in-law. "I had cast my lot, complaints were unavailing, and you and my other friends are ignorant of the many causes of uneasiness I have had." To her father, she wrote that she had had to move to a smaller house, "parting with my furniture, wine, and many other comforts provided for me by the indulgent hand of [Arnold's] affection." Arnold had paid a final compliment to Peggy's business acumen by making her sole executrix of his estate, an unusual step at the time. Once she had cleared up the mess he had left and could see that her children would be provided for, she thanked her father for her fine private education: "To you, my dear parent, am I indebted for the ability to perform what I have done."

Years of anxiety and illness had exacted a terrible toll, and Peggy Shippen Arnold's quarter-century ordeal in exile ended on August 24, 1804. She had, she wrote, "the dreaded evil, a cancer." She told her sister she had "a very large tumor" in her uterus. "My only chance is from an internal operation which is at present dangerous to perform." Peggy died at forty-four. After she died, her children found concealed among her personal possessions a gold locket containing a snippet of John André's hair. Family tradition holds that Benedict Arnold never saw it.

QUESTIONS FOR THOUGHT AND DISCUSSION

1. Why was the Shippen family unsympathetic to the American Revolution? Does it seem strange that Judge Shippen would entertain both Loyalists and rebels in his home?

2. What do you think was the primary motivation behind Margaret Shippen Arnold's work to promote her husband's conversion to the British cause in the American Revolution?

3. Was the treason of the Arnolds justifiable on any grounds? Do you sympathize at all with the reasons behind this famous "treason"? Was their support for the Loyalist cause more or less justified than that of William Franklin?

4. How did the Arnolds fare in their conversion to the British cause? Did their treason pay off?

SUGGESTED READINGS

Engle, Paul. "Peggy Shippen" in *Revolutionary Women*. Chicago: Follett, 1976, pp. 153–162.

Hoffman, Ronald and Peter J. Albert, eds. *Women in the Age of the American Revolution.* Charlottesville: U of Virginia P, 1989.

Klein, Randolph S. "The Shippens of Pennsylvania: A Generational Study in Colonial and Revolutionary Pennsylvania." Unpub. PhD. dissertation. Rutgers U 1972.

Randall, Willard Sterne. *Benedict Arnold: Patriot and Traitor.* New York: Morrow, 1990.

_____. "Mrs. Benedict Arnold." *MHQ: Quarterly Magazine of Military History.* Winter, 1992, pp. 80–91.

Smith, Paul H. *Loyalists and Redcoats.* Chapel Hill: Institute of Early American History and Culture, 1964.

10

Abigail Adams

People living in Massachusetts in the 1740s and 1750s knew where they stood in the domain that mattered to them most, in their relation to their creator. A time of greater than usual religious fervor, the spiritual revival known as the Great Awakening exposed the population to frequent and passionate reminders that their first duty was to live in a way that carried out God's plan. The entire culture repeated that message through the media that existed: sermons delivered to crowds and written sermons passed around as the most important form of popular reading.

Abigail Adams spent her childhood in that morally severe climate where she learned that, as a woman, her duty would be to follow and be the "help-meet" of her husband. The no-nonsense Puritan sermons of her girlhood had taught her to expect trials from life such as the loss of one's children in infancy or the early death of one's parents or even husband. Her upbringing had not prepared her for the subtler trials of a life filled with contradictions. While she would appear to be the ideal wife and mother, she would in fact live as a single parent in practical terms, shouldering most of the domestic responsibility in her family. Toward her husband she would come to feel great psychological intimacy, but it would be as a result of their prolonged separations. Her letters, in which she reflected on her experience, helped to create that closeness. Better educated and better off than many other women of her day, this founding mother used her time and leisure in writing letters that now show where all the moral rigor and all those sermons went.

ABIGAIL ADAMS cannot be thought of as typical of her time. While the majority of women in New England as late as 1780 could not sign their names, literacy counted among Abigail's privileges.

Because Abigail Adams had the lifelong habit of writing letters almost daily to her family and friends, she left behind a portrait of her personality and a record of her achievements. But her letters do not automatically show how much she represented other women of her time and how much her thinking set her apart. Her early life especially includes experiences that make her resemble other girls born in New England in the mid-eighteenth century. Abigail Smith's mother came from the respected Quincy family of Weymouth, Massachusetts. Yet Abigail never went to school. For some young women, that lack may have meant not having an education, but Abigail Smith came from a family that knew how to train minds. Her mother taught her to read and the family made sure she had access to books, with supervision. Her family attracted intelligent visitors, including Richard Cranch, from England. That young scholar conveyed to Abigail his own passion for literature and, apparently, an additional passion for her older sister, whom he married.

For a child trained at home, the influence of books she read, in her case under the guidance of Mr. Cranch, probably multiplied since it was not diluted by the experience of school. The moral formation of a young person, then considered the point of all education, could not allow for any harmful ideas in the private curriculum. In this vigilance her family could not have been more typical of the times. Many educated families of her time recognized the moral danger of novels. This new category of reading matter was aimed at women, especially young ones, and believed capable of corrupting them. The Smith family, because of its general level of education, culture, and sophistication, understood that a good literary education should include some novels chosen with discrimination. The works of Samuel Richardson, the most popular English novelist of the day, helped form the mind of Abigail because she read them so diligently during her adolescent years. While she would later refer to *Pamela* as a book she enjoyed, in her youth it was *Sir Charles Grandison* whose impression sank deep. Published in seven volumes, it was an epistolary novel, that is, written and arranged as a series of letters. The moral purpose of the book was to give the portrait of a man of honor. More than that, it offered the portrait of a good husband.

In the eighteenth century, people were only beginning to understand that women might hope for a good husband and for a happy marriage—a new idea. Up to that time, notions of marriage had centered on the importance of preserving a family by having children, who assured the continuity of a name, and of providing a decent material standard of living. This was especially important from a woman's point of view since no well brought up woman could expect to support herself in economic terms. But the new thinking saw a married couple as partners and companions, each offering help and friendship to the other. This possibility appealed to Abigail Smith, the young reader of Richardson.

Abigail's love of Richardson's novels may have deepened her fondness for letters, yet any well-bred person was expected to spend part of nearly every day writing letters. From general reading (there were books showing model letters, including manuals by Richardson), and from living in a family in which letters were read aloud when they were received, young people grew up with a sense of how letters were supposed to sound. Abigail Smith learned that, unlike poetry or sermons, letters could be written in the "familiar style," which meant less formal than other kinds of writing and closer to everyday speech. Letters could report conversations, offer news, and give personal opinions of that news. In other words, they could transmit written gossip. A good letter came as a gift because it brought, through its use of language, the personality of the writer. It worked to deny the often painful absence of friends and family members. Those two strong ideas, the possibility of a companionable lifelong relationship and the importance of letters, belonged to the intellectual formation of Abigail Smith even before she married.

On October 25, 1764, just before she turned twenty years old, Abigail Smith married John Adams from nearby Braintree. To marry a man nine years older than herself upheld the general practice of men marrying younger women. (Her own sister, after all, had married Mr. Cranch, nearly sixteen years older than she.) They had planned to marry in the spring of the year, but the arrival of smallpox in Boston forced them to wait. The danger of accidental or "natural" infection seemed so serious to her bridegroom that he took the risky step of having himself inoculated. People counted on the technique of applying a thread carrying a small quantity of pus from an infected person to induce a milder case of the illness than would be experienced if unsupervised infection occurred. Before being given the treatment, the patient had to follow a special diet and purgings under a physician's eye. In fortunate cases, the inoculated person had mild symptoms. Other times the choice to be inoculated left people with disfiguring scars or it could kill them.

Abigail Smith's father, Parson William Smith, had known young Adams for about five years by the time he gave him his daughter in marriage. The Smith family did not see in him the best possible husband material. They knew that he had first intended to enter the ministry, the profession of Mr. Smith, and then had given it up because of religious doubts. Now, as a young lawyer, he might not necessarily be a good provider for young Abigail since few men could make a living by practicing law in those days. Her family also realized that socially, very little prestige or respect attached itself to the legal profession.

The Boston epidemic of smallpox limited travel and kept the couple from seeing each other. For this reason, throughout their courtship they wrote letters. John Adams was living under a physician's care after his inoculation because the treatment required being kept isolated with other patients. Their very frequent early letters show a playful side of their relationship, but they also show decided differences in style and personality. Abigail's lightness and her quick wit comes through strongly. Her genuine desire to see her fiancé allows her to write urgent requests for his news. When he did not tell her enough of the kinds of facts she wanted to know, she helped him along by providing a list of questions to guide him in noting the particulars of his progress. Such gestures revealed her attitude about helping her future mate. Some young women of her time might have confused modesty with a hesitant passiveness, but no such quality marked her. Her request for frequent letters tells how much she valued the news since the letters themselves were considered dangerous. To handle paper that had been touched by someone infected with smallpox put her at risk. Before she could read them they had to be held over smoke to be decontaminated.

After John Adams came through his inoculation with only the mildest discomfort, they married and the couple moved to Braintree. They moved into a house he had bought for his bride that was a very short distance from his birthplace in the house where his mother still lived. Abigail Adams would remain in the new house, only yards away from her mother-in-law, as her husband began his career in public life. As a lawyer, John Adams had to travel to sessions of court. These sessions were typically in Boston or Plymouth, far enough away by horseback over bad roads to keep him away from home. During the first year of their married life he attended court most months. He may have been away from home on July 14, 1765 when their first child, Abigail, was born. (There was never any question of the Adams' improper conduct before their marriage. The baby was born slightly earlier than expected.)

Even Abigail Adams, who wrote down so many things about her inner experience, says nothing at all in writing about giving birth to this child. Like any woman of her day, she no doubt prepared for childbirth by acknowledging to herself that she faced the possibility of death in giving birth, not because of a morbid personality but from personal knowledge. In North America very few physicians could be found who had trained themselves to assist at the inevitably risky trial of childbirth. Women assisted other women in giving birth, relying on their own experience as mothers and as midwives. Abigail Adams recorded practically nothing of that aspect of motherhood in letters and likely would not have done so had she kept a diary. But her letters do record the great happiness she found in having a daughter and in having a child survive the first few months (another stage that could prove fatal to weak children or women who suffered infections associated with nursing).

Abigail's intellectual energy allowed her to come up with rigorous and rewarding reading programs to get through the lonely periods when she missed her husband's company and conversation. Her letters show that she did miss him, even though she did not find herself solitary in her house. Her mother-in-law lived close by, and within Abigail's house she had four servants. But winter weather lasted for many months and restricted travel, especially for a young woman with a baby. When the second winter of married life came, Abigail knew that she was pregnant again. Reading a series of sermons by a well-known preacher got her through those months of separation from her husband. In her letters, she did not disguise the fact that she would rather have had her husband by her side, day and night.

Possibly because she did not keep a diary, Abigail used her letters as a way of thinking out on paper things that she wanted to analyze, just as she had done before she had married. The moral questions that interested her concerned understanding the relation of what people believe to how they behave, the kind of analysis she had learned to love in the "letters" of Richardson's novels. Her letters let her think.

Mrs. Adams' mental energy found its outlet in writing not only to her husband but to other relations and friends, some of whom had been her correspondents since girlhood. But her children claimed any physical effort she could muster. Her second child, John Quincy (named for her grandfather who was dying when she had the baby) was born on July 11, 1767. A third child, a daughter, died at the age of thirteen months. A second son came in 1770, and a fifth child two years later. By the age of twenty-eight, Abigail Adams had given birth five times. During these years she also had the responsibility of moving her family to Boston—to Brattle Square, then to two other houses in Boston, then back to Braintree, and then back to Boston. In all, by November 1772, Mrs. Adams was moving her four children for the fourth time since 1768. And two years after that, her husband recommended that she move the children back to Braintree, where he would worry about her less.

All the moves, in fact, had been at his suggestion, usually to make it possible for the family to be together or for him to have his wife's advice and help.

Early in the American Revolution, during 1775 and 1776, Abigail Adams, in Massachusetts, had a great deal to tell her husband in Philadelphia. Her letters contained information of special value to the Continental Congress, details about British ships in Boston harbor and about troops. Because she understood what she was seeing, Abigail Adams knew how exposed she was to danger without her husband's help. At the start of the Battle of Bunker Hill, she climbed from the bottom of Penn's Hill, where she lived, to the top to watch with her seven-year-old son, John Quincy, the British burning the town of Charlestown. When she later described the ten month long siege of Boston, she wrote, "The constant roar of the cannon is so distressing that we cannot eat, drink, or sleep."

When John Adams visited his family in August 1775 in Braintree, he was returning from a visit to the American army, behind the lines in Watertown. When he left shortly after that to go back to the Continental Congress in Philadelphia, members of his family began to come down with dysentery, a disease caused by the erratic hygiene of army camps. (It appears that Mr. Adams brought the disease home with him.) When Abigail finally began to suffer its debilitating symptoms, including acute abdominal cramps and bloody bowels, she found it impossible to care for her small children by herself and sent for her mother to come and help. When Mrs. Smith did come, she contracted the ailment herself and died from its weakening effects. When Abigail had a daughter on July 11, 1777, whom she had planned to name for her mother, the baby was born dead. When John Adams returned home that November, Abigail hoped that he would make good on his promise: "The next time I come home it will be for a long time." He stayed for about three months.

For years Abigail Adams had known that her husband took seriously his plan to achieve renown by serving the young country they had worked to set on its course. Knowing that, she still felt bitterness when she found out only weeks after his return home that John Adams planned to go to France as American minister (the equivalent of ambassador, a post which had not been created). His plan included taking his ten-year-old son John Quincy to Paris with him. After her husband and son sailed for Europe in February 1778, Abigail Adams had no word to confirm their safe arrival for four months. Instead, rumors came her way, impossible to disprove or verify, of their capture and of the loss of their ship. That voyage merely began a pattern of foreign travel for the family. After their safe return in August 1779, John Adams and his son John Quincy, this time joined by a younger son, Charles, all left for Paris.

When her husband and two sons left Abigail Adams had no way of knowing that the brief spell of a few months that they had spent together would be all the time she was to have with her husband for six years. While he was away she took it upon herself to defend the reputation of John Adams from people who did not value him as she did. As the long absence grew, she came to believe that no one had sacrificed as she had, giving up so much personal happiness and years she might have spent with her husband, all for the benefit of the United States. She reasoned that because she allowed him to be away, he was able to do the important work of making treaties and protecting the interests of the new republic. In taking the position that her cooperation had been essential to his diplomatic work, Abigail Adams implied that she might have insisted that he stay at home and not devote those years to public service.

To help his wife endure their separation, John Adams tried to give her the illusion of closeness by reporting to her what occupied him. From letters, she knew that her husband and his associates were preparing papers to change the legal and political status of the British colonies in America. In response, Abigail Adams gave advice, warning him not to repeat what was sometimes omitted from such discussions: "I long to hear that you have declared an independancy—and ... I desire you would Remember the Ladies, and be more generous and favourable to them than your ancestors" (March 31, 1776). John Adams appreciated what her letters were worth; he encouraged her to keep copies of the letters she wrote, to read them to their children and to use them as lessons.

An overall view of her correspondence shows her vigorous intellect and her discipline in keeping at letter writing, reading, and discussing what she read as she kept up her efforts to develop the native strength of her mind. Her sense of decorum made it impossible for her to complain in society of how much she missed her husband. But in her letters to him she saw no reason to hold back. When he read his wife's version of her personal suffering because he remained far away, John Adams did not feel moved. The letters that apparently gave Abigail the satisfaction of having expressed feelings that tormented her, offered no benefit for her husband as he read them. Finding it impossible to know what to say, he put off answering and finally told her, bluntly, that he would prefer no news at all to her letters so full of what he called her "complaining tone."

Abigail probably did not imagine that as her husband spent more time in Europe, he would write to her less often. While he traveled in Spain in 1780 he sent a few reports of his work and life there, but less frequently as the year went on. In 1781, she received her first letter of the year in August, after a silence of eight months. For that period her husband neglected to tell her he had taken the children with him to Holland where they attended school. Not from her husband, but from other people she learned the whereabouts of her sons.

Because she had been brought up with the same attitudes as other young women in New England in the eighteenth century, Abigail Adams had no reason to expect from marriage the kind of life she found with her husband. She had no reason to imagine herself spending so much time alone, but neither had she seen ahead such a degree of independence. In her husband's absence, it fell to her to make financial decisions which would influence the material circumstances of her children. She had to sell property and had to manage the farm, the equivalent of running a small business. In those arrangements she openly opposed slavery. She may not have expected to move her household so frequently, or to have so little stability compared to most moderately well-off young married women, but neither did she anticipate meeting such interesting people as she would soon come to know. In getting her own daughter ready for an uncertain future, Adams supervised her education carefully, believing it could do a great deal to prepare a woman for responsibility.

New York State Historical Association, Cooperstown

Few portraits remain of Abigail Adams's face, while many letters preserve and project her character.

At the age of forty, when her youngest child was twelve, and after both her parents had died, Abigail Adams finally felt free to accept her husband's invitation to join him abroad. When she reached London she laid eyes on her younger son for the first time in five years. In August of that year she met her husband after an absence of four and a half years. With her husband and family she spent nine happy months in Paris where she acquired a great deal of experience entertaining as the wife of a diplomat. She observed the customs of a world quite unlike Braintree, Massachusetts. A quick observer, she understood that the representatives of the United States did not enjoy the same advantages as those of other countries. To entertain in the expected manner required the purchase of fine table linens, exquisite dishes, and all the necessities of high style, but on a limited expense allowance. New England simplicity or not, she knew that formalities had to be respected in order for her young country to be taken seriously in a European capital. Because of her upbringing, she had trouble at first appreciating the luxury of French fashions, particularly of the clothing of the ladies she saw. But she softened her judgment as she came to know some.

After living in Paris for nine months, Abigail Adams and her household moved to London. From there she maintained contact with Paris through her lively correspondence with a notable American whose company she had learned to enjoy during her stay in France. Thomas Jefferson saw in Abigail Adams the straightforward manner that must have reminded him of American women he had known. Because his own wife had died three years earlier, Jefferson welcomed Mrs. Adams's kind interest in his daughter, Patsy, age thirteen, who came to join him in Paris. Their letters show how fondly the two friends enjoyed each other. With Abigail Adams, Jefferson let himself joke and even show outrageous sarcasm, perhaps because he thought their letters were being intercepted. When he referred to an attempt to assassinate the English king, whom Jefferson considered contemptible, he insisted most excessively that the monarch had done a great deal to help the United States (he meant by massive ineptitude): "No man upon earth has my prayers for his continuance in life more sincerely than him. He is truly the American Messiah. That most precious life that ever God gave..." Through the same exchange of letters ran frequent requests for "favors," as each friend asked the other for things not easy to buy. From France, Abigail Adams never forgot that, as an ambassador's wife, she might be criticized for being too fashion conscious. But still she asked Jefferson to send her silk shoes of "any fashionable colour, orange excepted which is in high vogue here" (December 5, 1787).

While in England, Abigail Adams and her husband received news from America, sometimes finding it incomprehensible or distressing. Word of Shays' Rebellion in Massachusetts, for example, disquieted Abigail Adams, who seemed to be losing her original confidence in the wisdom of "the people." Whether it was absence from America that changed her thinking or her frequent contact with aristocratic circles within the orbit of a monarch, it is impossible to delineate exactly how it happened that the years in England left her somehow less convinced of the original revolutionary ideals. Along with her husband, she was coming to see differences between herself and the supporters of Jefferson, the stronger upholders of the wisdom of the people.

In the spring of 1788 the Adamses, parents and children, returned to North America. Daughter Abigail, recently married to Colonel William Stephens Smith, son of a New York family, remained for a short time in England. Toward the end of that same year, Abigail traveled alone from Boston to New York to visit her daughter who was getting ready to have her first child. The custom of the time did not allow her husband to go along on the journey because of his interest in being elected vice president. Prospective candidates for public office had to observe the propriety of doing absolutely nothing to go after the positions they wanted and he had to avoid any crowds he might have encountered along the way. But while Mrs. Adams visited with the in-laws of her daughter, supporters of her husband came to her to make known their support. John Jay among others called on her to encourage her husband in this indirect yet normal manner. So strong was support for Adams that at the time of the first presidential election, he received the second highest number of votes after George Washington, a distinction which entitled him to serve as Vice President in the nation's capital at New York.

Abigail Adams loved the year they spent in New York City before moving to the new capital at Philadelphia. She had a strong sense of having earned some recognition as a reward for the years she had spent deprived of her husband. The years 1790 and 1791 in the Quaker City brought an extremely rich social life which the sociable Mrs. Adams loved. But when her health weakened late in 1792, she moved back to Braintree where she lived for five years, again without her husband. In 1796, Adams was elected President. For much of this time, too, Abigail lived alone without him. When he lost his bid for re-election and she and her husband moved together to Quincy, Massachusetts (as their section of Braintree had been renamed) in early 1801, it was the first time they had managed to be together without expecting a long separation.

The simplicity of those years brought the companionable pleasure that Abigail Adams had expected so many years earlier in her marriage. Living as a country woman, she milked her own cows, tended her garden, and delighted in the tranquility of their new style of living. During these same years, however, her strength failed and her rheumatism grew more painful. She resumed correspondence with her old friend Thomas Jefferson, writing him when his daughter, whom she had known as a little girl in Paris, died in her twenties. Eventually after years as political enemies, Adams and Jefferson were brought together again by Abigail's tactful diplomacy.

In her letters to Jefferson and in his to her, the lightness of their days in Paris and London had been lost. Politics had chilled their friendship, a change which they were finally able to talk over in their mature letters, to make peace. In October 1818, just one month before she would have been seventy-four years old, Abigail Adams died. Her old friend Jefferson, writing through tears to her husband, felt such pain at losing Abigail that he could not write very much, but offered Adams what he had learned: " ... The same trials have taught me that, for ills so immeasurable, time and silence are the only medicines."

When Abigail Adams was an old woman and heard the proposal that her letters be collected and published, she found the idea laughable. The letters had been her way of discussing a demanding life with an often absent partner.

QUESTIONS FOR THOUGHT AND DISCUSSION

1. What sacrifices did Abigail Adams make in her personal life as the wife of a politician? In what ways did these sacrifices make her stronger? Would you describe her life as a satisfying one?

2. To what was Abigail Adams referring when she wrote to her husband to "remember the ladies"? From what you know about the actions of the founding fathers, did her plea have an effect?

3. How did the letters between Abigail Adams and her husband (and other correspondents) serve a deeper purpose than mere communication?

4. From the many bits of news discernible in Abigail Adams' correspondence, a historian can reconstruct the attitudes, sentiments, and daily activities in order to recapture what life was like and what people were thinking at that time. With letter writing now a nearly lost art, how will future historians reconstruct our times?

SUGGESTED READINGS

Akers, Charles W. *Abigail Adams: An American Woman.* Boston: Little, 1980.

Butterfield, L. H. et al. *The Book of Abigail and John: Selected Letters of the Adams Family, 1762–1764.* Cambridge, Mass.: Belknap, 1975.

Cappon, Lester J., ed. *The Adams-Jefferson Letters: The Complete Correspondence Between Thomas Jefferson and Abigail and John Adams.* Chapel Hill: U of North Carolina P, 1987.

James, Edward T. and Janet W. James. *Notable American Women, 1607–1950: A Biographical Dictionary.* 3 vols. Cambridge, Mass.: Harvard UP, 1971.

Ketcham, Ralph. "The Puritan Ethic in the Revolutionary Era: Abigail Adams and Thomas Jefferson," in Carol V. R. George, ed., "Remember the Ladies": *New Perspectives on Women in American History.* Syracuse: Syracuse UP, 1975, pp. 49–65.

_____. *John Quincy Adams, the Critical Years, 1758–1794.* New York: Bookman, 1962.

Levin, Phyllis Lee. *Abigail Adams: A Biography.* New York: St. Martin's , 1987.

Norton, Mary Beth. *Liberty's Daughters: The Revolutionary Experience of American Women, 1750–1800.* Boston: Little, 1980.

Smith, Page. *John Adams.* 2 vol. Garden City, N.Y.: Doubleday, 1962.

11

Thomas Jefferson

During the American Revolution, Thomas Jefferson predicted to his young friend, James Madison, that unless they rammed through the Virginia House of Delegates their entire radical reform agenda before the shooting stopped, it would be virtually impossible to rekindle revolutionary zeal and bring about any further change. His words were prophetic. The Virginia Constitution, passed in the first fervid days after the break with England, remained little changed fifty years later when Jefferson died. Despite all his efforts, the institution of slavery and a corrupt county judiciary were left virtually intact. It took ten years for Jefferson and Madison to win the battle for religious freedom and twenty for free public education.

In the backlash of the American Revolution, many of the states reverted to the control of conservative oligarchies. In less than five years of the cessation of hostilities, this ruling system chafed to curtail democratic tendencies and impose a stronger, more structured, and centralized government. The result was the Constitution of 1787. In Paris through most of this period as American minister plenipotentiary, Jefferson was not consulted about many of the changes. Aghast that the reform of "our dear old constitution" had been so sweeping, he nevertheless vowed to support the new form of government so long as Madison promised to work equally hard to enact a Bill of Rights. When Jefferson returned to America after an absence of five years and joined Washington's Cabinet as the first Secretary of State, he was well aware that the country he had left so recently was rapidly changing.

BY THE END of the First Congress in the spring of 1791, Thomas Jefferson, the first Secretary of State, badly needed a break from the power struggle that was wracking President Washington's government. Jefferson disliked the noise, dirt, and crowds of living in the capital at Philadelphia. He also disliked the boring routines of office work. The past year especially had taken its toll, since Jefferson had been suffering from recurring migraine headaches. He could find little peace in his rented house on the main wagon route into the city. But, worst of all, he was becoming increasingly embroiled in political controversies with Secretary of the Treasury Alexander Hamilton.

The in-fighting was about to become public. Jefferson opposed Hamilton's pro-British trade policies and was alarmed that his old friend, Vice President John Adams, writing in a series of columns in the pro-Hamilton *National Gazette* under a pen name, was advocating stronger ties with England. Jefferson therefore was elated to receive a copy of Thomas Paine's latest anti-British blast, *The Rights of Man*, just published in London. Jefferson wrote a note recommending publication and sent it off to a printer. He intended his comments to remain private. He was, after all, in Washington's Cabinet with Adams and Hamilton. He was chagrined when the printer published his signed letter as the introduction to Paine's tract. That spring, scores of newspapers reprinted Jefferson's letter. Overnight, Jefferson became the spokesman for Americans disenchanted with Washington's policies. "I am sincerely mortified," he wrote Washington, "to be thus brought forward on the public stage against my love of silence ... and my abhorrence of disputes."

Jefferson sorely needed to get away from a job he had only accepted after James Madison told Washington that, without Jefferson to speak for the farmer and for the worker, the new government would be in trouble. Returning to America in 1789 on home leave after five years as minister to France, Jefferson had expected to return to his diplomatic post in Paris. Only Washington's insistence made him accept an office job in the new federal government.

For a long time, Jefferson had wanted to visit Vermont. As champion of the frontier farmer, he thought of Vermont as the frontier ideal. It represented to him a sort of Virginia unspoiled by slavery and entrenched tidewater aristocrats, where every person would have a chance to own a home and land and make a good living by trading surplus crops for whatever else they needed.

Thomas Jefferson liked to think about things in new ways. In the strictest sense, he was not an inventor. The only device he actually invented was a new kind of plow. However, there were many other things in which his innovative spirit stopped little short of invention as he put his mind to think about age-old problems in new ways. Like time, how and where to spend it, and travel, and how and when to put time and travel together into something entirely new: the summer vacation. At a time when traveling for pleasure was almost unheard of (except for the once-in-a-lifetime grand tour of European capitals made by a small number of wealthy young Englishmen and even fewer Americans), Jefferson began to take annual trips away from the press of official business. (The word vacation had not even been invented yet.) On half a dozen sojourns away from Paris, Jefferson turned himself into a scientific traveler, always following a carefully arranged and timed itinerary and carrying out a complicated agenda of activities. Traveling without servants in a plain black suit in a carriage crammed with books and a portable writing desk, he made detailed notes of his studies of farming methods, soil conditions, weather, art and architecture, currencies, governments, trade, and nutrition. Shunning politicians, he interviewed farmers, merchants, shopkeepers, shipowners, and workers of all sorts as he traveled through England, France, Italy, the Netherlands, and Germany.

To his close friend, the Marquis de Lafayette, he wrote on the eve of the French Revolution his belief that to govern a country with any degree of enlightenment, officials needed to get away from their capitals and go "absolutely incognito" to see first-hand how people live:

> You must ferret the people out of their hovels as I have done, look into their kettles, eat their bread, loll on their beds under pretense of resting yourself but in fact to find if they are soft. You will find a more sublime pleasure ... when you shall be able to apply your knowledge to the softening of their beds and the throwing of a morsel of meat into their kettles of vegetables.

It had been seven years since Jefferson had made a long swing through the eastern United States en route to his diplomatic duties in France. To former aide David Humphreys he confessed, "I know only the Americans of the year 1784. They tell me this is to be much a stranger."

When Thomas Jefferson wrote the story of his life, he said his earliest memory was of being handed up, at age two, to a slave on horseback and being carried fifty miles on a pillow from his father's farm to a plantation he was to manage. Jefferson was born in a simple frame farmhouse on the Virginia frontier on April 13, 1743. His father, Peter, never went to school but taught himself accounting, surveying, and mapmaking. His small library included the Bible and Shakespeare. He became Albemarle County judge, militia commander, delegate to the House of Burgesses, and the man who surveyed and mapped Virginia's boundary lines.

Family legend has it that Jefferson read all of his father's books by age five before he began attending school. He already was aware of the differences between blacks and whites. While he went to school each day, his black friends couldn't. One of eight children, Tom was packed off to a boarding school at age nine where he learned French, Latin, and Greek. He taught himself the violin and he loved to ride horses. He liked to hike in the woods but not to hunt. When his father ordered him to go out and learn how to kill a wild turkey, he bought a live one at the market and shot it.

When Tom was fourteen, his father died, leaving him 7,500 acres of land, twenty-five slaves, his bookcase of forty books, his writing desk, and his surveying tools. His final wish was that Tom continue his studies. A guardian enrolled Tom in a small academy where he studied science, and his teacher took him on field trips in the Blue Ridge Mountains in search of fossils. He acquired a lifelong habit of copying out his favorite lines from his readings.

The first in his family to attend college, he spent two years studying at William and Mary College, then trained as a lawyer for six years (there were no law schools). A brilliant young teacher from Scotland, Dr. William Small, introduced Jefferson to the Age of the Enlightenment. "When I was young, mathematics was the passion of my life," he wrote in his autobiography. He also taught Jefferson to love rhetoric. He studied hard. A friend said his studying was "not only intense" but unremitting. Jefferson managed to study even when a college roommate rode a horse into his room to try to distract him.

Introduced to George Wythe, later the first American law professor, Jefferson decided to study law. Many colonial lawyers studied for only a few months before taking bar examinations. For the next five years, Jefferson walked from his rented rooms to the brick house on Palace Green in Williamsburg and took his place with other young clerks at the round table in the back room. There, he learned to admire written constitutions of laws and to loath dull, complicated language. He qualified to practice before the colony's highest court, rapidly emerging as one of Virginia's leading lawyers.

In 1769, at age twenty-six, he won a seat in the House of Burgesses. The very first bill he wrote would have allowed plantation owners to free their slaves. It took a special act of the Burgesses to free a single slave for extraordinary service and then he had to leave the colony without his still-enslaved family within one year. This first antislavery bill was shouted down. Yet that same year, Jefferson paid to advertise for the arrest of Sandy, a slave shoemaker who stole one of his horses and tried to run away. Jefferson wanted to be able to decide who would be emancipated and when. In 1770, he refused to defend a white overseer who whipped a black woman to death. His first public pleading that all men are created equal came in the case of *Howell v. Netherland*. He took Samuel Howell's suit "for freedom" without charging a fee. Howell's grandmother had been the child of a white woman and a black man. She had been enslaved for miscegenation. Rising before the General Court in April 1770, Jefferson stunned the jurors with his vehemence:

> Under the law of nature, all men are born free. Everyone comes into the world with a right to his own person, which includes the liberty of moving and using it at his own will. This is what is called personal liberty, and [it] is given him by the Author of nature.

Jefferson said he doubted Virginia's legislature could be "wicked enough" to extend his client's slavery from generation to generation. He was gavelled down. The case was dismissed.

Jefferson was also considered radical for representing the interests of settlers on the frontier against the Tidewater oligarchy. The bulk of his legal work involved trying to break the stranglehold of absentee landlords. His law practice came to an abrupt end when the revolutionary movement against the British shut down the courts.

In 1770, Jefferson helped organize the colonial boycott of British goods. He wrote the Virginia resolution establishing a standing House of Burgesses committee of correspondence coordinating protests with other colonies' assemblies. In 1774, after the Boston Port Act took effect, he served on the committee which rejected British conciliation. Prevented by illness from attending the Virginia Convention of 1774, he wrote *A Summary View of the Rights of British Americans*, denying parliamentary authority over the colonies and urging repudiation of all British claims to tax Americans. Elected in 1776 a Virginia delegate to the Second Continental Congress, at age thirty-three he was the youngest member of Congress, and was soon appointed to the committee to draw up a Declaration of Independence.

The genius of Jefferson's writing lay in his ability to take complicated concepts of history, law, and philosophy and clothe them in direct, simple language. It was not his task to educate but to use the power of reasoning to justify a revolution. His Declaration was one of the earliest attempts at political science. Jefferson spelled out "self-evident" truths he held most important: "All men are created equal ... they are endowed by their creator with certain inalienable rights... life, liberty, and the pursuit of happiness." This memorable phrase was the most succinct expression ever of American political philosophy. In this draft Declaration, Jefferson charged that the King was personally responsible for the slave trade. Jefferson's condemnation of the slave trade was cut out completely at the insistence of Georgia and South Carolina, still importing slaves. Returning to Virginia, he was elected to the new revolutionary assembly, the House of Delegates. He wrote 133 new laws in three years, including bills separating church and state and establishing a public school system. In 1778, he drafted a bill abolishing the foreign slave trade, "leaving to future efforts ... final extinction of slavery." Less successful in two one-year terms as governor, he found that his reforms had helped to make the governor's office too weak to be effective. When the British invaded Virginia in 1781, Jefferson was only able to mobilize 200 militia who fled before experienced British troops. Jefferson twice narrowly escaped capture.

After his wife gave birth to her sixth child in nine years, she died. Devastated, Jefferson left Virginia for six years. Returning to Congress, he devised a decimal monetary system and drafted the Land Ordinance of 1784 (forerunner of the Northwest Ordinance), which banned slavery in all states carved out of federal territory.

Elected by Congress to go to Paris to negotiate trade treaties with European nations, Jefferson succeeded Benjamin Franklin as minister to France in 1785. He became a literary sensation when he published his *Notes on Virginia* (Paris, 1785), his only book, a natural history. It contained Jefferson's strongest written stand against slavery. He denounced "the whole commerce between master and slave" as "a perpetual exercise of the most boisterous passions, the most unremitting despotism on the one part and degrading submission on the other ... I tremble for my country when I reflect that God is just." He hoped, he wrote "for a total emancipation with the consent of the masters."

Traveling widely in Europe, he established many American consulates and drafted a model trade treaty with Prussia. Witnessing the beginnings of the French Revolution, with his close friend Lafayette he helped edit early drafts of the French Declaration of the Rights of Man and of the Citizen. After five years in Europe, he went home on leave just as Washington was forming his first Cabinet. Worried about centralizing power under the new Constitution, he reluctantly joined the new government. Almost at once, he began using his new office as Secretary of State to oppose Hamilton's policies.

Jefferson had been working hard in the temporary capital in Philadelphia. In addition to his official duties as Secretary of State, he was designing the new nation's mint, establishing a system of weights and measures, and helping to choose the site and supervise the design of a permanent U.S. capital. A summer trip offered a welcome respite when, on March 13, 1791, Congressman James Madison wrote to propose that they make a tour as far to the north as they could go and return in a month. In his free time, Jefferson wore another hat: vice president of the American Philosophical Society, a circle of amateur scientists who included most of Jefferson's close friends. That spring, the society was pondering two questions: when does the opossum's pouch disappear and how to stop crop damages caused by the Hessian fly.

Jefferson had written his son-in-law, Thomas Mann Randolph, managing Jefferson's plantation, Monticello, to be on the lookout for opossums. On May 8, Jefferson wrote the Society that Randolph had observed that the "pouch of the opossum disappeared after weaning the young," and continued:

> Though a single observation is not conclusive, yet the memory remains strong with me that, when a boy, we used to amuse ourselves with forcing open the pouch of the opossum, when [it had] no young ... The sphincter was so strongly contracted it [was] difficult to find where we were to enter our fingers.

More serious was Jefferson's concern about the Hessian fly, which had been ravaging American wheat harvests. He asked his scientist friends to help him put together a list of questions he could ask along his vacation route. Such a questionnaire was quite advanced for the times. While the document does not survive, we can deduce its existence from the systematic way Jefferson recorded responses at every stop to questions he put to farmer, ferryman, local official, or tavernkeeper and to the report he later circulated in the newspapers. He would note the year and extent of each Hessian fly infestation, asking about each of the last six years. Jefferson, a man of the Enlightenment, believed that the use of reason when applied systematically could lead to human progress. He believed such questions of paramount importance, especially when they related to anything that endangered the crops of his largely agricultural country.

Jefferson believed that the American future should belong to the independent farmer, not the city-dweller. He not only was uncomfortable in cities, he thought they bred crime and disease. He envisioned the dark urban landscape of the Industrial Revolution after only a single visit to the grimy factories and crowded tenements of London. Instead, he wanted to endow Americans with enough land to provide high nutrition and crop surpluses that they could sell or barter for whatever they themselves could not grow or make. In addition to putting into practice a long-thought-out philosophy, he was combining his public and private offices. As Secretary of State, he was also secretary of the interior and secretary of agriculture, since there was none yet. Jefferson was using his unique position to carry out what was probably the first federal scientific study.

On May 9, 1791, Madison left Philadelphia for New York City to procure supplies and make travel arrangements. Jefferson sent him a proposed itinerary:

> When we tack about from the extremity of our journey, instead of coming back the same way, to cross over through Vermont to [the] Connecticut River and down that [river] to New Haven, then through Long Island to New York and so to Philadelphia.

Jefferson wrote to President Washington, touring the Carolinas, "I think to avail myself of the present interval of quiet to get rid of a headache which is very troublesome by giving more exercise to the body and less to the mind."

A note to son-in-law Randolph suggests a hidden political agenda. Jefferson sent him a copy of a Philadelphia newspaper, the *National Gazette*, which supported Hamilton, its editorial policy was:

> pure Toryism, disseminating [Hamilton's] doctrine of monarchy, aristocracy and the exclusion of the people ... We have been trying to get another weekly or half-weekly

[newspaper] excluding advertisements set up, so that it could go free through the states in the mails and furnish [our] vehicle of intelligence. We hoped at one time to have persuaded Freneau [Philip Freneau, a New Jersey journalist and poet], but we have failed.

Jefferson here was admitting in a private letter what he had been denying in public: that he was involved in an opposition faction within Washington's government and was backing his own partisan newspaper. His son-in-law was to forward Hamilton's paper each week via government mail to stops along his route. Jefferson and Madison would have the latest political news to discuss in the long days on the road, where they would have strictest privacy.

As usual, Jefferson was strapped for cash. He had to await arrival of four hogsheads of Monticello tobacco to sell for travel money. When the shipment finally arrived, it was worthless, already smoked in a fire. It "cannot be sold here at all," he bemoaned. At first, Jefferson had offered to pay all Madison's expenses, but Madison insisted on dividing them. As it turned out, Jefferson would run out of money on the road and end up borrowing from Madison. Jefferson's high, black carriage rolled out of Philadelphia on May 17. He wrote in a travel journal he kept on the back of his pocket almanac that he "heard the first whip-poor-will." Two days later, Madison, in New York, wrote his brother that "Mr. Jefferson is here." Jefferson checked into Mrs. Ellsworth's boardinghouse in Maiden Lane with journalist Philip Freneau and fellow Virginians Madison and John Beckley, Clerk of the House of Representatives. Their meeting fanned reports from Hamilton supporters of political intriguing, but Jefferson and Madison remained silent. One of Hamilton's friends was George Beckwith, unofficial envoy of Great Britain to the United States. "I am sorry to inform your Grace," he wrote to the British foreign secretary, "that the Secretary of State's [Jefferson's] party and politics gains ground here. [They] will have influence enough to cause acts and resolves which may be unfriendly to Great Britain to be passed early in the next session of Congress. The Secretary of State, together with Mr. Madison, are now gone to the Eastern States, there to proselyte as far as they are able a commercial war with Britain." Alexander Hamilton's son, John, had no doubt Jefferson was politicking. He flatly asserted the Virginians were meeting secretly in New York City with newly-elected U.S. Senator Aaron Burr, Hamilton's enemy, before going on to huddle with Governor George Clinton, a leading anti-Federalist, in Albany, the state capital. Aaron Burr had just unseated Hamilton's father-in-law, Philip Schuyler, from the Senate.

If Jefferson and Madison were merely on vacation, they had no reason to conceal *or* to comment on visits to New York politicians. But if they were engaged, as John Adams's son, John Quincy, later wrote, in "double dealing," there was good reason for silence. It is likely that Jefferson and Madison called on Aaron Burr. Instead of using his own distinctive Monticello-made carriage, which was recognizable, Jefferson's expense records show he hired a coach for one day while in New York City. Even the possibility of such an alliance worried Hamilton's supporters. "They had better be quiet," wrote Robert Troup to Hamilton, "for if they succeed, they will tumble the fabric of the government in ruins to the ground."

National Portrait Gallery, Washington, D.C.

After forty years in various public offices, Thomas Jefferson died bankrupt. His family sold Monticello and most of his slaves to clear his debts.

Intrigues aside, the first thing Jefferson did when he reached a large town along the road was to buy books. He also sent out his manservant, the mulatto slave, James Hemings, to buy fresh fruit and vegetables. In his years in Paris, Jefferson had placed James in the kitchen of the Prince de Condé to learn French cooking. In Paris, Hemings's younger sister, Sally, was the servant of Jefferson's teenage daughter, Patsy. James and Sally were the half-brother and half-sister of Jefferson's wife, Martha Wayles Jefferson. They shared the same father.

Shortly after Jefferson had married in 1772, his father-in-law, John Wayles, had died after importing a shipload of slaves from Africa. With Wayles's death, the task of selling off the newly-arrived slaves devolved on Jefferson, whose wife inherited one-third of them. He kept slave families together when he selected 135 slaves and brought them to Monticello in 1774. They included Betty Hemings, the mulatto slave concubine of John Wayles, and her family of five children, who became the favored house slaves at Monticello. James Hemings was nine when he arrived at Monticello. Months later, Betty Hemings gave birth again, this time to Sally, according to an older brother, "mighty near white." Sally was nearly the same age as Jefferson's second daughter, Polly, and was to be her body servant. According to a younger brother, Madison Hemings, interviewed after the Civil War, his grandmother Betty Hemings "had seven children by white men and seven by colored."

James Hemings, who spoke French fluently, shared Jefferson's travels for ten years. The next year, Jefferson set James free. He was becoming convinced, as he wrote to the black mathematician Benjamin Banneker, that "nature has given to our black brethren talents equal to those of the other colors of men." Jefferson entrusted James with his carriage and enough travel money for him to go ahead on the Post Road to Poughkeepsie, New York, where the touring party would rendezvous. For all their obvious and numerous presence, slaves are usually invisible in early American history. Jefferson's expense records prove Hemings' presence on his voyages and give glimpses of his duties. "James for expenses to Poughkeepsie six [dollars]."

As they sailed up the Hudson they made an overnight stop at Conklin's Tavern. In addition to writing down the price of breakfast, Jefferson began to rate the inns along their route: a nondescript inn got no comment or "middling," a good inn, a plus mark or star, a bad one, a minus. Jefferson passed on this record to family and friends: thirty-five years later his granddaughter went to New England on her honeymoon, using Jefferson's travel recommendations from his 1791 vacation. Back aboard Captain Cooper's sloop, Jefferson began to keep yet another journal on a single 7½ by 9 inch sheet of paper: a botanist's account of the tour. He recorded plants and trees he had not seen farther south. He wrote on his portable laptop desk:

> May 22. Conklin's in the Highlands. Found here the Thuya Occidentalis, called white cedar, and Silverfir, called hemlock.... Also the Candleberry myrtle.

Botany was the cutting-edge science of the late eighteenth century. Jefferson had been keeping detailed garden records at Monticello for nearly twenty years. Here, he was keeping a detailed traveling botanist's record for the first time.

After three days aboard ship, Jefferson and Madison were ready for the comforts of Hendrickson's Inn in Poughkeepsie. Jefferson appreciated a good roadside inn:

> A traveler retired at night to his chamber in an inn, all his effects contained in a single trunk, all his cares circumscribed by the walls of his apartment, unknown to all, unheeded and undisturbed, writes, reads, thinks, sleeps, just in the moments when nature and the movements of his body and mind require. Charmed with the tranquility of his little cell, he finds how few are his real wants, how cheap a thing is happiness."

The next day, they rode north. Jefferson noted there were juniper trees with "berries used for infusing gin." They drove sixteen miles before breakfast. In all, they rode thirty-seven miles that first exhilarating day on horseback, Hemings driving the carriage behind them. It was at Lasher's Inn that evening that Jefferson conducted his first interview on Hessian fly damage:

> The Hessian fly remains on the ground among the stubble of the old wheat. At plowing time for sowing the new crop, they rise in swarms before the plow horses. Soon

after the wheat comes up, they lay the egg in it.... [Conrad Lasher] supposes the old fly dies in the winter. In the spring they begin to grow. I saw them in the worm state, about as long as a grain of rye, and one third its volume. White, smooth and transparent. In June, the chrysalis bursts and the insect comes out, brown like a flax seed, a little longer, and with wings.... He has counted 120 on one stalk, always under cover of the blade.

Jefferson noted that farmers nearby "have found a remedy," using a "new sort" of white bearded wheat with "a more vigorous stalk." The new variety of wheat was undamaged.

Hurrying on toward Albany, Jefferson noted a variety of azalea he had never seen before. He used one flower to describe the fragrance of another. The azaleas were "wild-honeysuckle rose-colored, on stems four feet high loaded richly with large flowers, of a strong, pink fragrance." In other words, they smelled like pinks.

If the two tourists indulged in politics in Albany, there is no record they visited Governor George Clinton. The Albany *Register* of May 30 recorded:

On Thursday last, this city was honored with the presence of Mr. Jefferson, Secretary of State, accompanied by ... the celebrated Madison.... It is to be regretted that their short stay in this city deprived our principal characters from paying that respectful attention due to their distinguished merit.

Only John Hamilton insisted that Jefferson and Madison visited Governor Clinton and other anti-Federalists "under the pretext of a botanical excursion to Albany," where, he said, they were studying "Clintonia borealis."

One man in New York State was big enough to set politics aside when the two Virginians arrived. He was Major General Philip Schuyler, recently unseated from the Senate by Aaron Burr. Hero of the Revolution, Schuyler's family owned the land on which several battles had taken place. He welcomed Jefferson and Madison and instructed his son, a Hamilton partisan, to do likewise. In Paris, Jefferson had been a close friend of Schuyler's daughter, Angelica. Their daughters had attended the same school. For the next few days, Jefferson and Madison toured overgrowing battlefields where British, German, French, and Americans had fought for control of the continent. Jefferson described these "scenes of blood" in a letter to President Washington.

Riding north into the Hudson Highlands, Jefferson and Madison visited factories: a canvas factory, where sailcloth was made; a plant where "1,000 barrels of salted herring [are] exported annually; and a distillery from which 1,000 hogsheads of rum are annually exported." They "saw nails made by cutting them with a pair of shears from the end of a bar of iron." Making nails was a technology new to America: houses and furniture were still joined by wooden pegs. Jefferson was amazed to see "120 [nails] cut off in a minute" with "very simple tools." He later manufactured nails at Monticello.

Jefferson was struck by the serene beauty of what he called the "lake country." On May 29, 1791, Jefferson's journal burst with honeysuckle, wild cherry, black gooseberry, velvet aspen, cotton willow, paper birch, "bass-wood wild rose," and "abundance of sugar maple." Hemlock was draped with moss "a foot long" sometimes "four [feet]." Strawberries were in blossom, bearing "young fruit." His account of their two days gliding over Lake George on a sloop includes geography and geology: the lake was thirty-six miles long and "very clear"; "formed by a contour of mountains into a basin," and the climate was "healthy."

Jefferson and Madison did more than take notes: they went fishing. The "abundance" of fish "have added to our other amusements the sport of taking them," wrote Jefferson. They caught salmon-trout "of seven lb. weight," speckled trout, Oswego bass "of six or seven lb. weight," rock bass, and yellow perch. He noted wild ducks and sea gulls "in abundance." They found rattlesnakes, "two of which we killed." As any visitor to the north country in late May quickly learns, there were "swarms of mosquitoes and gnats, and two kinds of biting fleas." Swatting and picking off the insects, he carefully noted he had been bitten by two different kinds of fleas!

Sailing on Lake George with the right "kind of leisure," Jefferson wrote letters. To his daughter, Patsy: "Lake George is without comparison the most beautiful water I ever saw." It was "finely interspersed with islands, its waters limpid as crystal and the mountain sides covered with rich groves" of evergreens "down to the water edge." As they approached Lake Champlain, his only complaint was the weather: it was as "sultry hot" as "could be found in Carolina or Georgia:"

> I suspect indeed that the heats of northern climates may be more powerful than those of southern ones in proportion as they are shorter. Perhaps vegetation requires this .... Here, they are locked up in ice and snow for six months. Spring and autumn, which make a paradise of [Virginia], are rigorous winter with them, and a tropical summer breaks on them all at once.

What struck James Madison, who was also keeping a tiny diary, the hardest was to find a free black farmer, Prince Taylor, whose house in Ticonderoga township sat all alone at Lake George's north end, at what is still called Black Point. "He possesses a good farm of about 250 acres which he cultivates with six white hirelings." The "free Negro", a Massachusetts native and Revolutionary War veteran, had paid about $2.50 per acre

> and by his industry and good management turns [it] to good account. He is intelligent; reads, writes and understands accounts and is dexterous in his affairs....

They trudged over the ruined ramparts of Fort Ticonderoga and enjoyed a French-Canadian meal at Charles and Mary Hay's inn in the old King's Store, the only building left standing by the British. Their hosts had helped the Americans during the Revolutionary War attack on Quebec and fled with them. Another traveler in the 1790s found the Hays provided "a neat table and a comfortable light supper specially laid out for us." Jefferson's only comment was to rate the tavern "middling."

The next day, Jefferson and Madison sailed out onto Lake Champlain—into strong headwinds. Sailing on the mountain lake with its headlands, shoals, and crosswinds was tricky. After a full day of making only twelve miles' headway, they lodged at an inn at Chimney Point on the Vermont shore. The next morning, Jefferson "met with a small red squirrel, of the color of our fox squirrel with a black stripe on each side, weighing about six ounces generally." The squirrels were in such abundance ... that twenty odd were killed at the house we lodged in ... without going ten steps from the door ... We killed three which were crossing the lakes, one of them just as he was getting ashore where it was three miles wide and where, with the high winds then blowing, he must have made it five or six miles.

The next day, they attempted to sail north again, but the wind was still adverse and the sea was high.

Now nearly a week behind schedule, Jefferson and Madison cut short their cruise north the full length of Lake Champlain and their plan to cross the Green Mountains. Instead of sailing to the Canadian border, they came about at Split Rock, only thirty miles up the 110-mile-long lake. Jefferson vented his frustration on his journal: "Lake Champlain is a much larger but less pleasant water then Lake George." Yet he admired the Vermont scenery, the "champagne" country of wheat fields rolling up to the Green Mountains. He wrote daughter Patsy that his journey was "prosperous and pleasant."

Hurrying south sixty-two miles in the next two days by carriage, they retraced their route to Saratoga, then crossed the Hudson and came at Vermont from the southeast by way of present-day Hoosick Falls. Riding over a rutted, bone rattling dirt road to Bennington on horseback, they had to stop every day at blacksmiths. As they left New York, Madison noted that the terrain changed from flat pine barrens as they crossed into Vermont to "seven or eight [miles] of a fine fertile vale separating two ridges of low mountains." They were looking down on the close-packed rich farms of the Walloomsac River Valley. The ground was "rich and covered with sugar maple and beech." In Vermont, unlike the New York side of Lake Champlain, the countryside was "closely settled." The fields were full of corn and potatoes, flax to make linens, wheat and clover, and half a dozen grass crops for feeding livestock. From the sugar maples they now saw for the first time "some sugar is made and much may be."

That spring, Jefferson had been busy with an interesting agricultural question with political overtones. The British government's Rule of 1756 barred American ships from carrying British goods to and from British possessions in Canada and the Caribbean. Jefferson was determined to break American reliance on imports such as sugar grown on British plantations in the Caribbean. Sugar was the leading American import and a severe drain on hard cash. Americans drank many cups of tea a day, lacing it with expensive imported sugar. Searching for an American substitute, he came across maple sugar. Jefferson believed Americans could produce enough maple sugar on their farms to meet not only their own domestic needs but to export their surplus to Europe to compete with the British. And maple sugar could be tapped, boiled, and bottled by free men, women and children on the family farm, with no need for slave labor. In 1790, Jefferson had instructed his son-in-law to plant maple seedlings at Monticello, but he did not know enough about where to situate them or how to cultivate them and they all died. Before going on vacation, Jefferson wrote another Virginia farmer, President Washington, the latest news about "the sugar-maple tree." He was a little worried that farmers would distill the maple juice into alcoholic spirits, drink up the stuff and still need to import sugar. He had sampled the drink, "which is exactly whiskey."

As they crossed over into Vermont, Madison observed a fundamental difference: Vermonters owned their own land. You can see him poking his head into farmhouses, asking, "Do you own your own house or do you rent it?" Vermont farms, he recorded, "vary from fifty to two hundred acres; in a few instances, they exceed two hundred." The Vermonters' way of life was extremely plain and economical, particularly in the table and ordinary dress. Their expense is chiefly on their houses, which are of wood and make a good figure without, but are very scantily furnished within."

Stopping briefly at the scene of the revolutionary Battle of Bennington (near present-day Hoosick Falls, New York), the road-weary travelers rode on to Elijah Dewey's Tavern (now the Walloomsac Inn) in Bennington, Vermont, the afternoon of June 4. They stayed only one night. Vermont's first U.S. Senator, Moses Robinson, learned they had arrived in town and insisted they stay with him. Until now, they had kept to Jefferson's plan of traveling *incognito*, but they had not reckoned with Anthony Haswell, a fiercely-republican fan of Jefferson's who edited the *Vermont Gazette*. He had received his exchange copy of the previous week's Albany *Register* and he had broken the story of this visit of the two highest U.S. officials ever to come to the new state of Vermont the day before they arrived.

The town of Bennington was couched in the middle of the richest wheat-and-corn-producing area in the adolescent United States. Young couples who came to the Walloomsac Valley enjoyed probably the best opportunities for prosperity in the new nation. An average couple could buy land, build a house and barn, and pay them off in only five years, exporting their surplus crops by wagon to New York and rendering any scrap wood into potash and shipping it in barrels up Lake Champlain to Canada. It was the perfect forum for Jefferson's doctrine of life, liberty and land, and he was welcomed as a hero.

If the two Virginians had hoped to move on after a one night stopover, they had not reckoned with a new Vermont blue law that forbade travel on the Sabbath. As a high government official, Jefferson could claim pressing business and, by applying to a magistrate, obtain an exception. But, as Secretary of State he was also in charge of protocol: he decided to observe the newest state's newest law. They would again modify their route, staying over in Bennington until Monday morning.

Jefferson spent much of Saturday interviewing local citizens about the Hessian fly (there had been little damage this far north). In his memo for the American Philosophical Society, Jefferson noted, "Bennington. Had a few in '89 and '90. Have not heard if there are any this year." That afternoon, they moved to Senator Robinson's, where Jefferson was fascinated by a giant balsam poplar tree in Robinson's front yard. That evening, Senator Robinson gave a dinner and they were introduced to the local gentry. Several at the table that night had represented Vermont as agents to the Continental Congress in its decade-long effort to enter the Union.

But this night, according to journalist Haswell, it was Thomas Jefferson bending Vermonters to his point of view. In his low, slow voice, he urged them to consider seriously a new cash crop—maple sugar. Haswell enthusiastically reported Jefferson's idea to make money from the sugar maples that abounded in Vermont.

Bringing to the maple-tree-rich, cash-poor Vermont frontier a promise of dripping prosperity, Jefferson gave birth to its maple syrup industry. The next year, as Jefferson promised, a Dutch company set up maple sugaring operations in nearby Rutland. That autumn, using techniques long ago developed by Native Americans, Vermont settlers began their annual mid-winter harvests.

Visiting Bennington on the Sabbath meant going to church. The "zealously pious" Senator Robinson took Jefferson and Madison along to the great gambrel-roofed Congregational meeting-house and ushered them to his family pew as the choir sang its favorite hymns. That afternoon, at Senator Robinson's house, Jefferson found peace for his favorite activity, writing letters. He took out several slips of birchbark he had cut from trees along Lake George and wrote his son-in-law a long letter describing the first four hundred miles of their tour. "The laws of the state not permitting us to travel on Sunday has given me time to write to you." He listed their battlefield tours and botanical discoveries, especially "an azalea very different from the nudiflora with very large clusters of flowers, more thickly set on the branches, of a deeper red, and high pink fragrance. It is the richest shrub I have ever seen." When he returned to Philadelphia, Jefferson confirmed with botanist friends that he had discovered an as-yet-unclassified variety of azalea.

Jefferson wrote another letter—to President Washington. Probably at dinner the night before, he had learned that the British, violating the Treaty of Paris of 1783, had built a blockhouse "something further south than the border," on North Hero Island, five miles south of the Canadian line. They had stationed a sloop-of-war, the *Maria*, there, and were forcing American ships to heave to, even in storms, causing two of them to sink. Vermonters were nervous; 200 militia had occupied a stockade nearby and Vermont officials expected trouble.

With a clock ticking now, before sunrise on Monday morning Jefferson and Madison slipped out of town, riding fourteen miles before breakfast. Madison's horse was becoming lame: they stopped at a blacksmith's. Jefferson tried to make light of the problem to Washington: they were having "cavalry troubles." They rode on, south along the Connecticut River, making overnight stops at Northhampton, Hartford, and Guilford. Crossing to the North Shore of Long Island, they toured farms and stayed in comfortable inns for five nights, arriving in New York City on June 16. In all, Jefferson calculated, they had traveled 900 miles, 236 by water, and 664 by land.

In those last days on Long Island, Jefferson paused long enough to interview three old women of the Unquachog tribe, writing down 250 native equivalents for English words. It was the first of fifty brief tribal glossaries he gathered, hoping in retirement to publish a systematic study of Native-American languages. He also shopped for trees at a nursery at Flushing, ordering, at the top of his list, sixty maples for Monticello. They never produced any syrup or sugar, but Jefferson had learned another use for trees during their five weeks on the road. From that time on, when politics oppressed him, he took afternoon rides along the Schuylkill River in Philadelphia or the Potomac in Washington and sat a spell under a shade tree. Thomas Jefferson had finally learned how to relax.

Jefferson served as Secretary of State until 1794. He resigned when it became clear that Washington was increasingly adopting Hamilton's views. Jefferson opposed Hamilton's fiscal policies on the grounds that they exceeded the powers delegated to the central government by the Constitution. He believed these policies were contrary to the interests of the majority of the people and represented a threat to republican institutions. The two men also clashed on foreign policy, Jefferson leaning toward France and Hamilton toward Great Britain. Their disagreements led to the formation of national political parties. Jefferson retired from the Cabinet near the end of Washington's first term and Hamilton left a few years later. Each became the principal spokesman for the emerging parties: Jefferson for the Democratic-Republicans and Hamilton for the Federalists.

Persuaded by Madison to seek the Presidency in 1796, Jefferson ran a close second to John Adams, advocating less federal power. As the second-highest vote-getter, he became vice-president, a post with no real authority. Jefferson spent much of his term at Monticello where he wrote *A Manual of Parliamentary Practice*, the rulebook still used by the Senate. He resisted many of the administration's efforts, especially the Alien and Sedition Acts. The Sedition Act was used to suppress Democratic-Republican criticism of the Federalist-controlled government. Some twenty-five pro-Jefferson printers, newspaper editors, or writers were tried, convicted, fined, or jailed for questioning government policies. Jefferson believed the act contrary to the First Amendment guarantee of freedom of speech, and therefore unconstitutional, a position he articulated in the Virginia and Kentucky Resolutions of 1798–99 which he wrote. Jefferson argued that the states have the authority to reject Federal laws they consider unconstitutional (under the name of nullification, this state's rights doctrine was later to divide the Union).

In the bitter presidential campaign of 1800, Jefferson's religious views (he had just become a Unitarian) were a key issue. Federalist campaigners urged voters to choose "God—and a religious President" over "Jefferson ... and no God." Federal authority, not religion, Jeffersonians argued back, was the real issue. Jefferson defeated Adams seventy-three to sixty-five electoral votes but, because Jefferson and vice presidential candidate Aaron Burr received the same number of votes, when Burr refused to concede, a runoff was thrown into the House of Representatives. After thirty-five ballots, Jefferson was declared the winner and Burr became Vice President.

Jefferson's presidency was full of contradictions. He did not attempt to reverse all the Federalist policies of the past twelve years—at times, he was more Federalist than the Federalists. While he made deep cuts in American military spending, he sent a squadron of thirty American warships to the Mediterranean in the victorious Tripoli War and established a professional officer class by founding the U.S. Military Academy at West Point. An ardent nationalist, he exceeded his constitutional powers as president and secretly arranged the Louisiana Purchase of 1803, for $15 million, or only three cents an acre, doubling the size of the United States, never consulting Congress and using a congressional slush fund. Yet he remained enormously popular and won congressional support for the first U.S. funded scientific expedition by Merriwether Lewis and William Clark to map and explore the Purchase, advancing American interests to the Pacific Rim for the first time.

Dumping Aaron Burr as Vice President, Jefferson easily won re-election in 1804. He spent much of his second term trying to convict his former vice-president of treason for allegedly plotting with Spain to set up an empire in the Southwest. (Burr was ultimately acquitted.) Increasingly after 1806, Jefferson was engaged in a futile struggle to keep the U.S. out of the Napoleonic Wars between England and

France. One of his rare successes during the second term came in March, 1807, when Jefferson signed into law the bill that banned the importation to the United States of any more African slaves. But his Embargo Act barring all imports and exports the same year, intended to keep America strictly neutral, not only proved economically disastrous but ruined Jefferson's popularity in much of the country, especially in New England. His hounding of Aaron Burr on unproven charges of treason further weakened his party. By replacing every high Federalist officeholder with a Democratic-Republican, he became increasingly unpopular, as he initiated the winner-take-all spoils system. Refusing a third term, he turned the Presidency over to his friend and protegé, James Madison.

He devoted his last years to completing Monticello and writing thousands of letters—sometimes all day. His most important retirement project was to found the University of Virginia at Charlottesville. Jefferson designed the buildings, brought stonecutters and Carrara marble from Italy, directed construction in his leather apron, drew up the curriculum (pointedly omitting religion), handpicked the faculty and served as first rector, and banned all servants and slave labor from the campus. He pioneered the system of student electives "to leave everyone free to attend whatever branches of instruction he wants and to decline what he does not."

As Thomas Jefferson lay dying, in the aftermath of the financial Panic of 1819 all over Virginia, the farms of cash-poor, land-rich planters who could no longer sell their lands were going under the gavel. On the day of his death, Jefferson was $107,000 in debt (over $1 million today). This debt was partly the result of two loans he had co-signed for a political lieutenant who went bankrupt and partly because, every year of his public career, he had sunk deeper into debt by living beyond his meager government salary. After forty years of public office, he received no government pension. When he could no longer pay the interest on loans and couldn't sell his land after the 1819 crash, his estate was put into receivership and taken out of his control. He could no longer free his slaves but his bank receivers could and did sell them off. He was increasingly disturbed by slavery and, during the acrimonious Congressional debates that produced the Missouri Compromise in 1820, he foresaw the Civil War. To Jefferson, the slave question was:

> like an alarm bell in the night, awakened and filled me with terror; I considered it as the knell of the Union. I regret that I am now to die in the belief that the useless sacrifice of themselves by the generation of 1776 to acquire self-government and happiness to their country is to be thrown away by the unwise and unworthy passions of their sons, and that my only consolation is to be that I live not to weep over it.

Using his political influence to have the Virginia legislature allow a lottery to pay off his debts posthumously by selling off Monticello, its furnishings and its lands, Jefferson wrote his will. Five slaves, all members of the Hemings family, were to be freed. Two Monticello slaves had walked away in 1822 and Jefferson had made no attempt to bring them back. He had already arranged for the University of Virginia to provide the Hemings' house slaves jobs and build them houses. His daughter, Patsy, would have to vacate Monticello a year after his death. For fifty years, Monticello was to pass out of the Jefferson family. Patsy bought Sally Hemings at the auction and freed her. She lived with two of her sons until she died.

The sons then moved to Ohio, part of the Old Northwest Territories that Jefferson had pushed Congress to make free half a century earlier. After he died, Jefferson's family admitted privately that Sally Hemings' children were fathered by one of Jefferson's nephews. Yet a tradition survives that they were really the offspring of Thomas Jefferson and Sally Hemings. Such stories are hard either to prove or disprove although Jefferson specifically denied there was any truth to the rumors.

In retirement at Monticello, Jefferson had renewed his old friendship with his former political enemy, John Adams. They wrote scores of letters to each other. On July 4, 1826, both men died. It was the fiftieth anniversary of the Declaration of Independence.

QUESTIONS FOR THOUGHT AND DISCUSSION

1. Name some of Thomas Jefferson's many personal interests. How do you account for his multi-faceted character and broad range of interests?

2. How did Jefferson's trip to New York and Vermont with James Madison reflect Jefferson's political philosophy as well as his other varied interests? Can you imagine a significant American politician today making such a trip *incognito*?

3. Given Jefferson's belief in a limited government, how does one account for his secretly arranging, as president, for the Louisiana Purchase?

4. What event did Jefferson refer to in his retirement as "like an alarm bell in the night"? In what ways were he and his founding father colleagues responsible for setting off that alarm bell?

SUGGESTED READINGS

Cappon, Lester J. ed. *The Adams-Jefferson Letters.* Chapel Hill: U of North Carolina P, 1988.

Cunningham, Noble E., Jr. *In Pursuit of Reason: The Life of Thomas Jefferson.* New York: Ballantine, 1987.

Malone, Dumas. *Thomas Jefferson and His Times.* 6 vols. Boston: Little, 1948–81.

McLaughlin, Jack. *Jefferson and Monticello.* New York: Holt, 1988.

Peterson, Merrill. *Thomas Jefferson and the New Nation.* New York: Oxford U P, 1970.

Randall, Willard Sterne. *Thomas Jefferson: A Life.* New York: Harper, 1994.

Smith, James Morton. *The Republic of Letters: Correspondence between Thomas Jefferson and James Madison, 1776–1826.* 3 vols. New York: Norton, 1995.

12

Tecumseh

A reasonable person might believe that contact between whites and Native Americans moved from being a rare but recurring event to an aspect of everyday life in America. In fact, all such contact kept its novelty for both sides for generations because the people involved kept changing. Much subtler than the meeting of two, big, stable populations, American settlement put together newly arrived Europeans with natives from different tribes, from places farther and farther west. But, on each side, people told stories about the other, and over time the fact of prolonged contact did change how each thought about its opposite. The Native Americans slowly learned that all whites were not the same. The British, they knew, strived at dealings that were correct in diplomatic and legal terms, trying to find old agreements and documents to uphold their claims. The French, whom the natives had known over many generations, left the culture of North America undisturbed for the most part so long as they could hunt and trap to promote their flourishing fur trade. Then new people came, settlers who would promise anything to get land.

Gradually, and in many cases reluctantly, the Europeans had to change how they saw the natives. In the Southeast, in particular, where the Cherokees developed a system for writing down their language and had their own newspaper, the cliché of portraying them as uncivilized no longer described what many whites saw and knew. But even as their knowledge of the Native Americans changed, some whites felt no less greed for their land and saw themselves as entitled to seize it. Whites did not question or doubt what they expected as the result of their contact—to defeat the natives and take their land.

On their side, the natives showed new ideas that evolved within their own societies because of contact with whites. Some of their leaders took lessons from the generals sent to deal with them, other Native Americans gave lessons. When the Shawnee chief Tecumseh went to talk with William Henry Harrison, Military Governor of the Indiana Territory and future president of the United States, he addressed the general as nearly his equal. "How can we have confidence in the white people?" he asked.

"When Jesus Christ came upon the earth, you killed him." Not confident that translation could convey his message, he later relied on corporeal expression, as he used his body to transcend language. He and Harrison sat on a bench. The native steadily leaned against the general, finally crowding him so much he nearly fell on the ground. Without a word, Tecumseh had eloquently conveyed to the officer that he understood what was being done. He made plain that white settlers were humiliating his people and that no one could be expected to put up with it.

IF HE HAD NOT been a Native American, Tecumseh would likely be remembered as a revolutionary leader and political thinker of vision and daring. In the proud and sad memories of his people, he was and remains a hero. Tecumseh ("Tecumtha" before whites changed it) was born a Shawnee and became an Indian. That shift gives clues to the extraordinary man who came close to achieving an Indian state within the still expanding United States. One of his most bitter enemies, William Henry Harrison, governor of the Indiana Territory and later president of the United States, understood the greatness of this warrior with "one of those uncommon geniuses which spring up occasionally to produce revolutions and overturn the established order of things." What he had seen of Tecumseh made Harrison speculate that if he had not lived within the territory of the United States, "he would perhaps be founder of an empire that would rival in glory that of Mexico or Peru."

For a time during the short life of Tecumseh, Native American people had greater hope than they had known before or since. Tecumseh gave them a consciousness of themselves as one people more than members of just one tribe. He taught them that all tribes shared the challenge he saw, just as all tribes shared the native history he taught them. No one before Tecumseh preached the tragedy of the Pequot and the Narragansett, of tribes who were simply gone as all Native Americans would be, he warned, if they did not unite.

Tecumseh, whose name means "panther lying in wait," was born in March 1768 in Old Piqua, near Dayton, Ohio. Puckenshinwe, his war chief father, and Methoataske, his mother, had come to eastern Ohio after wandering great distances. The Shawnee ("southerners") had migrated so much that they could be found all the way from South Carolina, where Europeans called them Savannahs, to Pennsylvania. Besides migrating, these tribes divided and subgroups went to new regions. Because Native groups in disparate places called themselves Shawnee, white settlers and soldiers could not easily understand that they were one coherent people or nation. Because some Shawnee groups had settled in Alabama, Tecumseh's father did nothing unusual in having as his wife Methoataske, a Creek woman from the eastern part of Alabama. By the time they reached Old Piqua in eastern Ohio where Tecumseh was born, the couple already had four children. In all there would be nine children.

As a boy, Tecumseh learned that treaties could not be counted on for land and that white people could not be counted on for honor. Because he was born in 1768,

Tecumseh always knew war, and especially border war. In 1774 friction between white settlers and the Shawnees worsened to the point of being called a war, Lord Dunmore's War, named for the Royal Governor of Virginia who led about 2,000 settlers into Ohio and Kentucky. Many Shawnees and settlers died before the Shawnee leader Cornstalk decided to make peace. His main concern was to preserve Shawnee villages in Ohio. Making what he saw was a sensible bargain, Cornstalk gave up Shawnee lands that were south of the Ohio River and consented to open Kentucky to whites. In return he understood that his people retained their land north of the Ohio River.

The older males in Tecumseh's family, his father and his oldest brother Cheeseekau, both fought at the side of Cornstalk and knew what the treaty promised. They resented the settlers who ignored the agreement and kept on coming into Shawnee land. Far worse, a group of whites found Puckenshinwe in the woods alone and shot him through the chest. He was not yet dead when Methoataske and her young son Tecumseh found him. Only a few years later Tecumseh lost Cornstalk, a hero to the fatherless boy. He, too, died violently, murdered by whites the Shawnees saw as lawless liars. No one had to teach Tecumseh hatred.

Tecumseh would inevitably become a warrior, but not like his father. Part of his great intelligence expressed itself in very lucid self-awareness: "I am a Shawnee. My forefathers were warriors. Their son is a warrior. From them I take only my existence. From my tribe I take nothing. I have made myself what I am." The adult who characterized him so starkly had in mind perhaps his unusual beginning of warrior life. Even before he could fight Tecumseh witnessed violent conflicts. Land-seeking whites burned Old Piqua where he was born. The Shawnees of that settlement moved to the west on the Miami River to build a new settlement named Piqua ("village that rises from the ashes"). That happened in 1780, when Tecumseh was only twelve. Just two years later he came close to fighting himself for the first time. In Ohio he and his brother Cheeseekau were in a small engagement with settlers when his brother was wounded. In horror the young Tecumseh ran away. Later that same day he suffered shame and disgust at his own cowardly reaction. He vowed to himself that he would not show fear again.

While he honored the promise to himself, Tecumseh insisted on the difference between courage and brutality. As a teenager he did what other Shawnees did in attacking boatloads of settlers on the Ohio River. One day after a river attack, the Shawnees burned at the stake a settler they had captured. Tecumseh felt such revulsion that he took a stand and publicly spoke out against their barbarism. Winning had to do with honor and with land. And the speech worked. He humiliated the Shawnees with him. That ability to move people with his words would develop as he matured into an orator of legendary power.

Because white settlers filled up land so quickly and had the protection of soldiers, some native tribes thought that resistance made no sense when there could be treaties. Aware of this reasoning and also aware of his own powers to convert people to his thinking, Tecumseh traveled great distances to win the support of more tribes. He went east to Tennessee, then south to what is now Mississippi, Alabama, Georgia, and all the way to Florida. But while he was away from Ohio, a new army under Anthony Wayne headed north from Cincinnati. Wayne planned to stay. Rather than accompany soldiers or protect boats on the Ohio, he set out to build frontier fortresses. He spent nearly a year in one of these at Greenville, Ohio before heading northwest in the direction of the Maumee River. In late August 1794, the tornado season, Wayne was advancing with 3,000 men. Shawnees under their chief Blue Jacket decided that they would go against Wayne's forces. The place where they fought was along the Maumee River, an open place where men could fight because so many big trees had been knocked down by a tornado. Later, that encounter would be referred to as the Battle of Fallen Timbers. The Shawnees under Blue Jacket gave a good fight, but against cavalry and bayonets in superior numbers, they ended by fleeing. Tecumseh fought in Blue Jacket's forces that day and inspired others to fight.

Not until the following spring did the natives hear from Anthony Wayne. This time he called for a peace meeting. In answer to his gesture, leaders and representatives of as many as twelve different tribes went to see what was being offered. Blue Jacket went but Tecumseh refused. Two months later the chiefs of the different tribes accepted the terms of what would be known as the Greenville Treaty. The United States won a great deal of land as a result of Fallen Timbers. Places important to the Shawnee, including Old Piqua, passed to American hands. Most of what is now Ohio became the property of the whites, as did good settlement locations that would in time become Detroit, Toledo, Peoria, and Chicago. For their part, the natives were given promises, money, and goods worth nearly $20,000. They were also promised annuities that would amount to $9,500.

The chiefs at the conference saw these terms as valid, or at least they signed. But Tecumseh, still furious, refused to acknowledge the agreement as legitimate. From his experience, he was counting on whites not to respect their own terms. But what bothered him and many other Indians, including no doubt some who had been at the conference at Fort Greenville, had to do with treaties in general, not this one in particular. By the reasoning of the Natives, treaties made no sense. The idea that words on paper could alter the relation of people to land struck them as foolish. For one thing, they had no concept of having acquired the land they called theirs. They belonged to it as much as it belonged to them, and that relationship was far more spiritual than legal. They lived from what the land gave them in their hunting and fishing. The bones of their ancestors belonged to the land. How could words on paper change any of that? Even chiefs who signed treaties did not necessarily understand that once they had deeded land over that they were expected to leave. If a paper opened land to whites, then whites were free to belong to the land as they did. Why could they not both belong to it? They probably wondered how it had been possible for so many whites to leave their own land on the other side of the ocean. What about the bones of their ancestors?

Tecumseh, with his talent for articulating what others believed, gave this terse analysis: "Sell a country. Why not sell the air, the clouds, and the great sea, as well as the earth? Did not the Great Spirit make them all for the use of his children?" Even while the concept of owned land remained incomprehensible, Tecumseh could see the tide of settlers advancing from east to west, and he moved west.

Not all the tribes of the Northwest had sent representatives to Fort Greenville, and not all tribes accepted the treaty. Their discontent suited Tecumseh's plan to put himself at the head of a force of warriors from many tribes. He did not want to be a Shawnee war chief but a leader of red men. His gift for speaking depended on his ability to hold the attention of a gathering of people of any race. Almost every eyewitness account of him says close to the same thing, that he was an unusually good-looking man. His fine features, light hazel eyes and superb physique helped the tall Shawnee create a strong visual impression. To address a crowd he would sometimes stand before it in only his moccasins and breech cloth, displaying his strength. Then, when he began to speak, a powerful voice conveyed the great conviction with which he spoke and most of all, his authority. Even through the clumsiness of translations that survive, his poetic language comes through.

When he was around thirty Tecumseh met a well-read farmer living in Ohio named Galloway who recognized and appreciated Tecumseh's language and curiosity. More dramatically, Tecumseh also met Galloway's daughter Rebecca, young, fair-haired, and beautiful. She tutored Tecumseh, read to him and with him. In time, Tecumseh's admiration for the young woman moved him to ask her father for her hand in marriage. Her wise father wanted the choice to be his daughter's. She told Tecumseh that she would gladly be his wife, provided that he leave his people and live with her as a white man. She wanted him to stop being Shawnee. Tecumseh recognized a grave decision and would not be rushed. A month later he gave Rebecca Galloway the answer that cost him much agony: he had to turn her down. He knew that he could not abandon his people.

Quite often chiefs who were talked into signing treaties, the old and the weak in particular, ceded land that was not theirs. In his response to that injustice, Tecumseh showed the suppleness and originality of his thinking. Rather than resent the trickery of the ploy or the arrogance of the white view in which *any* Indian could sign off any Indian land, he seriously considered the notion of seeing all Native Americans as the same race. That change in his thinking gave Tecumseh a vision that no native leader of his time had expressed. He recognized that if Natives saw themselves not as Creeks and Sioux and Choctaw and Miami, but as one people resisting the whites, they had a strong chance of succeeding. The tribes he visited recognized the power of this new, revolutionary idea. They must have had a sense of urgency about the new thinking because they knew that the United States government was organizing ways to prepare land to be settled. In particular, they were preparing the territory west of Ohio being referred to as Indiana. The question for Tecumseh, and it remained a question for everyone, was what kind of state would Indiana be—white or Native American?

One strategy of preparing land for settlers used a new element in the white arsenal for weakening Native-American resistance. At the very end of the eighteenth century the whites found that alcohol could bring willing chiefs to the negotiating table very quickly. In this campaign, tribes that stayed farthest from contact with whites withstood the best. Others, such as Chippewas, Piankashaws, and Weas quickly sank from proud, socially coherent groups to pitiful, miserable stragglers living in poverty. When Natives held their own land, poverty did not exist as a social curse. From hunting and fishing and from knowing the forest, people could provide for themselves and take care of their families. Tribes could grow.

Without land, families were made homeless, unemployed, and alienated with astonishing speed. Naturally, in no time the profound sense of loss led to hopelessness. The demoralized Natives could be counted on to sign white men's papers.

For the most part Tecumseh kept alcohol from his Shawnee people by the force of his personality and by keeping white contact minimal. But his brother did not show the same strength. His shiftless one-eyed brother who made no attempt at hunting and fishing was given the degrading name of Laulewaskia ("the idler"). The outcast showed no resistance to alcohol. But after white culture diminished him, it also offered him a way out. Contact with the Shakers, a Protestant sect whose followers swooned, trembled, and writhed in a spiritual dance, impressed Laulewaskia with the possibility of saving himself. Before long he experienced trances which left him with the conviction that he must and could stop drinking

The Field Museum, Chicago, A93851

Tecumseh's unusual vision of a union of all Native American peoples made him dangerous to whites and legendary in his own culture.

because he had met with the "Master of Life." The radical change in him the Shawnees saw convinced them of his spiritual powers so much that they freed him from his demeaning name and started calling him Tenskwatawa ("The Prophet").

Tecumseh needed no help in seeing the value of a brother with powerful medicine to help him in his cause of converting tribes to unified resistance to whites. Since "treaty chiefs," as they were called, tended to be old and tired of fighting, the warriors most easily convinced to join Tecumseh were the young, strong, and fierce warriors of many tribes; the Sioux, Blackfeet, Arikaras, and Mandans wanted to follow the Prophet. The combination of a powerful new idea and strong spiritual backing needed to be controlled. The desire to get rid of chiefs of tribesmen who had too easily cooperated with whites created what modern times would recognize as a revolutionary purge. Only the faithful and the pure could be tolerated. The zeal of Tecumseh's converts started a massacre of Natives by Natives which he had to stop personally.

News of the Prophet and his brother Tecumseh spread through Natives to whites. Thinking that he could fight words with words, the Governor of the Indiana Territory, William Henry Harrison, started his own campaign to discredit the Prophet by mocking him. Sure he had found a way to defeat an unimportant rival, Harrison sent a written challenge to a group of Indians. In effect he was asking for proof. A real prophet, said Harrison, would be able to "cause the sun to stand still, the moon to alter its course, the rivers to cease to flow, or the dead to rise from their graves. If he does these things, you may then believe he has been sent from God."

Because he had a low opinion of Natives in general, Harrison had never considered that other whites, including the British, talked to important Native-American leaders. It was probably from them that Tenskwatawa knew what a solar eclipse was and that there would be one on June 16. Staging it as an answer to the written challenge, the Prophet let all the Natives know that he wanted a large gathering at Greenville on June 16. (That location where a broken treaty had been signed, enhanced the propaganda value of what he intended to do.) With a large crowd around him, Tenskwatawa let it be known that he would make darkness at mid-day. Just after 11:30 A.M. he called out with a large pointing gesture and ordered the sun to stop shining. Within minutes the thin disk, the shadow of the moon, started to conceal an edge of the sun and then moved across its face. Dumbstruck, every Native American there knew a challenge had been met. Before the awed assembly, the Prophet then summoned the Master of Life to make the light of noonday return. Moments later the moon's shadow passed. As news of that day spread, it was not individual warriors but entire tribes who came over to the side of Tecumseh and the Prophet. When Tecumseh went to speak to tribes, his riveting style usually assured his success. The Potawatomis of Illinois joined his cause; the Sauk and the Foxes and great numbers of Menominees and Winnebagos in the North promised to help him. Some tribes said that in case of war they could be counted on. These included the Ottawas and the Kickapoos. Tribes weakened and ravaged by alcohol took heart in the message of Tecumseh: Piankashaws, Chippewas, Weas, and all the Wyandots.

During Tecumseh's absence the Shawnee lost land through a treaty with William Henry Harrison, but worse, it included some of their most valued hunting ground. From reports he had heard, Harrison thought that the Prophet led the uniting tribes. He did not know that his war chief brother Tecumseh had first gathered and then led the thousand warriors who now stood ready to keep new settlers from coming into Indiana. Making what he saw as a concession, Harrison sent word that the Prophet was invited to Washington to meet the president. Tecumseh and his brother sent word that they would come to see Harrison in August 1810 at Vincennes.

Mutual distrust surrounded the meeting of Harrison and Tecumseh. Arriving with several battle-ready warriors, Tecumseh gave no hint of being intimidated. In his mind, they met as equals. Tecumseh, who could speak English, made his address in Shawnee. According to reports from witnesses, he spoke with such conviction and speed that the translator could not easily keep up with his pace. His words can accurately be called a speech, even a lecture. Not at all what Harrison would have expected, Tecumseh gave a well-reasoned argument based on a careful chronology of grievances between Indians and whites. He recounted the many injustices and broken treaties the Native peoples had suffered because of whites. His most important point had to do with unity. "The way, the only way to stop this evil [of the whites] is for all the red men to unite in claiming a common and equal right in the land, as it was at first, and should be now—for it never was divided, but belongs to all. No tribe has a right to sell, even to each other, much less to strangers."

Harrison's reply could not have shown more contempt. His words gave the impression that he had not even been listening to Tecumseh. He spoke as if he had just arrived in the room, having heard nothing. He objected strenuously to Tecumseh's claim, saying that Shawnees came from Georgia, so how could he have any say about land in Indiana? Insulted, Tecumseh accused Harrison of lying and nearly lost control of himself as he reached for his tomahawk. To avoid a violent conclusion to the meeting, Harrison announced the meeting was adjourned and left. The next day Tecumseh sent his apologies. As further proof of how poorly he understood the stature of the leader he was facing, Harrison later felt sure that all his troubles with the Shawnees could be explained by the meddling efforts of the British in Canada. He could not imagine an intelligent Native.

In November 1811, Harrison and an army of some 1,000 soundly defeated the Prophet's forces in what came to be called the Battle of Tippecanoe. The notoriety from this success earned Harrison the nickname, "Tippecanoe." In 1840, he won the presidency campaigning on the slogan, "Tippecanoe and Tyler, Too." Having been away when the battle was fought, Tecumseh was enraged over his brother's decision to fight this battle for which their people were unprepared. Tecumseh banished his brother the Prophet, and saw his own dream of a Pan-Indian resistance fade.

Meanwhile, the United States and Great Britain went to battle again with the outbreak of the War of 1812, and Tecumseh was quick to side with the British. In fact, Tecumseh had excellent relations with the British, partly because they listened to him. When a British officer astutely asked for Tecumseh's help, the result benefited both sides. Major General Isaac Brock, the Lieutenant Governor of Canada, got along well with Tecumseh, perhaps because they were alike and understood each other. When Brock arrived at Fort Malden, near present-day Detroit, he did not rely entirely on his officers. The tall and confident Brock acted on Tecumseh's advice (and against that of all his officers except one), and attacked Detroit at daybreak and sent a message to General William Hull, the American commander, asking him to give up. Hull, an aging hero of the Revolution, refused at first. Then Tecumseh and Brock proved brilliant collaborators. Arranging for a scout to be captured, they planted the false information that 5,000 Indians were on their way from the lakes to the north to reinforce Tecumseh. To make the lie credible, Tecumseh went with his men to the woods, then marched them single file past a small convoy of Americans under Captain Henry Brush. Then he took them back through the woods and marched them a second time, and then a third. The trick worked. Men in the fort believed that the reinforcements had arrived. At that point, Hull did give up. Tecumseh and Brock were victorious without a fight.

That partnership, had it gone on, might have made the critical difference for Tecumseh and his cause. But meanwhile Brock had been killed in fighting near Niagara. His replacement, or his successor more accurately, could not have been worse, in Tecumseh's eyes. Colonel Henry Procter, the new commander at Malden, resembled Harrison rather than Brock in his low opinion of the Native Americans. Tecumseh wasted no time in letting the obese and arrogant Procter know that the low opinion was mutual.

When Indian warriors won a solid victory at the River Raisin against men from Kentucky, Procter was on the scene to assure the Americans that he would guarantee the safety of prisoners who had been captured. But he did nothing. Because Tecumseh was not there, alcohol transformed tension into violence. While Procter remained absolutely passive, drunk Native Americans butchered unarmed captives. Indignant, Tecumseh criticized Procter severely. Besides the loss of life and his revulsion at such brutality, he knew that the massacre had set back his cause.

Inevitably, the River Raisin Massacre, as it was known, helped white settlers justify uncontrolled vengeance against Natives. Harrison came back to get even. Again, the Native forces defeated the whites, this time near the very recently built Fort Meigs, on the site of Fallen Timbers. After their victory, and once again in Tecumseh's absence, the Native Americans started a massacre of captives. This time, however, Tecumseh was nearby so that word could be sent to him. While the massacre was still going on, after twenty murders, Tecumseh arrived and stopped it. Immediately he asked Procter why he had not stopped the killing. His inept answer blamed the Natives: "Your Indians cannot be controlled." Procter's incompetence continued to hurt Tecumseh by eroding the confidence of his people. Procter lifted the siege of Fort Meigs. As Harrison advanced, his response was always the same, to retreat. In disgust, Tecumseh finally called him a "miserable old squaw."

Tecumseh knew exactly what would happen next. As he prepared his men to follow Procter retreating toward the Thames River, he told his men, "We are now going to follow the British, and I feel certain that we shall never return."

In his final battle at the Thames River, Tecumseh faced Kentuckians whose battle cry "Remember the River Raisin" must have pained the humane Shawnee. Outnumbered more than two to one, the Native Americans and the British lost to the American forces. Most of the day Tecumseh fought in the woods and could be heard, roaring like a wild animal and inspiring his men. By the end of the day, having been severely wounded after continuing to fight with blood running from his mouth and from wounds, Tecumseh stopped. The following morning Harrison's men felt disappointed, mystified, and afraid when they could not find his body. For years after that battle of October 4, 1813, white settlers still believed that Tecumseh roamed the woods.

The Native Americans and the Shawnees had lost much more than a brilliant and gifted leader. They had also lost a dream.

QUESTIONS FOR THOUGHT AND DISCUSSION

1. What early experiences of Tecumseh's gave rise to his distrust and utter hatred of white settlers and the U.S. government? Was his attitude justified or an overreaction?

2. What became Tecumseh's principal strategy in the early 1800s to halt white settlers from taking over more Indian lands? How successful was Tecumseh?

3. Why did William Henry Harrison's meeting with Tecumseh in 1810 fail to halt the deteriorating relations between the U.S. government and Tecumseh and his followers?

4. In comparing the stories of Teedyuscung and Tecumseh, was there ever a legitimate possibility that white settlers seeking lands further west could have reached some peaceful accommodation with the many Native tribes who already peopled these territories, or was the result we now know always inevitable? Explain.

SUGGESTED READINGS

Billington, Ray Allen and Martin Ridge. *Westward Expansion: A History of the American Frontier* (5th edition). New York: Macmillan, 1982.

Edmunds, R. David. *Tecumseh and the Quest for Indian Leadership.* 1984.

Josephy, Alvin M., Jr. "Tecumseh, the Greatest Indian," in Josephy, *The Patriot Chiefs: A Chronicle of American Indian Leadership.* New York: Viking, 1961.

_____. *500 Nations: An Illustrated History of North American Indians.* New York: Knopf, 1994.

Milner, Clyde A. et al. *The Oxford History of the American West.* New York: Oxford UP, 1994.

13

Charles Grandison Finney

In the Jacksonian era, American society underwent drastic and rapid changes. Its market economy expanded rapidly through a revolution in transportation that brought farm produce from the interior of the United States to New York City and New Orleans, and much of it on to Europe. The ships came back laden with new immigrants and luxury imports. The revolution in America's markets brought another kind of competition for status and wealth through the new gospel of democratic individualism.

Fortunes were won and lost almost overnight and reformers such as Charles Grandison Finney sought to bring some stability and moral order through religious revivals. An intermittent but steadily growing revival movement spread from the raw frontier clearings of Kentucky to the "Burned-Over District" of New York and New England, where revivalists concentrated their fire-and-brimstone along a line that corresponded to the 42nd parallel running through the raw Erie Canal port towns and teeming southern Massachusetts mill towns. The first Great Awakening of the 1740s had brought a boisterous new multitude of evangelical Christians who abandoned the sedate Calvinism of New England. The Second Great Awakening set off shock waves of reform that reverberated all the way down to the Civil War.

CHARLES GRANDISON Finney had never been a very religious young man. He came from an old New England Puritan family, but two years after he was born on August 29, 1792, his father Sylvester, a Revolutionary War veteran, moved the family to Oneida Country on the central New York frontier where there were no churches. The land around Kirkland had been taken from the Six Nations Iroquois during the Revolution. In Finney's *Memoirs*, he says he grew up in what was "to a great extent a wilderness" where "no religious privileges were enjoyed by the people" and where "no Sabbath schools had been established." The settlers, mostly New England veterans of the Revolution, saw the urgency of setting up elementary schools but there was "very little intelligent preaching" and where "very few religious books were to be had." He lived the rugged life of a boy on the frontier. He loved sports and prided himself on being able to out-run, out-jump, out-row, out-swim, and out-wrestle all his friends. He also managed to get a good schooling. Later, he was proud he could go to school "summer and winter until he was sixteen years old, an unusually good schooling for the son of a farmer." He seemed destined to become a schoolteacher, not a preacher. Very few of his neighbors professed any religion and the few sermons he heard, "when I heard any at all," were "some miserable holding forth" by an "ignorant preacher" that left people with "irrepressible laughter" on their way home from meeting "in view of the strange mistakes" and "absurdities" they had heard. Just as a meeting house was built and young Charles began attending regularly, his father decided to move again.

For two years, Finney was able to go to a private high school, the Hamilton Oneida Academy. He walked four miles each way to the school. There, the principal, Yale-educated Seth Norton, spotted in the tall, blue-eyed pioneer boy great intellectual potential. Six-feet-two, spare, and athletic, Finney had a natural gift for music and for classical studies. Norton urged him to go to Yale.

When his parents moved again to start over in Henderson, New York on the Lake Ontario shore, the sixteen-year-old Finney taught school for two years. Then he took a teaching job in his parent's home town of Warren, Connecticut, living with an uncle, while he attended Warren Academy and prepared for Yale. He supported himself by working on his uncle's farm and running a singing school. A skilled cello player and choir director, he also taught music at the academy. On the advice of his Warren schoolmaster, a Yale student, Finney decided not to enroll at Yale but to study privately. He became persuaded that so much of college time was wasted that he could do all the work himself in two years. He moved to Mount Pleasant, New Jersey, and began teaching school in November 1814, a job he held for two years while he mastered his studies. He had learned Latin at Warren and taught himself Greek and subsequently Hebrew. His self-teaching was effective enough to qualify him to study law, but he never received a college diploma.

In those days, it was still possible to be admitted to the bar by serving a clerkship in a lawyer's office to prepare for the bar examination. Finney seems to have decided half-heartedly to study law. His New Jersey headmaster wanted him to join him in going south to start their own academy. Finney had not seen his parents in about four years and when he wrote them his plans, his parents came after him and urged him to come home to Jefferson County, New York, and clerk in a law office in the town of Adams. He entered the law office of Benjamin Wright in 1818 at age twenty-five.

It was at this point that he began to study the Bible—as a law book. "In studying elementary law," he afterwards wrote, "I found the old authors frequently quoting Scripture and referring especially to the Mosaic institutes as authority for many of the great principles of common law. This excited my curiosity so much that I went and purchased a Bible, the first one I had ever owned." Finney began to take an interest in the Bible beyond his legal studies. He not only read it but began to meditate on it; "however, much of it I did not understand."

He also began to attend church services in Adams, where the pastor was George Washington Gale (later the founder of Galesburg, Illinois and of Knox College). Finney liked Gale personally but not his preaching. One Sunday, after church, Finney said to Gale, "You don't believe what you preach. Were I in your place, holding the truth you declare I would ring the church bell, and cry in the streets, Fire! Fire!" Reverend George Washington Gale got in the habit of dropping in on Finney at his law office and asking him what he thought of his latest sermon. Finney "sometimes criticized his sermons unmercifully." Finney was just as outspoken in his critiques of the dogmas Gale taught: he found that his clergyman-friend was just as mystified by his preaching as his congregant. He went on with his legal studies and was admitted to the bar, but as Finney attended church, listened to Gale, and studied the Bible more and more, "I became very restless." Something about religion "was of infinite importance." He became convinced that the teachings of the Bible had little to do with all the sermons and prayers at church. He refused to allow the congregation to pray for him because none of their prayers seemed to be granted. He was popular enough to get away with openly criticizing the church services: "You have prayed enough since I have attended these meetings to have prayed the devil out of Adams if there is any virtue in your prayers." Studying the Bible more and more, he came to believe that his neighbor's prayers weren't answered because they didn't expect them to be.

In October, 1821, Finney relates in his memoirs, he had a two-day struggle with himself. He stopped by the church on Monday night, October 7th, where Gale said to him, "You want to get something to make sport of." But Finney surprised him: he declared he had decided to "be a Christian." Years afterward, Finney asked Gale if the church had shaken as he knelt down with the others. "He trembled so that he thought the house shook," Gale recalled. "The next night," Finney said later, "I felt almost like screaming." He went to the law office anyway, but later took a walk in a grove of woods north of town where he often strolled, but he could not relax. That evening, after work, he went into a darkened conference room at the law offices after everyone left. There, his conversion took place. He wrote in his memoirs that he then and there met God:

> face to face and saw him as I would see any other man .... The Holy Spirit ... seemed to go through me, body and soul. I could feel the impression like a wave of electricity, going through and through me. Indeed it seemed to come in waves and waves of liq-uid love ... as the breath of God .... Immense wings ... literally moved my hair like a passing breeze.

The next day, Finney went to work and began to ask the senior partner about "his salvation." The lawyer looked at him "with astonishment." Then a client came in and asked him if he was ready for his court case. Finney told the man, "I have a retainer from the Lord Jesus Christ to plead his cause and I cannot plead yours."

Finney left his law practice and decided to prepare himself to become a minister. His own dramatic conversion experience at age twenty-nine led him to become a powerful preacher with a plain, direct message and style. Refusing to go to Princeton seminary to study theology as Gale urged—even when he was offered a scholarship to Princeton—he applied to the St. Lawrence Presbytery as a candidate for the ministry but said he did not want to be put under the same theological influences "as they had been under." His friend, Reverend George Washington

Gale, and the Reverend George S. Boardman were appointed to supervise his private studies, which lasted nearly three years. "After a great struggle with [Rev.] Gale," Finney finally was examined by the St. Lawrence Presbytery and licensed in March 1824. Once again, Finney had proven extremely independent, aggressively opposing Gale's views on original sin and atonement, working out his own theology from his own study of the Scriptures. Gale's health was broken in the effort and he toured the South to recover before leaving for the West.

Three months after his ordination in July 1824, the thirty-two-year-old lawyer-turned-minister married Lydia Andrews and began immediately to carry out his promise—to convert everyone else, starting with the state of New York. Tall, handsome, with strikingly intense eyes and a powerful voice, he could project and modulate over a great distance. Finney introduced a new technique of preaching, what he called "new measures." His hold over an audience was so strong that when he described the descent of a sinner into hell, people in the back rows of a church stood up to watch the final fall. He singled out a poor "sinner" and called him by name to come and sit on the "anxious bench," the front row under the pulpit on stage, and berated his sinfulness in personal terms as the entire congregation witnessed the conversion struggle.

Religious revival meetings had been sweeping the country for a quarter-century, but Finney subjected them to rules and order. "A revival is not a miracle, it is a purely scientific result of the right use of constituted means." Casting aside the usual conventions of preaching, he used expressive language and colorful illustrations. Finney was shockingly direct and personal in his appeals to the conscience and in his prayers, so much so that he was threatened with tar and feathers and even with death. Emphasizing the terrible guilt and consequences of disobeying divine laws, he terrified his hearers. Rejecting the Calvinistic doctrine of predestination, he preached that everyone was responsible for his, or her, own salvation and, moreover, for the welfare of the community. Even writing a training manual for other revival preachers, he began a ten-year-long campaign of confrontation and conversion in the Middle and Eastern States that attracted nationwide attention.

His methods and his message were so controversial that, in July 1827, Presbyterian and Congregational ministers from all over New York attended a convention called to consider his views. His followers, however, seemed to win out and he was permitted to go on preaching. But the revival movement was not new and other practitioners objected vehemently to Finney's aggressive techniques and popularity. When Finney met Lyman Beecher at the New Lebanon Convention, Beecher warned him to stay out of Massachusetts. If he dared bring his message of free will and salvation to all, his style of revival, to Massachusetts, "I'll meet you at the state line and call out the artillerymen, and fight you every inch of the way to Boston."

The religious revival that became known as the Second Great Awakening began, if it can be traced to any one location, on the Kentucky frontier in 1800, and reached its climax at the Cane Ridge Meeting of August 1801. The meeting was attended by an estimated 24,000 and resulted in a schism in the Presbyterian Church. In New England, the virulent Presidential campaigns of 1800 and 1804 in which eighty percent of the newspapers and most of the Congregationalist clergy attacked Thomas Jefferson as a Deist masked a revival and great struggle between

Congregationalists and Unitarians. Unitarian scientist Joseph Priestley was one of the first to prophesy a millennium, which became a standard feature of the nineteenth century revivals.

The revival movement had swept the nation's college campuses in 1802. Many Yale undergraduates boasted that they read deist books like Thomas Paine's *Age of Reason*, which mocked Biblical "superstitions." Yale President Timothy Dwight challenged the campus radicals to debate, and by his eloquence won students over. One of those students was Lyman Beecher, the son of a Connecticut blacksmith. By the time of Charles Finney's ordination a quarter-century later, Beecher was the most famous evangelical preacher in the nation. Father of eleven children (including Harriet Beecher Stowe), he brought an almost fanatical energy to almost every aspect of his life. His religious routine at home included taking his family to hear him preach twice on Sundays, to a weekly prayer meeting, and to a monthly "concert of prayer" where they prepared for the conversion of the world. By 1810, Beecher's evangelism would result in the formation, with help of other born-again Protestant ministers, of the American Board of Commissioners for Foreign Missions; in 1816, the American Bible Society; and in 1826, the American Tract Society. Together, they spread Bibles and tracts all over America. Soon, benevolent societies sprang up in hundreds of churches to promote Sunday schools and to provide ministries for sailors and for the poor.

In 1826, Beecher became pastor of Hanover Street Congregational Church in Boston, where he attacked Unitarianism and its upper-crust Boston Brahmins. Unitarian theology, which denied the divinity of Christ and saw him only as a teacher and redeeming role model, was far too liberal and rational for Beecher, who called it a "halfway house on the road to infidelity." Beecher vilified the comfortable lives of Boston merchants, bankers, lawyers, and Harvard professors, and denounced as sinful their card-playing and gambling. He crusaded to outlaw lotteries popular with lower class Bostonians. He roundly condemned drinking and campaigned to shut down the grog shops on Boston Common. He also attacked Roman Catholics beginning to throng Boston in the late 1820s, calling their priests and nuns operatives of the "Antichrist."

What Beecher advocated was the "New Haven theology" of his friend Professor Nathaniel Taylor of the Yale Divinity School. Like Finney's, this set of beliefs rejected the Calvinist doctrine of original sin, which held that the sin of Adam and Eve tainted human nature. Men and women sinned, Taylor said, but they were rational beings with free will who could choose to resist evil. The new evangelical theology rejected the predestinarian views of John Calvin and Jonathan Edwards, the belief that God sat in judgment on every human being before its birth and decided its eternal fate: to the democratic American this was a harsh and unbelievable God.

The new evangelical theology, which Finney and Beecher popularized, preached that it was the duty of ministers to persuade sinners to choose by their own free will to accept God's gift of salvation. Over and over again, Finney insisted to his millions of listeners from Rochester, New York to Glasgow, Scotland, that they were "moral free agents" who were "responsible for your own salvation" and for that of others around them. To the squirming occupants of the "anxious bench"

The Bettmann Archive

Handsome and endowed with a powerful voice, Charles Grandison Finney spellbound multitudes as he preached personal responsibility for America's ills.

and the teeming, crying, and mooning congregations looking on, he thundered, "Do it!" Emotion was not only central to the new American religion, it was paramount. And if Beecher and his fellow ministers questioned his methods at the 1827 New Lebanon Convention, he argued that the emotional outbursts of the sinners were preparing them to accept conversion. His success became his justification. If everyone cooperated with him, "if the church would do her duty, the millennium may come in this country in three years." Urging "the complete reformation of the whole world," Finney pushed onward his revivalist crusade, preaching not only personal progress but human "perfectionism." Christians should "aim at being holy and not rest satisfied until they are as perfect as God."

Finney's aggressive brand of optimism was nowhere more successful than in his attempt to convert the entire new city of Rochester, New York, during six months of daily preaching from 1830–31. Growing from a farming community of a few hundred people to the largest town in the American interior at the completion of the Erie Canal in 1824, by the time Finney arrived on a canal boat in the autumn of 1830, some 20,000 people made their living from the half-million barrels of flour milled and exported as far as England every year. As the Genesee valley became one of the world's leading grain producing areas, merchant fortunes were made in Rochester and expressed in Grecian Revival mansions and tall-spired churches.

But there were two Rochesters: the one of prosperous church-going middle class merchants and proprietors of family businesses, and the other a brawling frontier town of bars and brawls and poverty-stricken wives and children who watched helplessly as pay envelopes were emptied on whiskey and cards before wages made it home each week. In both Rochesters, there were thousands of men who had lost their moral bearings since they had left their New England homes to strike it rich in America's latest boomtown.

Between September 1830 and the spring of 1831, Charles Grandison Finney and a team of four fellow evangelists waged daily war on sin in Rochester. They attacked alcohol, the circus, the theater, and other working man's entertainments that wasted time and money and distracted and delayed the coming millennium. Ignoring sectarian boundaries, Finney and his assistants mobilized the entire religious community and tapped its enormous economic power. While Finney was in Rochester, his rich evangelical converts organized a church for canal workers, transients, and the poor—the Free Presbyterian Church. Starting with forty-five members, the church grew to 237 in one year. Church membership in general doubled in Rochester as a result of Finney's crusade. There were financial rewards to conversion: two-thirds of the workers who became church members improved their job status in the next seven years as employers insisted on hiring only God-fearing, church-going men.

Aiming his crusade at women as well as male sinners, Finney grasped that the factory system was depriving women of income and status as such cash-paying traditional home crafts as weaving were destroyed by the power looms. Women gained a new status in Finney's revived churches, where they were urged to form women's associations to promote temperance, prison reform, abolition, and other reforms. Finney not only appointed women as the guardians of the new morality but gave them a church sphere in which they were freed from their husband's domination. Men and women were urged to pray together—and women could lead the congregation in prayer.

This new power and moral authority was a dangerous novelty for many men, implying equality between the sexes. One Rochester gentleman was especially unhappy about Finney's practice of going door-to-door and handing out tracts to women. After a Finney visit, he complained, "He stuffed my wife with tracts and alarmed her fears and nothing short of meetings, night and day, could atone for the many fold sins my poor, simple spouse had committed." But what really bothered him was that "she made the miraculous discovery that she had been unevenly yoked. From this unhappy period, peace, quiet, and happiness have fled from my dwelling, never, I fear, to return." When men resisted Finney's blandishments, not all women were persuaded to accept their own salvation. Finney records in his memoirs that one woman refused to be saved because she didn't want to go to heaven alone while her husband went to hell without her.

Finney's well-publicized Rochester revival—he introduced the use of newspaper advertising in advance of his sermons and visits—led to his call to a prosperous church of his own in New York City the next year. In 1832, he became pastor of the Second Free Presbyterian Church in New York City, which held its services in the Chatham Street Theatre. Finney had attracted the backing of millionaire abolitionist Lewis Tappan, who leased the theatre and helped him organize his own church, the Broadway Tabernacle. Withdrawing from the Presbyterian Church in 1836, Finney joined the Congregationalists and preached the New Haven Theology with his own variations to a huge audience fed not only by his sermons but by his own newspaper, the *New York Evangelist*, which published his lectures. He also printed his lectures in best-selling book form. By 1835, as his books sold widely, he took a decided antislavery stand in public for the first time, but he was careful not "to make it a hobby or divert the attention of the people from the work of converting souls."

His antislavery views attracted young seminarians who left Lane Seminary because of restrictions placed on discussing slavery. At first, he agreed to teach them in a makeshift seminary, one room in his tabernacle. But then the newly-founded Oberlin College in Ohio invited him to establish a theology department. Guaranteed financial backing by the devoted Tappan, Finney left for Oberlin. He imposed only one condition: that music be established in the curriculum. He also insisted on retaining his pastorate in New York City, but after two years of divided ministry, his health suffered and in 1837 he resigned his New York City charge.

For the next forty years, the second half of his vigorous life, Finney based himself at Oberlin, where he trained hundreds of ministers to carry his Christian crusade all over America and the British Isles, where he preached during tours of England and Scotland in 1849–50 and again in 1859–60. Carrying on his evangelistic work part of each year, he also spread his views far and wide through the *Oberlin Evangelist*, the newspaper he founded in 1839 to disseminate his views on doctrine and practical matters. As he increasingly espoused perfectionism, holding that sin and holiness could not co-exist in a person, he came under increasing attack from Calvinists who long held "Oberlin theology" in disrepute.

But Finney clung to an exalted idea of what a Christian should strive to attain and insisted that churches should always be kept at revival pitch. He became the champion of an evangelical strain of American Christianity that opposed popular amusements which might hinder salvation and take time away from his reform agenda. His temperance campaign—he was opposed not only to alcohol consumption and the use of tobacco, but even drinking coffee or tea—led in large part to the first prohibition movement that swept the North in the 1850s.

The visible fruits of Finney's brand of evangelism were phenomenal. The proportion of church members in America increased from one in fifteen in 1800 to one in seven in 1850. The college-founding movement, almost exclusively evangelical, increased the number of permanent Christian liberal arts colleges from twenty-five in 1799 to 182 in 1861. Finney went on writing until his death in 1875. Because of his work, thousands of voluntary associations were formed to promote reforms including temperance, abolitionism, women's rights, co-education of the sexes, health and prison reform, peace, and Sunday schools. Further, as historian William McLoughlin puts it, "both as motivation and as rationale" Finney's evangelical religion "lay behind the concept of rugged individualism in business enterprise, laissez faire in economic theory, constitutional democracy in political thought." It became "the Protestant ethic in morality and the millennial hope of white, Anglo-Saxon Protestant America to lead the world to its latter day glory."

QUESTIONS FOR THOUGHT AND DISCUSSION

1. What gave rise to Charles Grandison Finney's emergence as the leading evangelist of his era? Do you get the sense that he was a sincere believer or a charlatan?

2. What were the controversial methods used by Finney in his revivals in order to persuade sinners to change their lives? Were these techniques appropriate to achieve noble goals, as entertainment, or both?

3. What role did Finney see for women in his revivals and in church activities in general?

4. How was Finney's evangelical message of universal salvation and his promotion of the Protestant work ethic tied to more secular currents in nineteenth-century American society?

SUGGESTED READINGS

Carwardine, Richard J. *Evangelicals and Politics in Antebellum America.* New Haven: Yale UP, 1993.

Finney, Charles Grandison. *Memoirs: The Complete Restored Text.* Ed. by Richard A. G. Dupuis and Garth M. Rosell. Grand Rapids: Academic Books, 1989.

Hamilton, James E. "Finney: An Appreciation." *Christianity Today,* 19(No. 22, 1975), 13–16.

Hardesty, Nancy A. *Women Called to Witness: Evangelical Feminism in the Nineteenth Century.* Nashville: Abingdon, 1984.

Hardman, Keith L. *Charles Grandison Finney, 1792–1875: Revivalist to Reformer.* Syracuse: Syracuse UP, 1987.

Johnson, Paul E. *A Shopkeeper's Millennium: Society and Revivals in Rochester, New York, 1815–1837.* New York: Hill and Wang, 1978.

McLoughlin, William G., *Modern Revivalism: Charles Grandison Finney to Billy Graham.* New York: Ronald, 1959.

McLoughlin, William G., ed. *Religion in America.* Boston: Houghton, 1968.

14

Sam Houston

If there had to be a Texas, then there had to be Sam Houston. The confusion around the one gave mystique to the other. Many Americans believed that Texas belonged to the United States as part of the Louisiana Purchase. The exact boundaries of Texas had not been set, even when Louisiana passed from Spanish to French possession. The government of Mexico encouraged its people to settle in the state of Texas so that they would outnumber Americans there, just in case the United States decided to assert ownership. This unique relation to other states meant that Texas acquired a distinctive identity and history before its statehood in 1845. Because it had been a republic of respectable size and had negotiated with the United States, it did not follow the model of other states. For a short time, Northerners expected Texas to remain an independent country. The man who helped to achieve its political independence would have been the national hero had it remained autonomous, would have continued to serve as its president.

Few Americans moved across cultures with the ease of Sam Houston who had learned how to leave the United States without leaving North America when he became a member of the Cherokee nation. The possibility of expansion, the leading national concern during Houston's lifetime, proved a boon and a curse to the young nation. A tendency to expand in experience and reputation also describes the character of Sam Houston. Observers from outside America could not possibly understand his flamboyant presence. A visiting French aristocrat, Baron Alexis de Tocqueville, after meeting Houston, called him one of the "unpleasant consequences of popular sovereignty." A fellow American described what a later age would call charisma: "Two classes of people pursued Sam Houston all his life—artists and women."

THE UNITED STATES remained for generations an unfinished project. Its boundaries seemed to exist for the purpose of being changed. White Europeans continued to arrive, and not all of them wanted to remain in Eastern cities. The promise of land,

a commodity so scarce in the old world, lured boatloads of people with few certain-
ties left except a solid expectation of finding more land than they could have hoped
for back home. Sam Houston understood that even though his family had arrived
early in North America (in the 1730s), they had continued to move in the direction
of open land from the beginning. For reasons having to do with his style as much as
any of his considerable achievements, he acted on that family ambition in ways that
inspired legends. He likely viewed his own life, like the United States, as an unfinished project for years on end.

Sam Houston's Scots-Irish immigrant ancestor Robert Houston led his family
to America, where he arrived in Philadelphia, but he did not stay there for long.
Preferring the freedom of the frontier, the Houston family moved to rural Virginia,
east of the town of Lexington. Stories put the birth of Samuel Houston, his father's
namesake, in a log cabin, while the record shows that he came into the world in
1793 in a proper two-story house, built by his great-grandfather. The older Samuel
Houston, a veteran of the American Revolution, remained in the army and worked
at inspecting militia frontier forts. Because of this work, he spent a great deal of
time away from his wife and large family.

His very capable wife, Elizabeth Paxton Houston, mother of his nine children,
could have married whomever she chose. Her prosperous father knew that the
whole valley considered his beautiful daughter to be the best kind of wife. Her
family had money enough to "help out." Time and adversity brought out an
admirably stalwart side in Elizabeth Houston, whom her famous son would call
"extraordinary." Of the nine children she raised while her husband's work kept him
away, her fifth son, Samuel, was Elizabeth's favorite. When her husband died in
1807, she decided that she would follow a plan the couple had in mind and move
her family across the mountains to eastern Tennessee where cheap land could be
had. With so many children, especially those six sons who would be expected to
own real property, she saw in Tennessee land a way to keep her children near her
as adults. Packing up her entourage, she successfully crossed the Allegheny mountains and relocated the Houstons to eastern Tennessee where she helped build
their new home with her own hands.

Strength of personality and strong resolution passed through Elizabeth to her
young son Sam (as he called himself), but also deflected him from a conventional
path in life, again and again. When he was a teenager, for example, Sam Houston
showed great enthusiasm in school for one book in particular, Alexander Pope's
translation of Homer's *Iliad*. Heroic characters, war in the name of honor, man-to-
man combat, and memorable speeches full of dramatic flourishes thrilled the young
man who had recently lost his soldier father. He committed long passages of it to
memory. In particular, the book inspired him to want to learn classical languages in
order to read Homer in Greek. When his Tennessee schoolmaster told Sam Houston that he would never be able to master Greek, the boy quit school. His family saw
that decision as freeing him to work to help out. Losing no time, they used local connections to find him work in a local store, the worst possible match for a young man
fired by heroic visions. Rather than tell his family he wanted to do something else,
Sam decided on a more dramatic gesture. He ran away from home and went to live
with the Cherokee Indians, not far from his family, on Hiwassee Island.

To live among the Cherokee did not represent a radical departure for Sam. When they counted themselves among the "Five Civilized Tribes" the words described their aspirations but also their way of life. More than any other tribe, the Cherokee had adopted European ways, deliberately appropriating some elements of the culture that they saw taking root around them. Many Cherokees were literate, usually as a result of missionary efforts. But with their literacy, they had evolved a system for writing down their own language. They had a newspaper. Not nomadic, Cherokees had plantations and some owned African American slaves. Their tribal leaders lived in a way sometimes more prosperous than neighboring European settlers. Impressive-looking two story houses stood in some Cherokee settlements. Not infrequently local traders, particularly Scots in that part of Tennessee, married Cherokee women and remained in their villages. The Cherokee chief, Ooleteka, who welcomed the young runaway into his family, could not fairly be described as "savage," in any sense. When the teenager, quite a tall boy, had come to him looking for epic heroes, the respected leader understood that he could trust and teach Sam Houston.

Following the Native American custom of giving a name that described a man's character, Ooleteka gave Houston the new name of Kelanu (sometimes recorded as Col-oh-neh), "The Raven," a fitting designation for a large, noisy, and unusual visitor. For three years Sam lived with Ooleteka's people, long enough for an eager student to learn their language, their ways of hunting and fishing, and of being in the woods. From time to time he would go and visit his mother, and then return to his close friends on Hiwassee Island.

Although he quit school because he felt insulted by a teacher, Sam Houston did not end up less educated than other young people who grew up on the frontier. Schooling had to be sporadic because of the need for help with the hard work of frontier life. Nor was it so unusual that when Sam Houston finally moved back from Hiwassee Island, his mother found him a job as a teacher. He had as much training as some rural teachers. He could read, write, and do sums. And from his time with Ooleteka, he had no doubt assimilated many lessons in behaving as a leader, and in speaking with authority. Or Sam Houston's Cherokee experience merely enhanced an ability he would have shown anyway. His teaching career lasted a very short time, but it no doubt gave him even more of a taste for the pleasures of being listened to and of being taken seriously.

After this unconventional interlude, Sam Houston took a step that most people on the frontier considered natural, especially for the son of a soldier. He joined the army to fight with Andrew Jackson, who intended to clear more land for white settlement. People in his family, on the other hand, found it hard to swallow that the son of an officer would sign up as a common soldier, forgetting who he was, they would say. But in his style of fighting no one could call Sam Houston common.

With Jackson and 2,000 soldiers, a quarter of whom were Cherokees, Sam Houston fought the Creek Indians at Horseshoe Bend, the War of 1812 engagement that broke a Creek alliance with the British. A Creek arrow got Houston in the thigh, a wound that cost him a considerable loss of blood. Before Houston could recover, Andrew Jackson asked for volunteers to get a small number of Creeks out of an improvised fortress. No one could keep Houston from volunteering, wounded or not. In that second round, he was wounded again, this time by two rifle balls in his right shoulder. The battlefield surgeon who treated the shoulder poked around long enough to yank out one of the rifle balls. But when he looked at the unconscious man and saw how badly his leg had been wounded, the surgeon made a judgment call. Rather than spend time removing a second shot from a soldier who most likely would die soon, he left Houston in order to go and treat other soldiers whose chances of surviving looked stronger. For Jackson's army, the battle marked a success: the Creeks ceded twenty million acres of land to the United States. For Sam Houston, that engagement changed what he could expect from life.

Two months later a very weakened man was brought to Elizabeth Houston, still in her log house in eastern Tennessee. Loss of weight had made her son unrecognizable. A thigh, grotesquely torn by the violent removal of the Creek arrow, would have been enough to make recovery difficult, but the clumsy probing of the battlefield doctor left Sam Houston's shoulder a scarred mess that never healed properly. An account by a man who knew Houston claimed that the wound continued to "discharge" every day for over thirty years. No one records how it smelled.

Horseshoe Bend marked Houston's future in another way even more obvious than his wounds: he had met Andrew Jackson. Houston did not stand out necessarily for having been wounded that day, but he did have a special relationship with the Cherokee, which soon made him of special value. In 1817, Jackson knew that the time had come to tell the Cherokee they had to leave, to move west to Arkansas. Settlers still arrived and had to have land. By now the edge of settlement reached land inhabited by Cherokees, by Creeks, and other Native American tribes. With Jackson, Cherokees had fought at Horseshoe Bend, yet now they were asked to relinquish land as the Creeks had, as losers of that battle. The peaceful method, when possible, entailed "removal" of Native Americans through negotiation. The United States proposed conditions and promised good terms, the government thought. In return for leaving their land, the Cherokee were promised the protection of the United States Army. As they moved farther west, sometimes to land already inhabited by other tribes, that protection seemed even more necessary and more valuable in the eyes of Washington.

To complicate these dealings, the conflict had begun over the authority of Washington versus the local authority of individual states. Washington, bound by treaties, had to declare Native-American land as simply off limits to settlers. But when settlers left their own states to claim better land farther to the west, the local government held them innocent of any charge. Custom if not law in individual states made it legal for whites to arrive, to declare land to belong to them, and to require Indians to leave. Whites took over land as well as houses from Native Americans who could not count on federal help. Their refusal to abandon what they considered their ancestral birthright, their material and spiritual essence, counted as belligerent conduct to Washington. Profound cultural differences made it hard for the Native American population to acknowledge the notion of land being owned at all. Over time, as land became more scarce and more valuable, government practices slipped in their ethical correctness. As "pay" for their land, Cherokees and others were not given gold, as they expected, but script money, or vouchers. Before long, the symbolic medium invited abuse.

Against this background of mutual mistrust, Andrew Jackson saw the need for a negotiator the Cherokees would trust. In 1817 he assigned Sam Houston the job of going not just to the Cherokee but to Ooleteka himself to talk him into moving his people west. Recovered from his wounds enough to travel, Houston did the job that his commander had said was his duty. We can imagine how half-heartedly he must have argued with the chief. While he spoke as Andrew Jackson's representative and won agreement from Ooleteka, Houston lobbied Washington to get more blankets and supplies for Cherokees about to emigrate.

At this point Houston could have thought that his military career was on track. No obstacle existed on his path to advancement. Nothing that Sam Houston did ever got in his way. Yet an accusation clouded his record in a way that made him feel so defeated that he quit. Unfounded charges, maybe from a political rival of Jackson, said Houston had disobeyed orders and had used his position to profit from illicit slave traffic. He proved his innocence, but the vicious plan had worked. He was fed up. Whenever things seemed not to be working out, Sam Houston did not wait. He tried something else. This time, at age twenty-four, he quit the army.

Considering his flair for speaking, something which must have helped him as a teacher, Sam Houston turned to a line of work that used his gift and did not require much training: he decided to become a lawyer. To practice law in America, not just on the frontier but in cities as well, young men ordinarily apprenticed themselves to a lawyer to prepare for the bar. Because his family had good connections in Tennessee, he was able to work with a Nashville judge. Sam Houston worked hard and learned quickly, and after a few months passed the bar. At about the same time he let himself pursue another activity that might have been seen as amusement, but that also amounted to practical training for his future work. In joining a dramatic society in Nashville, Sam Houston as an actor found expression for a streak in his character that others must have recognized. He had already started his habit of showing up in unusual costumes, even for the frontier. At a time when most men in public life wore black suits, only black at all times, the appearance of a large man in fringed trousers and a colorful Cherokee shirt or turban must have cut a figure. In fact, his personality was so "large" that people overestimated his height. Both War Department records and a passport he was issued gave Houston's height as six feet two inches, but people who knew him said that he was six-foot-six.

The imposing young lawyer with a flair for theater quickly attracted attention and also clients. His practice soon made him popular enough to be named district attorney for Nashville. His popularity went beyond his clients, far enough to get him elected to the United States Congress where he seldom spoke up but made his flamboyant presence noticed when he did. His rhetorical flourishes could have come from all the sermons of Presbyterian ministers he had listened to or from the imposing and dignified style of Ooleteka, observed so closely during Sam's formative years. Even without knowing exactly why, listeners recognized that Sam Houston could charm an audience.

With a prospering law practice, and a start in public life as a congressman, Sam Houston surprised no one when he was elected governor of Tennessee at age thirty-four in 1827. People interested in his career, including Andrew Jackson, saw what he lacked and gave him advice. Sam could not easily continue on the road he was on without a wife. The advice no doubt reflected sincere concern and good will; the result could not have been worse. The young and refined Eliza Allen whom Sam Houston chose, with help, as his wife struck everyone as perfect for the young governor. Rich, beautiful, and from a good family, she had been brought up to function in a polite circle as the wife of an important and respected man. For reasons not clear outside their intimate relationship, the twenty-year-old Mrs. Houston chose to return to her family home less than three months after her conspicuous marriage. One of the more plausible suggestions concerns her reaction to her bridegroom, and to his body in particular. The wounds he had received as a very young man had disfigured one thigh and left a shoulder permanently oozing. Nothing in her delicate background had prepared her for accepting such gross realities as normal. Although he wrote a letter to her parents, as honor required, Houston did not attempt any public explanation, respecting the silence expected of a gentleman and certainly of a public official. Even while he observed the appropriate protocol, Sam Houston felt publicly humiliated and could not stand it. He resigned as governor and chose to derail his public career, at least for a while.

On April 23, 1828 Sam Houston moved away from Nashville. As he crossed the river toward his old friends the Cherokee, he thought he could count on Ooleteka to take him back. During this stay with his old friends, Sam Houston came to know a woman who belonged to Ooleteka's family and, therefore, considered herself Cherokee. Tiana Rogers, whom Sam married, was the daughter of a Scottish Indian trader, which would have made her half white. But her mother, in turn, was only one-eighth Cherokee herself, which made Tiana Rogers one-sixteenth Cherokee. Rogers would have been outstanding in any community of her time because of her unusual beauty and intelligence. The Cherokee community had recognized her talents early and had provided her an excellent education both from private tutors and at a school in Nashville. Because he had turned his back on his old life, Sam Houston saw no reason not to marry among the people he now considered his own. In addition to marriage Houston took other steps to integrate himself with the tribe that had adopted him. He made himself a citizen of the Cherokee nation.

During his time with the Cherokee, Sam Houston tried to make use of his earlier experience in Washington. As a Cherokee who had formerly sat in the House of Representatives, he expected to be able to help his fellow citizens. During this time Washington had to discuss Native American questions for practical reasons because of Jackson's overall Indian removal plan. For this large, organized migration to work, there would have to be supplies, and the government would have to provide them rations for the journey from the east to the Indian Territory (Oklahoma). Bids had to be submitted before the contracts could be awarded. Inevitably, corrupt officials saw in this deal the potential for a huge profit. Rumors and inside trading marked the preparations. One rumor put it that Sam Houston participated in an attempt at getting a contract for a friend. While Houston visited Washington to represent the Cherokee nation, a Congressman insulted him on the floor of the Congress, which meant that by law the untrue claim could not be treated as libel. Houston, a lawyer, knew that he could not bring charges against his accuser, Congressman Stanbery from Ohio. But by saying nothing he could not

challenge the assertion. Stanbery knew enough about Sam Houston by reputation
to expect hearing from him, so much so that the congressman started carrying
weapons, two pistols and a small dagger, as he went around Washington. It happened on Pennsylvania Avenue that Sam Houston saw Stanbery and decided to
take the law and the congressman into his own hands. The record makes it impossible to know who provoked whom, but when their meeting ended, Sam Houston
was standing up and Stanbery was not, and where Stanbery sat he had acquired a
few bruises in indelicate places. Because a congressman was involved, Sam Houston's trial for assault had to take place before the House of Representatives. Not its
importance but its flashiness prolonged the trial and reminded people that Sam
Houston was working for the cause of the Native Americans. Houston hired the
Washington lawyer Francis Scott Key. After a debate that lasted four days, the
House found Houston guilty, by a vote of 106 to 89. The reprimand was light.
Meanwhile the project of Native American removal turned out to be irreversible.

In time, Sam Houston (Kelanu) ran for a place on the ruling tribal council. His
self-destructive habit of heavy drinking, which had overtaken him even more since
he left Nashville in disgrace, now reduced his credibility in another nation. Members of Ooleteka's tribe would not vote for the man they had started to call by the
new name of Big Drunk. Never having recovered from his earlier public humiliation, Sam Houston could not stay among people who had rejected him. Rejection
must have felt like a pattern to him: school, the Army, his first wife, and now his
adopted community had all told him he was unwanted. Full of internal pain, Sam
Houston showed up at the home of someone he wanted to think well of him, Elizabeth Houston. Her practical nature and truthfulness did not let her spare her son.
He returned to the Cherokee where he did business as a trader at the Neosotho
Wigwam.

Late in the summer of 1831, Sam Houston was summoned to go back to the
log house quickly, in time to see his mother for the last time. Knowing that she
would not live long, Elizabeth Houston let her favorite son know how much he had
failed her expectations. Two of his siblings had already died, one brother had taken
his own life, and a sister had turned out to be mentally ill, but no child had disappointed the dying woman as much as her favorite son, Sam. With no hope of
changing his life by going back to the Cherokee, Houston knew that he had to look
in a different place.

During the years when the federal government looked for land to resettle
Native Americans, the national political debate more and more concerned the status of new states entering the Union. The question focused on slavery and whether
new states would be allowed to be part of its spread. The Missouri Compromise of
1820 had allowed one new slave state to be admitted for every new non-slave state.
At the same time, to the south of the United States, settlers were finding land more
wide open than the largely Indian land of Tennessee and Georgia. While these territories to the Southwest belonged to Mexico, many Americans, including President Andrew Jackson, had always thought of Texas as part of the Louisiana Purchase. In other words, they saw it as already belonging to the United States. But
when Mexico gained its independence from Spain in 1821, all land claims were in
some way contested. Individual settlers thought they had clear title to property

from the Spanish government, but Mexico asserted that such claims had no legal status. Legislation to slow down the flow of immigrants from southern states into Texas had the bad effect of encouraging outlaws, but no one else, to continue to go to the vast territory.

Sam Houston, meanwhile, worked with New York land speculators to try to protect large investments in large tracts of land. Houston, like anyone else who wanted land in Texas, had to become Catholic, technically, in order to be granted the standard tract of 640 acres. But Sam Houston, like no one else, picked the same time he became Catholic to file for divorce from his first wife. His hopes were rising, and he wanted to be free to marry again. At this same juncture, Houston understood that Texas was finally the place he would not leave. His experience as a lawyer helped him establish himself in Texas, but he did not expect the law to make him rich. Land, on the other hand, could. But he had other experience that was equally important. He had, after all, been a major general of the Tennessee militia. His experience in battle and his personality easily made settlers understand that Sam Houston was someone to follow, especially into battle.

The new leader of Mexico, Santa Anna, had made many Americans think of him as a democratic leader, a friend. But land disputes had called that friendship into question. Sam Houston understood that only armed conflict would settle questions of property possession. He had seen what happened to Cherokees who counted on negotiation to settle disputed ownership. Needing a place to make a new life for himself and believing that he could, Sam Houston fought the forces of Santa Anna.

Besides the practical problems connected with crossing Texas during an unusually wet season that left many creeks and rivers swollen, Houston had to lead his Texas army faster than the advancing troops of Santa Anna, who were more numerous and better equipped than Houston's "troops." Under Santa Anna's orders, armed Texans could be treated as rebels and traitors, an order that discouraged men from signing up to fight under Houston. (Estimates now show only about one-fourth of men who might have fought actually did.) But armed Texans felt more loyalty to Houston as they started to learn about recent Mexican insults. On February 23, 1836, Santa Anna led 3,000 troops to start a siege that lasted until March 6, when 187 Texans could not hold out any longer. The men inside the old mission near San Antonio, known as the Alamo, were then massacred. At the Alamo, after Mexicans killed Davy Crockett and his companions, they stacked their corpses like firewood and burned them. At the battle near Goliad, Mexican atrocities continued. By reminding his men of these indignities, Houston got them to march through awful conditions, finally arriving in East Texas just ahead of Santa Anna. By the time the armies could camp near the San Jacinto River, Houston's men had not eaten anything for forty-eight hours and had not slept enough to keep up their strength. On the morning of April 21, 1836, it was a kind of showing off that made Houston sleep until nine in the morning (or appear to be asleep) to convey confidence to his men.

Santa Anna was camped close enough for the Texans to notice comings and goings in the Mexican camp. When word spread that Mexican reinforcements had come and swelled the numbers of Santa Anna's forces (which was true), Houston

The Bettmann Archive

Sam Houston's theatrical flair riveted listeners to him and at times disguised his serious political agenda.

understood that he must keep up the morale of his Texans. He put out the word that Santa Anna was marching the same men around and around to trick the Texans. Houston knew that he was up against the commander who gave himself the title "the Napoleon of the West," but as the day wore on Houston also observed that the commander was spending the afternoon in his tent, maybe for a siesta, maybe with female company. Using boldness to compensate for his many disadvantages, Houston attacked the Mexican army late in the afternoon. He did find them unaware and so confused that the battle started and ended within eighteen minutes. The Texans had followed the battle cry of "Remember the Alamo!" so literally that they kept fighting to satisfy their desire for vengeance, even after the enemy was beaten.

Santa Anna left the battle scene and escaped in disguise. In Texas, people tell the story that he was dressed in women's clothes, a detail that degrades a defeated opponent, but that wanders from the record. A Texas private found Santa Anna walking and picked him up as a prisoner. When other Mexican prisoners saw him and saluted their commander, he was brought before Houston. Before the would-be Napoleon could talk, he asked for opium to help calm his nerves. In fact, Houston found some for the commander, possibly because Houston was using it himself, as he was reported to do, especially after he gave up drinking alcohol—but not for good. In their bargaining, Santa Anna was given his life on the condition that he order Mexican troops to withdraw back across the Rio Grande, which he agreed to do. Houston had won Texas.

This critical battle, which won Texas its independence from Mexico, would be referred to as "San Jacinto." Besides the fact of victory against a superior enemy, the story of San Jacinto included details that enhanced the reputation of Sam Houston. In the battle his men killed 838 Mexicans, and sacrificed only eight Texan lives. The grateful Texans who followed him ended up winning what they had been after. Glory, maybe, but most of all their victory meant land. Texas was independent as a result of the famous battle won by a man who had already inspired legends.

When the territory that had been a state of Mexico organized itself as an independent republic, Texas counted itself as a free political entity. Some, including Sam Houston, saw its independence as viable. To others, independence was a stage on their way to becoming part of the United States. The complication of the Missouri Compromise meant that Texas could not apply to be admitted as a state because no corresponding northern state was at the gate to balance it. But if the United States were to annex or claim the territory, all sides would have to acknowledge a political solution. While it remained independent, Sam Houston served as the first president of the Republic of Texas from 1836 to 1838 and from 1841 to 1844. When Texas did become a state, Sam Houston served as one of its first two senators from 1846 to 1859. He was then elected governor in 1859. Beginning still another new life, Sam Houston remarried. Margaret Moffett Lea, a religious woman much younger than Sam, helped him to cut down on his drinking. They had eight children and stayed married for the rest of his life.

Sam Houston remained a believer in the federal government of his long-time supporter Andrew Jackson, at the cost of his own popularity. Discontent came to a crisis in Texas surrounding the Presidential election of 1860. The question had already been raised of whether or not Texas should remain in the Union. Governor Houston could not see strong reasons to leave. The worst thing that could happen, he pointed out, was a victory for the Republican candidate, Lincoln; but even so, there were still Democratic majorities in the Senate and the House.

After Lincoln won, the Texas legislature wanted to have a special session to argue the pros and cons of staying in the Union. The other Southern states were doing exactly that, as Houston and Texans could see. In the Texas legislature, the proslavery faction won control. When members of the legislature recognized Houston's trick of going as slowly as he could, in his hope that the whole trouble would settle itself, they started working around the governor. Opponents of his called for a meeting in late January to talk about leaving the Union. By that date, Texas was the only state of its neighbors not to secede. On December 20, 1861, South Carolina had taken the lead, followed by Mississippi, Florida, Alabama, Georgia, and Louisiana. Keeping up his tactics of delay, Governor Houston dug in his heels and said that such a grave decision should be brought before the citizens of Texas. The Texas legislature accepted that idea and thereby gave Texas the distinction of being the only state to present the question to an open and direct vote. The day the vote took effect was March 2, 1862, which happened to coincide with the twenty-fifth anniversary of the independence of Texas, and with Sam Houston's birthday. Ultimately, he could not continue to hold the office of Governor because he refused to swear an oath of allegiance to the Confederate States of America. By his reasoning, when Texas left the Union it went back to its status as a republic. He did not think that it automatically belonged to a new country.

The conflict that erupted between North and South during the Civil War marked the end of his life. Right after Vicksburg, before the war's final outcome was known, with the Union in the balance, Sam Houston's life, his own unfinished project, ended. He died in Huntsville, Texas in 1863 at the age of seventy.

QUESTIONS FOR THOUGHT AND DISCUSSION

1. How do you account for Sam Houston's frequent moves and "fresh starts"? What do his numerous "fresh starts" say about opportunities in American society at the time?

2. How did Houston's life prior to migrating to Texas reflect a contradictory attitude toward Native Americans? How do you explain his behavior in this regard?

3. Why was Congress unwilling to allow Texas immediate admission as a new state following Santa Anna's surrender?

4. Why was Houston unable to convince his fellow Texans to remain in the Union after Abraham Lincoln's election?

SUGGESTED READINGS

Campbell, Randolph B. *Sam Houston and the American Southwest*. New York: HarperCollins, 1993.

Day, Donald and Harry Herbert Ullon, eds. *The Autobiography of Sam Houston*. Norman: U of Oklahoma, 1954.

De Bruhl, Marshall. *Sword of San Jacinto: A Life of Sam Houston.* New York: Random House, 1993.

Gregory, Jack and Rennard Strickland. *Sam Houston with the Cherokees 1829–1833.* Austin: U of Texas P, 1967.

Hopewell, Clifford. *Sam Houston: Man of Destiny.* Austin: U of Texas P, 1987.

James, Marquis. *The Raven.* Indianapolis, 1929. New edition, Austin, 1988.

Michener, James A. *The Eagle and the Raven.* Austin: U of Texas P, 1990.

Williams, John Hoyt. *Sam Houston: A Biography of the Father of Texas.* New York: Simon, 1993.

15

James Forten

*N*ever was the anomaly of slavery and freedom more clear than during the early days of the American Revolution. The British offered freedom to enslaved Americans who would fight against their masters, who at first only held out the prospect of continued slavery if white Americans won their independence from England. For many of the Founding Fathers, the slavery they fought against was their enforced connection with the Mother Country, England. The freedom they fought for did not extend to African Americans, who had no rights at all.

But there were African Americans who had bought their freedom and to them American freedom and independence were literal. Many blacks fought on each side, expecting their freedom and the full rights of citizenship at war's end.

For James Forten and other free blacks, the prospect of full citizenship in a free and independent United States was worth the risk of being captured and sold into the slavery their forefathers had escaped once before. No one risked more in the American Revolution or had such cause for disenchantment as slavery not only survived the struggle for liberty but rapidly grew in the early nineteenth century.

JAMES FORTEN WAS a marble-shooting boy of ten when the Revolutionary War came crushing down on his native Philadelphia in 1777. The young African American, second generation of his family born free in America, marched off proudly as a drummer boy with militiamen who, like him, believed they were defending their homes and liberties against British invasion.

Both Forten's grandmother and grandfather had been born free in Africa and then kidnapped to America. Forten's grandfather had worked many hours beyond his required slave labors to buy first his own, and then his wife's freedom. James's father, Thomas, had evidently been born in Philadelphia, where the first antislavery movement, planted by the Quakers, was taking root. Thomas Forten had a good job as a skilled sailmaker in Robert Bridges' sail factory and he owned his own home.

When James Forten was born in 1767, there were still slaves working plantations across the Delaware River in southern New Jersey, and slaves in the households of prominent Philadelphians like Benjamin Franklin. But there was more and more moral pressure being brought to bear by Quaker reformers. In 1750, Anthony Benezet, a Quaker schoolteacher of French Huguenot descent whose family had fled persecution in France, had opened a free evening school for African American children in his own home. Benezet's writings against slavery reached London, where his pamphlets profoundly influenced such humanitarians as William Wilberforce and Granville Sharp to roll up their sleeves and work to abolish slavery. By 1770, Quaker societies in England and Philadelphia raised the money for a school building for free African-American children. The school opened in 1770 and James Forten enrolled at age eight in 1775, at the time of the Second Continental Congress.

In his only year of formal schooling, James learned to read, to write, and to do sums in his arithmetic book *Dilworth's Assistant*. His schooling stopped abruptly in 1776 when he was nine and his father fell into the Delaware River and drowned. James had to work in a grocery store to help support his family. The chance to make a lot more money came in July 1781, when James, now fourteen years old and a robust six feet two, was recruited by the mate of the new Pennsylvania-built privateer, the twenty-two-gun *Royal Louis*. Its crew of 200 was commanded by Stephen Decatur, Sr., a famous privateer who had already captured eight British ships on commerce-raiding voyages.

By this time, many free African Americans were serving aboard American vessels. In all, about 8,000 blacks were fighting on the American side, twice as many, at least 16,000 on the British side. At first, slaveowning American leaders like George Washington had been reluctant to recruit black troops. Yet, when the British proclaimed that any African-American slave who ran away from his master to join the British army would be given his freedom and a grant of land in the American states, all but South Carolina and Georgia had countered by accepting black recruits, with most states integrating African Americans into white units.

On July 31, 1781, taking a chest of clothes, his Bible, and a bag of marbles with him, fourteen-year-old James Forten, one of twenty African-American recruits, climbed aboard the *Royal Louis*. His new job: powder boy. It was his extremely hazardous job in battle to carry canvas buckets of water, gunpowder, and cannonballs from the powder magazine below decks up a ladder to his gun crew, and then race down for a fresh round under heavy (and explosive) enemy fire. Between engagements, he was a cabin boy, mostly working in the galley helping the cook.

He got his first taste of war at sea almost at once. In Delaware Bay, the *Royal Louis* overtook the British brig *Active:* after a single deadly broadside at close range, the British ship surrendered. Sent back to Philadelphia to be auctioned off, the *Active* and its cargo became prizes of war, with their value to be divided into shares. Even a lowly young powder boy would share in the booty. Life would become a little easier in the Forten household.

But James's luck did not hold. In her next engagement, the *Royal Louis* was surrounded by three British men-of-war and forced to surrender. Now, James Forten faced a fate far worse than he had ever known. Under the international rules of war, African Americans captured on the high seas were part of their captors' booty and were usually sold into slavery to work the rest of their lives on Caribbean sugar plantations where heat, work, and disease often killed them in a year or two. Almost never did the British treat blacks as prisoners-of-war. Yet young Forten again had incredible good fortune. On the *Amphyon,* where he was taken a prisoner, William Beasly, the young son of the captain, Sir John Beasly, spotted Forten's sack of marbles and asked him to play a game. The two boys became fast friends and the British youth pleaded with his father to spare the black youth from sale into slavery.

Exercising his virtually total and arbitrary power as a British naval captain, the *Amphyon's* captain gave James and the other African American prisoners the choice of joining the Royal Navy or being held as prisoners until the war ended. Young Forten declined the invitation: "I am here as a prisoner for the liberties of my country. I cannot prove a traitor to her interests."

Taken off the *Amphyon* and taken by another ship into New York harbor, James joined a thousand other prisoners confined below decks in a squalid, rotting prison ship, the dismasted hulk of the former man-of-war *Jersey.* Moored in Wallabout Bay off Brooklyn, she became the tomb of 11,000 Americans who died of disease, starvation, and maltreatment by British warders. More Americans died on the *Jersey* than in all the battles of the Revolution.

Locked below decks in total darkness in a foul, lice-infested, loathsome cell, roasting in summer and freezing in winter, James probably only survived because he found another ship's boy his age from the *Royal Louis,* Daniel Brewton, a white boy who would remain a lifelong friend. Brewton's health was deteriorating, however, and when an American officer being exchanged for a British prisoner offered to slip Forten out hidden in his trunk, Forten asked him to take Brewton instead. After seven months on the *Jersey*, Forten, too, was released in a general prisoner exchange at war's end. In bare feet and rags, he walked across New Jersey to his home. More than half a century later, Daniel Brewton, steward of Philadelphia's free public hospital, told a black historian, "with tears raining down his face," how his friend Forten had saved his life.

A hero on the Philadelphia waterfront, Forten surprised many people the next year, 1784, when he signed on as an able-bodied seaman aboard the *Commerce,* bound for England, so recently the enemy and now America's largest shipping client. Forten must have been confused by the treatment of African Americans after the Revolution. Many African Americans found themselves returned to lives of servitude or re-enslaved after the struggle for freedom as one state after another refused to affirm the civil rights of blacks. At least 6,000 African Americans who had fought with the British sailed for Caribbean islands.

In Pennsylvania, during the Revolution, where the Declaration of Independence had first stirred sympathy for enslaved peoples, the first statewide abolition society had been founded and had put pressure on the revolutionary government to end slavery. In November 1778, the state's ruling Council requested the Pennsylvania Assembly to pass a law to free infant blacks born to slaves. After a two year procedural impasse, Pennsylvania became the first state to abolish slavery, "to extend a portion of that freedom to others which has been extended to us."

Abolition was not outright: slaves in Pennsylvania were not freed, but when the children of slaves reached twenty-eight years of age, they would become free. Just across the Delaware River, slavery would continue in New Jersey until 1847, long after James Forten died an old man with increasingly conflicting emotions about the promises of the Revolution.

Now that there was peace with England, seventeen-year-old Forten made a fateful decision. When his sister, Abigail's, husband signed on the *Commerce,* he told Forten the ship was sailing for England in two weeks if she had a full crew. Forten lugged aboard his Bible, his Shakespeare, and his warmest clothes. One wintry day in February 1784, the *Commerce* dropped down the Delaware and set sail for Liverpool, where Forten landed four weeks later. Liverpool was the center of the booming British slave trade. Forten found work as a stevedore on the Mersey-side docks and took a room in a boardinghouse owned by a West Indian-born black man. He soon introduced himself to local Quakers and attended his first antislavery meeting. He was pleased to learn that English Quakers had been stirred to action by the writings of his old Philadelphia teacher, Anthony Benezet. In the daytimes, he worked provisioning ships that he soon learned were preparing to take more human cargo from Africa to the Caribbean. At night, he listened to the stirring words of Quaker disciples of Granville Sharp, a low paid English civil servant who had put Benezet's words into action and had organized the fledgling English antislavery movement that would eventually, after a sixty-year campaign, win over Parliament to abolish the slave trade and to enforce its ban with the Royal Navy. Sharp's first victory had come as early as 1772 when all slaves in Britain had been declared free by the Chief Justice, Lord Mansfield. A black man named Somerset had been brought by his master from Virginia to England, had escaped, been recaptured, and put on a ship to sail to Jamaica to be resold. Granville Sharp and his Quaker friends had hired a lawyer and briefed him with his own legal research. After a trial, Lord Mansfield decried the fact that slavery was still legal overseas:

> The state of slavery is of such a nature that it is incapable of being introduced on any reasons, moral or political, but only by positive law.... It is so odious that nothing can be suffered to support it but positive law. Whatever inconveniences, therefore, may follow from the decision, I cannot say this case is allowed or approved by the law of England; and therefore the black must be discharged.

Since no law had ever established slavery in England, slavery was illegal there. Fourteen thousand slaves were instantly freed.

The success of the abolitionists in England inspired James Forten. He left Liverpool, where five-sixths of all commerce still centered around the slave trade, and traveled to London to meet Granville Sharp in person. Using Quaker contacts, Forten wangled an invitation to a meeting where Sharp was to speak. There, he also saw for the first time products made in Africa by free Africans—ivory, dyes, beeswax, palm oil, fine cloth, leather goods, iron, and gold. Stunned by the evidence of a higher black culture than he had seen in America, the eighteen-year-old black seaman slipped out of the meeting too shy to introduce himself to Sharp, too moved to ever forget the experience.

Returning to Philadelphia in 1786, James Forten at age nineteen signed articles of apprenticeship to Robert Bridges, sailmaker, in whose sail loft his father had worked for many years. Here, in a vast space above Thomas Willing's waterfront warehouse, the largest of eight in Philadelphia, Forten learned all the skills required to fit out the sails of ships built nearby. Inside two years, he was promoted to foreman and had the new experience of supervising some forty white and black workmen. In the next ten years, as he learned how to manage the business, the elderly Robert Bridges turned over his business to Forten's stewardship, finally offering to sell it to him in 1798. Forten was surprised when Thomas Willing, business partner of financier Robert Morris and one of the wealthiest men in America, bankrolled him on condition that he make the sails for his trading fleet. Forten promptly announced that he would not take orders for sails of ships in any way engaging in the slave trade. Forten was well on his way to becoming wealthy himself. Much of his income would come from a new labor-saving device for hoisting sails he invented, the hand-cranked winch. Its patent and his sailmaking business helped him amass assets of $300,000 by the time he drew up a will in 1830. In modern terms, he was the first black American millionaire. But his influence went far beyond his wealth. He became one of a handful of the most influential African Americans in pre-Civil War America.

In 1787, at the time a new U. S. Constitution was being drawn up in Philadelphia (one that tabled all discussion of slavery by Congress for another twenty years), Forten joined two black clergymen, the Reverend Richard Allen and the Reverend Absalom Jones, in forming the Free African Society, a beneficial society organized to help free blacks in times of illness, unemployment, or other emergencies. The FAS was the first society formed for African American Philadelphians who were even barred from membership in the all-white Pennsylvania Abolition Society. One of its early tasks was to form black churches in Philadelphia after an incident at St. George's Methodist Church in 1791. As more and more African Americans attended the Methodist Church, elders had a new gallery built and tried to force African-American members to attend separate early morning services apart from white members. When Reverend Allen, Forten, and other blacks insisted on sitting in the lower pews, they were roughhandled by elders who tried to drag them from their knees. The African Americans walked out in a group. Over the next three years, not one but two black churches were built, Mother Bethel African Methodist Episcopal Church, presided over by Reverend Richard Allen, and the African Episcopal Church of St. Thomas, which James Forten helped to build and served as a vestryman for the rest of his life. While Allen's church would become the mother A.M.E. church that spread nationwide, Forten did not want to belong to a church that was only for African Americans. He believed that, in a black church within the larger Episcopal church, both whites and blacks would benefit. He had thus made his first integrationist decision.

After the nation's first Fugitive Slave Act was passed in 1793 encouraging the use of bounty hunters to track down slaves who had escaped to the North (sometimes resulting in free blacks being kidnapped and sold into slavery), Forten began to devote his money and his efforts to buying freedom for slaves and asserting himself politically to protect their rights. So widespread had the abductions become by

1800 that Forten helped to circulate a petition to Congress to end the slave trade as a first step toward emancipation. "We are happy and grateful to live in freedom under the American government," the petition began, asking Congress to relieve "the hard condition of our race," especially the "700,000 blacks in slavery." The Petition of the Free Blacks of Philadelphia presented to Congress by Quaker Robert Waln prompted an angry debate during which John Rutledge of South Carolina insisted that some states would not have come into the Union if they had not been promised that Congress would never legislate on slavery. The debate raged for two days. Late the second day a pro-slavery congressman presented a counter-resolution stating that the Free Blacks Petition invited Congress to act illegally and had "a tendency to create disquiet and jealously." Voting 85–1 in favor of this resolution, Congress deftly avoided ever taking up the Free Blacks Petition.

At a meeting of dejected black leaders in St. Thomas Church, Forten, now thirty-three, refused to be discouraged. "At least we have one steadfast friend in Congress [George Thacker of Massachusetts]. "While one voice speaks for justice, there will be those who hear." He went home and wrote eloquently to Representative Thacker:

> We, sir, Africans and descendants of that unhappy race, thank you for the philanthropic zeal with which you defended our cause .... Though our faces are black, yet we are man ... Judge what must be our feelings to find ourselves treated as a species of property ... A deep gloom now envelopes us ...

One bitter cold morning in January 1807, Forten the sailmaker, nearing age forty, was standing on a wharf near his sail loft gazing out at the river before going on to the day's work. It was near this spot some thirty years ago that his father had fallen into the fast current and drowned. Today, large chunks of ice were jostling in the gray water and a small boat was trying to pick its way through them to the dock. Suddenly the oarsman screamed and disappeared into the water. Forten plunged in after him, grabbed his hair as he began to go under, hauled him back with one arm, swimming with the other. Wrapping him in his cloak, Forten carried the man up to his sail loft, laying him on a pile of canvas near a fire.

Over the years, James Forten by one count saved a dozen people from drowning. In 1821, one rescue prompted the Humane Society of Philadelphia to honor him at a ceremony for "rescuing, at imminent hazard of his life," so many drowning victims. Yet no one was keeping count of how many blacks Forten was rescuing as he became America's first civil rights leader, the voice and pen of freed blacks, escaped slaves and the growing number in bondage. Sometimes, he personally rescued many slaves by buying their freedom, but he also was emerging as the spokesman for African Americans. When the ban on Congressional action on slavery imposed by the Constitutional Convention of 1787 expired in 1807, President Thomas Jefferson and his Democratic-Republican majority pushed a law through Congress prohibiting further importation of slaves after January 1, 1808. James Forten was among the African American leaders who sent a resolution of thanks to Congress.

It was to be one of the last unanimous acts of the African American leadership. In 1810, Granville Sharp's African Institution in London decided to launch a colony for freed blacks in Sierra Leone on the west coast of Africa. A close friend of Forten's, the black ship's captain, Paul Cuffe, of Newport, Rhode Island, also decided to launch a movement to transport freed blacks to Africa. His plan for "the redemption of Africa" was for "sober families of black people in America to settle among the Africans." On New Year's Day 1811, Cuffe, in his new ship *Traveller* sailed for Sierra Leone with the permission of British colonial authorities to plant a settlement there. The War of 1812 soon broke out, interrupting the colonization movement and postponing the rift among African American leaders.

During this war, James Forten emerged as the leader of the 7,400 free African Americans who made up ten percent of the city's population. In the Quaker City, blacks were admitted to free public hospitals and poorhouses. While they were barred from white schools, hundreds now attended Benezet's free school. But trouble arose as the city became the magnet for more and more blacks fleeing surrounding slave states. In January 1813, some white Philadelphians introduced a petition to the Pennsylvania Legislature to require "all Negroes to register with the state" within twenty-four hours or be fined and jailed. The measure would have given the state the power "to sell for a term of years the services of those Negroes convicted of crimes" and would have levied a special tax on free blacks to support poor blacks. The bill's chief aim was to prevent further black immigration into the state.

The measure and the growing animosity behind it shocked Forten into writing *A Series of Letters By a Man of Color,* beginning with his anguished question, "Why are we not to be considered as men?"

> Has the God who made the white man and the black left any record declaring us a different species? Are we not sustained by the same power, supported by the same food, hurt by the same wounds, wounded by the same wrongs, pleased with the same delights and propagated by the same means? And should we not then enjoy the same liberty and be protected by the same laws?

The authors of Pennsylvania's constitution had not differentiated between white and black, he argued, "because they never supposed it would be made a question whether we were men or not."

Forten marshalled evidence that black Pennsylvanians already paid more in property taxes than poor blacks cost the state. And he poured scorn on the proposal for making African Americans register with police and carry identity papers: "The constable, whose antipathy generally against the black is very great, will take every opportunity of hurting his feelings." And he reserved this eloquence until the end:

> Many of our ancestors were brought here more than 100 years ago: many of our fathers, many of ourselves, have fought and bled for the independence of our country. Do not expose us to sale. Let not the spirit of the father behold the son robbed of that liberty which he died to establish.

With his own money, James Forten published his letters to the Legislature and blanketed its members with it. After reading his powerful appeal, Pennsylvania's lawmakers defeated the Registration Bill of 1813. At the peak of the War of 1812, nearly twenty percent of all American naval crews were black. Scarcely more than a year later, when the British attacked Baltimore and Washington, Forten recruited 2,500 Philadelphia blacks to defend the city, forming an all-black battalion that marched to Gray's Ferry and fortified the city's western approaches. But the attack never came. The black citizens of New Orleans had helped Andrew Jackson to repel the last British invasion on the United States.

The struggle that pitted black against black in America now began. Southern white leaders formed the American Colonization Society to relocate freed blacks (and blacks they chose to free) to a new African colony fifty miles north of Sierra. To be named Liberia, the colony was to be purchased with private American funds. Blacks were to be transported free on American warships loaned to the society, which had the warm support of President James Monroe, a Virginia slaveowner: indeed, the society, presided over by Judge Bushrod Washington, nephew of

The Historical Society of Pennsylvania

Son of a freed black and a rich inventor himself, Philadelphian James Forten helped to bankroll the abolition movement.

George Washington, named the capital of the new American colony Monrovia in his honor.

At first, when his friend Paul Cuffe asked James Forten's support, he called a meeting of Philadelphia blacks to present his proposal. But when some 3,000 anxious blacks crowded into tiny Mother Bethel Church, Forten wrote Cuffe of their fears and his that the society's plan was actually a scheme to deport freed blacks and remove the incentive of Southern slaves to revolt or escape to the North. Moreover, Forten was not convinced that all American slaves would be freed to go to Africa. Only free people of color had been mentioned in the proposal. The plan might also mask the slaveowner's intention to "free" troublesome blacks and deport them to Africa.

On January 25, 1817, Forten wrote Cuffe:

> Esteemed friend,
> ... The whole continent seems to be agitated concerning the colonization of the People of Color ... Indeed the People of Color here was very much frightened at first. They were afraid that all the free people would be compelled to go, particularly in the Southern states. We had a large meeting of males at the Rev. Richard Allen's Church ... Three thousand at least attended and there was not one soul that was in favor of going to Africa.

Forten, who had been asked by Allen to chair the mass meeting, spared Cuffe an exact description of the hysterical meeting at Mother Bethel as the city's freedmen looked to him for help. "They think the slaveholders want to get rid of them so as to make their property more secure," he added, noting that he was able to calm the meeting enough to win support for a petition drive against the colonization society's plan "to exile us from the land of our nativity."

Forten had come prepared to the meeting. Now, he read in his strong, clear voice:

> Whereas our ancestors (not of choice) were the first successful cultivators of the wilds of America, we, their descendants, feel ourselves entitled to participate in the blessings of her luxuriant soil, which their blood and sweat manured ... any [measure] having a tendency to banish us from her bosom would not only be cruel but in direct violation of those principles which have been the boast of this republic.

Forten's resolutions, unanimously adopted by the crowd, condemned the "unmerited stigma" cast by Southern whites on the reputation of hard-working, law-abiding free blacks, and reminded the nation how recently they had enlisted in the war during America's "hour of danger." They further vowed "that we will never separate ourselves voluntarily from the slave population in this country."

The protest meeting at Mother Bethel Church did not deter the colonizers from going ahead with their plan. The organization opened an office in Philadelphia and asked Forten to swing over his support in exchange for being appointed the Chief Justice of Liberia. Outraged, Forten refused. More and more, Forten feared that the influential colonizers would persuade Congress to pass a law to deport all freed blacks to Africa. When the colonization society set up its Philadelphia auxiliary, thousands of free African Americans crowded into a schoolhouse on August 10, 1817. Forten, drafted to chair this first avowedly anti-colonization protest meeting, read to the quiet assemblage his "Address to the Humane and

Benevolent Inhabitants" of Philadelphia which he had worked out with other African American leaders.

Condemning colonization on behalf of both freed and enslaved African Americans who could not speak for themselves, Forten called the African colonies a constant danger. Any black who showed a tendency to stand up to whites would be deported and only submissive African Americans would remain in America in ever-worsening bondage:

> Parents will be torn from their children—husbands from their wives—brothers from brothers—and all the heartrending agonies which were endured by our forefathers when they were dragged into bondage from Africa will be again renewed, and with increased anguish .... Let not a purpose be assisted which will stay the cause of the entire abolition of slavery in the United States and which may defeat it altogether.

Soon afterward, Paul Cuffe, the black mainspring of the colonization movement died. In the first seven years of the Liberia colony, only 225 freed African Americans emigrated. Of these, only 140 remained alive there; forty died, the rest went to Sierra Leone or returned to the U.S. Forten's lonely stand had slowed the colonization movement long enough for most blacks and whites to take a second look.

Yet many whites still feared the presence and increasing number of freed African Americans. In 1813, there had been an estimated 14,000 blacks in the city of Philadelphia: by 1830, there were 40,000 black freemen, comprising ten percent of all Philadelphians. White hostility toward African Americans deepened after the bitter congressional debates over the Missouri Compromise of 1820 and after a series of slave uprisings in the 1820s and '30s. The uprising in Charleston, South Carolina, in 1822, led by a free black from San Domingo named Denmark Vesey, evoked all the horror among slaveowners of the mass killings of whites by blacks a generation earlier. A harsh legislative reaction also set in. In 1824, Virginia passed a law imposing a year in prison on anyone, black or white, who assisted a slave's escape. It was already illegal to teach slaves to read and write, and Virginia now made it a crime to teach free blacks to read and write. Everywhere the slave-catchers grew bolder.

By the late 1820s, a new antislavery movement based on education and literacy arose even as race relations deteriorated. In 1827, John B. Russworn, the first black college graduate of Bowdoin College, Maine, launched *Freedom's Journal.* An initial subscriber, James Forten, agreed with its call for education and job training. For the forty years since he had returned from England, Forten had given free classes first in his home and then in St. Thomas's Church, teaching black children to read, write, and do arithmetic. When Pennsylvania opened free public schools in 1818 and African American children were excluded, he had brought pressure that resulted in the donation of a building by the Pennsylvania Abolition Society and state funds to supply teachers. He had also helped to launch the Infant School for Colored Children, forerunner of the modern Head Start Program, in 1828. In an unsigned article he no doubt wrote in *Freedom's Journal,* Forten warned that black children needed to be prepared for school for two years.

Yet Forten continued to worry about the colonization scheme and when Russworn continually endorsed it in his pages, Forten withdrew his support, shifting it soon afterward to a new and far more radical paper, *The Liberator,* edited in Boston by William Lloyd Garrison, who had served two years in prison for libelling a slave trader.

On December 15, 1830, Forten wrote Garrison, sending along the money from twenty-seven badly needed subscriptions he had personally sold and his wish that *"the Liberator* be the means of exposing more and more the odious system of slavery .... May America awake from the apathy in which she has long slumbered." By 1830, Forten was ready to endorse Garrison's militancy, his breathtaking call not for the gradual end to slavery that had eluded so many moderate black and white leaders, but for total abolition now. After one of many visits to Forten in the 1830s, Garrison wrote, "There are colored men and women, young men and young ladies, who have few superiors in refinement, in moral worth and in all that makes the human character worthy of admiration and praise." He expressed his shame at being part of a race which "has done you so much harm."

The very next year, 1831, Forten launched a series of annual African American conventions in Philadelphia and invited Garrison to address the free African American leaders he also summoned from seven northern states. Forten had already won the endorsement of other Philadelphia black leaders for this new white champion of abolition. Eventually, Forten would lead other African Americans to provide eighty percent of *The Liberator's* subscriptions and he became Garrison's number two financial backer, his generosity outdone only by Arthur Tappan, a nephew of Benjamin Franklin.

Now the leading African American in Philadelphia, Forten urged the Pioneer Black Convention of 1831 to launch a black college at New Haven, Connecticut. But the plan came just before the news broke of a massive slave insurrection led by Nat Turner in Southhampton County, Virginia, in which seventy slaves killed sixty white men, women, and children. In the ensuing wave of panic, militant statements about emancipation and moderate calls for black education were drowned out by demands for harsher laws to control both slaves and free blacks. In New Haven, Forten's plan for a college was voted down 700–4 by a town meeting. In Pennsylvania, the state legislature passed two repressive resolutions. The first called for passing a law to protect whites from "the evils arising from the emigration of free blacks from other states;" the state called for a state fugitive slave law harsher than the existing federal law.

In January 1832, Forten, now sixty-five, called a mass meeting to launch a statewide petition drive. Free blacks had long depended on Pennsylvania to provide protections denied by the federal and slave state governments: why this harsh new code now?

> Why are her borders to be surrounded by a wall of iron against freemen whose complexions fall below the wavering and uncertain shades of white ... ? It is [no longer] to be asked, is he brave, is he honest, is he just, is he free from stain of crime, but, is he black, is he brown, is he yellow, is he other than white?

Once again, Forten's powerful reasoning and rhetoric—and his ability to mobilize thousands of reputable, tax-paying African Americans, repulsed repressive laws. But there was now, added to the fear of black rebellion, increasing unemployment among a rising tide of unskilled immigrants arriving in northern cities from Ireland and Germany and perceiving African Americans as competition for unskilled as well as skilled jobs.

The new surfeit of white labor deprived the blacks of construction work, mechanical jobs, carpentry, sail making, and other skills. The prosperity that had drawn Europeans to the mills and farms was fading as overspeculation in Western lands and Jacksonian banking practices led to the terrible depression and bank failures of the late 1830s that especially hurt Philadelphia, then the capital of the national banking system. Soon there was widespread unemployment and fierce competition for even the menial jobs so long held by freed blacks. Soon the African Americans clashed with the newly arrived and equally impoverished Irish in the fetid slums along the Schuylkill River. Unlike any of the earlier waves of immigrants, the Irish were determined to stay in the cities—and not head west to farmlands on the prairies. Indeed, they were encouraged by their religious hierarchy not to disperse across the land, but, instead, to remain a cohesive political and economic force. At the same time, the abolition movement made Philadelphia the center of its national organizing efforts. In 1833 Garrison formed the American Anti-Slavery Society there while he boarded with the family of an African American dentist and barber. The stage was set for ten years of the bloodiest confrontation in Philadelphia history.

What began as a scuffle between gangs at a carousel in August 1834 flared into widespread riots by the next night. That summer in Boston and New York, club-wielding crowds had broken up antislavery rallies. In New York City, the homes of leading abolitionists were targeted, while the homes and churches of African Americans were burned as hundreds fled the city. In Philadelphia, large numbers of boys and young men armed with sticks and clubs assembled. They marched downtown to a vacant lot on the edge of Society Hill, then a black neighborhood. From here they moved through alleys, smashing windows, breaking down doors, throwing furniture into the street, and mercilessly beating any African Americans they caught.

The neighborhood watch (there was still no central city police force) was helpless. After several hours of unchecked rioting, the mayor of Philadelphia, John Swift, the city constables, and a large body of the city's watchmen arrived and charged the rioters, taking twenty prisoners and dispersing the mob. On the evening of August 9th, when one of Forten's sons was on his way home from doing an errand for his father, he was attacked "by a gang of fifty or sixty young men in blue jackets and trousers and low-crowned straw hats." The boy was able to escape in time to warn his family. Three nights later, one of the most conspicuous targets of the Philadelphia mob was the large brick townhouse of James Forten at 92 Lombard Street where, according to the 1830 census, he lived with twenty-one relatives, guests and, servants who helped him fight off the rioters.

An undeterred Forten helped organize another national African American convention the next year. In December 1833, sixty-two black and white delegates from ten northern states came to Philadelphia to attend the first National Anti-Slavery Convention, openly supported and organized by Forten and his Philadelphia friends, and publicized in Garrison's *Liberator*. One of the delegates, twenty-six-year-old poet John Greenleaf Whittier, described most of his fellow delegates as "little known, strong only in their convictions and faith in the justice of their cause." To accommodate future abolitionist meetings, Forten raised funds for a lecture hall for visiting activists called Pennsylvania Hall.

When abolitionists gathered there in May 1838, for a three day convention featuring speeches by Garrison and the Grimke sisters, the mayor refused them police protection and asked them to disband their meeting. On May 16th, as Angelica Grimke rose to speak, a white mob crowded into the hall, hissed her, and then stoned the audience as their compatriots smashed the windows. The frightened women cut short the meeting. Appeals to the mayor failed to produce a constable's guard for the third and final night's meeting. By 10 P.M., a mob of 3,000 gathered, extinguished the street lights, battered down the doors, broke the blinds, turned on the gas, and set fires that quickly engulfed the building. Across the street, James Forten stood by helplessly with John and Lucretia Mott. Philadelphia, so long the City of Brotherly Love, he said, had become the city of mobs. When the volunteer fire companies arrived, they confined their efforts to hosing down surrounding buildings. The mob did not deter their efforts: they moved on to burn the Quaker-run Shelter for Colored Orphans.

The racially motivated riots were not confined to Philadelphia. Each summer they grew in intensity. The entire freed black quarter of Cincinnati burned and some 2,000 black Ohioans were forced to flee to Ontario province, where Forten helped them resettle. In 1835 alone, *The Liberator* recounted more than 100 mob attacks on abolition speakers such as Garrison, who was twice mobbed in his native Boston. Between 1830 and 1860, *The Liberator* counted 209 race riots in the United States; historian Richard Maxwell Brown has counted some thirty-five major race riots in Philadelphia, Baltimore, New York, and Boston during that time. So frequent and disquieting had the violence become that a young Illinois lawmaker, Abraham Lincoln, wrote in 1838:

> There is even now something of an ill omen amongst us .... Accounts of outrages committed by mobs form the everyday news of the times. They have pervaded the country from New England to Louisiana; they are neither peculiar to the eternal snows of the former nor the burning suns of the latter; they are not the creatures of climate, neither are they confined to the slaveholding nor the non-slaveholding states ... Whatever their causes be, it is common to the whole country.

A further setback came in October 1838, when the Pennsylvania Legislature amended its constitution to strip African Americans of the voting rights they had enjoyed since 1780, ignoring Forten's final public plea in his passionate *Appeal of Forty Thousand Citizens*. No black voted again in his beloved home state until 1873. By this time, James Forten had decided to use much of his fortune to help his final cause, the Vigilant Committee of Philadelphia, founded in 1839 to guide and finance slaves escaping along the Underground Railroad, as it became known, to Canada. Early committee records in Forten's handwriting show that he had in old age relented somewhat on the subject of African-American emigration. Case thirty-one, for instance, shows, "woman from Virginia, emancipated on condition of going to Liberia." Case forty included "eight persons from Virginia. A very interesting family. Sent to Canada."

James Forten never recovered from being stripped, along with 40,000 free African American citizens, of their coveted state citizenship. He worked so hard now to give away his money to help blacks and white abolitionists that his fortune dwindled by eighty percent in his last ten years. As the elder statesman of black America, he also supported a moral reform movement, and was elected in 1835 as president of the American Moral Reform Society. One of its chief aims was to seek equal rights for women as well as African Americans and to support the growing temperance movement. At age seventy-five, he went to bed one day in February, 1842, quietly reading his Bible and from time to time reciting his favorite poems to his five-year-old granddaughter, Charlotte, daughter of his son, Robert Bridges Forten. On February 24, he summoned his wife, Charlotte, and all of his eight children. His last words were to extend his love not only to his family but to all his abolitionist friends, "especially to Garrison."

He was buried in the graveyard of St. Thomas's Church. The Philadelphia *North American* noted the passing of "the leading sailmaker" of the city under the headline "Death of an Excellent Man," but did not mention that he was America's first civil rights leader. Some 5,000 people marched behind his coffin, "white and colored, male and female, about one-half white," noted the amazed *Philadelphia Public Ledger.* "Among the white portion were seen some of our wealthiest merchants and shippers, and captains of vessels." In recent years, it had been dangerous for whites and blacks to walk together through the streets of Philadelphia. James Forten's funeral, wrote Lucretia Mott, was "a real amalgamation." Then, James Forten, the last of its original members to die, was buried beside the first African American church in America.

QUESTIONS FOR THOUGHT AND DISCUSSION

1. As a free young black in Philadelphia at the time the American Revolution began, why did James Forten side with the rebels against the British? Was he fighting on the side best suited to advance his interests? Was the revolutionary rhetoric ironic to someone like Forten?

2. Why did Forten oppose colonization efforts to return blacks to Africa? Was he too optimistic in promoting racial integration in the United States?

3. What gave rise to the racial violence in Philadelphia in the 1830s?

4. Given the fact that Forten and all other black Pennsylvanians were stripped of their citizenship by the state legislature in 1838, was Forten's lifelong effort in vain? What was the principal legacy of his life?

SUGGESTED READINGS

Billington, Ray Allen, ed. *Journal of Charlotte L. Forten.* New York: Norton, 1953.

Davis, Burke. *Black Heroes of the American Revolution.* New York: Odyssey/Harcourt, 1976.

Douty, Esther M. *Forten the Sailmaker.* Chicago: Rand McNally, 1968.

Dubois, W. E. B. *The Philadelphia Negro.* Philadelphia, 1899. Repr. New York: Arns, 1967.

Litwack, Leon F. *North of Slavery: The Negro in the Free States, 1790–1860.* Chicago: U of Chicago P, 1961.

Quarles, Benjamin. *The Negro in the American Revolution.* Chapel Hill: Institute of Early American History and Culture, 1961.

Winch, Julie. *Philadelphia's Black Elite: Activism, Accommodation and the Struggle for Autonomy.* Philadelphia: Temple UP, 1988.

16

Harriet Beecher Stowe

Early in the nineteenth century, when Harriet Beecher Stowe was born, New England could still hold center stage in America. When there were only seventeen states, New England claimed twelve of thirty-four senators. In areas of life that all Americans considered supremely important, namely religion and education, New England had to be acknowledged as the cutting edge, claiming the oldest universities and the most famous preachers and teachers of theology. What many Americans may not have seen coming was the period of reform that would be created in part by those same forces, religion and education, that people easily associated with preserving the status quo.

In New England women were educated. They did not go to universities, but neither could women anywhere else. Because of their educations, New England women read books, they talked to people—not publicly, of course—they wrote, and they had ideas.

Harriet Beecher expected to die young, as her mother had, but also expected to make a difference. Her very good education changed her life by making her demand a great deal of herself. Her high standards let her give herself the task of expressing America's outrage with an unjust law. When he considered what she achieved with Uncle Tom's Cabin, *Henry Wadsworth Longfellow, the New England poet, wrote, "At one step, she has reached the top of the staircase up which the rest of us climb on our knees year after year."*

FROM THE STERN training that Lyman Beecher supervised for his eleven children, the sense of duty, the obligation to serve God, and the expectation that they would be highly educated and have public careers, all of it, they understood, followed from the supremely significant fact that they were Beechers. Their father, who never stopped considering himself the most important Beecher, did work that held unchallenged prestige in the ordered world of early nineteenth century Connecticut. As Congregational minister of Litchfield when Harriet was born, he preached what he esteemed the most important truths ever revealed to man and expected that through his success at saving individuals, one by one, he was making progress toward improving the entire society in which he raised his outstanding offspring.

Such lofty ambition corresponded to the results that Lyman Beecher witnessed: of the Beecher children, only one, Mary, did not make a name for herself. The sons eventually followed what had been presented as their inevitable path and became preachers, some of them famous. Henry Ward Beecher, the phenomenally successful pastor of Plymouth Church in Brooklyn, would become known in a particularly outrageous adultery scandal. Edward Beecher, besides being a minister, would also become president of Illinois College. Catherine, who never married, wrote numerous books of advice on education, child-rearing, and household management, which was the printed version of endless advice she could not help giving people. Lyman, who had a huge reputation, teased his serious-minded daughter Harriet that she would become more famous than her father.

When the delicate Harriet Beecher won a prize for a school essay, an occasion she would later rank as the happiest moment of her life, Lyman confided to a friend that he would give a hundred dollars if she were a boy. Like her father, Harriet saw at times disadvantages in being female, but her power to shake America's conscience ultimately changed more lives than the sermons of all the other Beechers.

In 1811 Lyman Beecher and his first wife, Roxanna Foote, had their seventh child and second daughter, Harriet. Because of the reputation of her father as a learned man and gifted preacher, Harriet surprised no one in being unusually bright at her lessons. But her father, who judged her in relation to his other children, recognized her as his genius, especially when he considered her in the same breath as her brother Henry, who struck him as a charming child and quite ordinary. Reading held a strong attraction for Harriet, maybe as an escape at first for the sad and "odd" child whose mother died in 1817 when she was five years old. Her father then married Harriet Porter in 1817, with whom he produced three more children. Harriet did not replace, or even try, the warmth and affection the older children had lost with their own mother's death. To help make ends meet both Beecher wives had to cooperate in taking in boarders including John Brace. Brace was the energetic and impressive teacher at the Litchfield Female Academy where Harriet started classes when she was eight, rather than at age twelve as most students did.

In New England as in England in the 1820s and 1830s, belief in progress made people count on education as a means of improvement. Because Americans could see so much growth and prosperity around them, they came to believe that things would continue improving. And in some vaguely understood way, the character formation and moral training at the core of the education of women, the mothers of the next generation, would ennoble the whole society. This reasoning proved persuasive because it matched people's experience of progress in their own lifetime. By 1840, for example, literacy in New England was just about universal as the region continued to develop along a different path from that of the rural south. But Beechers held themselves to a higher standard than literacy.

To console herself after her fiancé drowned and in a project of self-reformation, Catherine Beecher, Harriet's older sister by six years, decided to start a school for young women to save them from what she judged as the conventional and pointless education she had undergone. When Catherine moved to join her brother Edward, a school principal in Hartford, she took along thirteen-year-old Harriet as a student for her Hartford Female Seminary. For eight years Harriet stayed at the school where she too taught after completing her own training. Part of what students learned connected their moral education with politics. When the United States government told the Cherokees to quit their own lands in the South in 1827, the move inspired a lively campaign of petitions and letter-writing at the school. Catherine Beecher, with a temperament inclined to bossiness, took pains to create a curriculum that engaged Harriet's academic gifts. She made sure, for example, that her sister studied Latin and theology, subjects that very few young ladies were pushed to master quite so rigorously, but that all well-taught young men had to survive. Possibly from her study of Roman oratory or maybe just from being a Beecher, Harriet understood the connection between her first-rate education and what she nervously joked about as her life's work: in a letter she told her brother George she would preach in writing.

If Harriet wanted to preach it would have to be in writing. She knew as well as any young woman in the 1830s that women, educated or not, could not preach in any other way because women did not speak in public, and certainly not before an audience. But Harriet knew her own ability after she first preached at age sixteen during an experiment at Hartford Female Seminary. The students showed great enthusiasm for her words and Harriet found it disturbingly satisfying.

Circumstances took care of Harriet's choosing a career to make use of her background. The West was opening and needed moral leaders as much as it needed farmers, and the Beechers wanted to be sure that these leaders were the right kind. In Ohio, for example, a new seminary was being started to train ministers to be sent even farther west. In 1832 Lyman Beecher accepted the invitation to serve as first president of Lane Seminary in Cincinnati, a city growing faster than any other American center at the time. Boston, where he had gone to take over the Hanover Street Church, had become an unfit place for the convinced Calvinists. The throngs of immigrants from Catholic Europe, both Irish and German, made Beecher and many Bostonians fear being outnumbered. Just as menacing, the growing numbers of Unitarians who did not even accept the divinity of Christ made Beecher see himself as more and more unwelcome. When Boston citizens watched his church burn rather than work to save it, he knew he would answer a call to go West. There was no question that twenty-one-year-old Harriet would do anything but go with her father.

While the Beechers saw themselves as moving West when they left Connecticut for Cincinnati, in reality they were about to live on the rim of the South. Located on the Ohio River just across from Kentucky, Cincinnati expanded because of river traffic. Its port unloaded goods coming up from New Orleans and carried farm products back down. Stories arrived along with other cargo that came by boat, stories about the very different culture that existed to the south. A place that Harriet knew only in a story-book way, like the land of Canaan in the Bible, the South now lay in sight, just across the Ohio River, whose far shore belonged to slave territory. Harriet soon learned that Cincinnati also lay within reach of slaves. In

Cincinnati she first heard stories of Josiah Henson, of Henry Bibb, and of other slaves in Cincinnati, stories that would reappear after years of ferment in Harriet Beecher's highly developed moral consciousness.

While in Cincinnati Harriet continued her intellectual work with less teaching but more writing. As a teacher she knew the need existed for useful classroom books; she started with her favorite subject. Her textbook called *Geography* must have struck many teachers as practical because it sold 100,000 copies and was adopted by schools throughout the West. The experience of earning money for her writing changed radically the way that Harriet Beecher answered the practical question of how to help her family. Her taste for writing found more encouragement even in frontier Cincinnati, or rather partly because she happened to be in Cincinnati. Unlike New England, the unchallenged center of American literary life where traditions existed and formality mattered, the West could do things a little more loosely. While in New England literature was gradually being entrusted to serious writers (men) who organized themselves to create serious journals such as the *Atlantic Monthly* to set the standards of taste and legitimacy for American writing. In places like Cincinnati men and women could still get together and have fun with what they wrote. As part of the Semi-Colon Club, a group of friends who liked books and liked to talk, Harriet wrote stories that she read aloud to delight her friends.

Occasionally, even as they adjusted to being away from the center, the Beechers had to acknowledge that Cincinnati was far from their spiritual home in New England. In the summer of 1834, for example, Harriet along with a female friend, Mary Dutton, traveled to Massachusetts to be at her brother Henry Ward's graduation from Amherst College. In years before the bits of railroad were connected, the trip required travel by barge, steamboat, and stage, which made the journey take nine days. But they might have counted themselves fortunate to have a reason to be away from Cincinnati that summer because of the raging cholera epidemic that drove many residents to flee the city. When the Beechers returned, Harriet learned that the disease had killed a member of the Semi-Colon Club, Eliza Tyler Stowe, wife of the scholarly Calvin Stowe, another New England Calvinist displaced to Cincinnati to teach theology at Lane Seminary.

Because Calvin Stowe had so little regard for social conventions, his close friends could not tell whether he was getting ready to marry Catherine Beecher or her younger sister, Harriet. Even after he married Harriet in an extremely private ceremony at her home in January 1836, he did not change his way of life much to allow for his new young wife, any more than any other young scholar would have done. When the Ohio Legislature asked Calvin Stowe to travel to Europe to study public schools and Lane Seminary chose him to go and buy the books that would create the seminary library, there was no question of declining the offer, although it meant leaving a pregnant wife who would give birth to their first child months before her husband's return. When Calvin Stowe did return to Cincinnati, he found Harriet with twin girls, Harriet and Isabella. His first fatherly gesture was to change Isabella's name to Eliza Stowe, giving him two baby girls named for his two wives, one living and one sainted.

The spirit of self-sacrifice that allowed Calvin Stowe to accept the assignment to travel without his wife at a critical time, considering how commonly women died in childbirth, also allowed him to work for a salary that could not match what his family needed. Soon Harriet Stowe found herself with five children under the age of seven. Like her mother and stepmother and many other women like herself, Stowe attempted to cope with her increasing load of work by hiring domestic help. Even when the dynamic five-foot Mrs. Stowe could find suitable helpers, money had to be found to keep the household going while Calvin's salary changed only by shrinking. Each time that Lane Seminary experienced a rocky year, the Stowes felt it.

As part of one effort to bring in more money, Harriet tried taking in boarders, another measure she had lived with as a girl. For the considerable disruption it brought to family life, after a household manager was hired, the small returns proved insufficient. Some people worked out such arrangements successfully, but Stowe had no training and less aptitude for tracking expenses and recording accounts, although she kept believing she could bring in money on her own. By writing, she eventually proved she could earn just enough money to get the domestic help she acutely needed. Contributing to three different periodicals at one time gave Stowe a respectable way to exercise and maintain her intellectual strength and increase the family income, a task that usually remained impossible for her high-minded husband.

When a Boston publisher who had seen her essays and stories asked Stowe to consider writing a book in 1842, she did not equivocate but left almost immediately to meet and talk with the people at Harper Brothers, after consulting with Thomas Perkins, her attorney brother-in-law. Stowe knew that her growing family needed money when she bargained for the best possible contract. Apart from his generous encouragement, her husband made an altogether sound suggestion. She should stop signing herself H. E. Beecher Stowe and use the more straightforward form of Harriet Beecher Stowe.

The book brought out in 1843 included stories from *Godey's Lady's Book*, the *New York Evangelist*, and *Western Monthly*, along with pieces first read to the Semi-Colons, collected now under the title *The Mayflower; or Sketches of Scenes and Characters among the Descendants of the Pilgrims*. The time would have been perfect for her to follow up with another book right away to keep her name before her readers, if only Harriet Beecher Stowe could have found the time—and the peace. In 1843 her older brother George, with whom she had grown up in a close relationship, committed suicide. Just two years later, still living in Cincinnati, she found herself with cholera and nearly died from it. By then she had had five children within seven years (she would have seven in all), but had enough innate physical strength, despite her small size, to survive this very serious illness. To recover her usual stamina, Stowe thought of a favorite nineteenth-century remedy, namely, to send the patient on a trip. Probably any trip would have helped so long as it took the mother of five away from the demands of family and household, but Stowe believed what she had been reading about a new, regimented kind of rest that incidentally required a return to New England. In 1845 she spent the summer in Brattleboro, Vermont, to take a Water Cure, a method that had been imported from Europe where spas were considered fashionable and efficacious in restoring strength.

The event that stirred Stowe to write her next book did not involve her personal experience in the usual sense so much as her intellectual and moral outrage in response to a law. When the United States Congress debated the Fugitive Slave Bill, it forced Americans in the North as well as the South to take sides on the question of slavery. There had been race riots as early as the 1830s when white immigrants fought to uphold slavery and thereby protect themselves from having to compete with freed blacks for the bottom-rung jobs that were keeping them alive. At Lane Seminary as early as 1834, two debating clubs opposed each other on whether the remedy to slavery lay in converting to Christianity then deporting black Americans to Africa, or in abolishing slavery altogether. Because Lyman Beecher, president of Lane, could not entirely grasp why his students saw these variants as antithetical to each other, most of his enrollment walked out to go and study at Oberlin under Charles Grandison Finney. By 1840 Beecher enrolled five students. His daughter, Harriet, agreed that slavery could not be defended, but she called the abolitionists "ultras," a word that she used to mean they were going too far. But since that time, her brother Henry Ward Beecher had become one of the most outspoken and famous abolitionist preachers, and other Beechers were evolving as well.

In 1850 the Bill became the Fugitive Slave Law, part of the series of measures pushed through Congress as the Compromise of 1850. This law, which required an aggressive pursuit of runaway slaves, made a huge change in American life. Northerners now had to help maintain slavery by capturing and sending back to his or her master any runaway slave found anywhere, even outside the South. In its enforcement this law threatened the well-being of black Americans everywhere, even outside the slave states. Virtually any African American, once captured, could be treated as "guilty" of having escaped because blacks could not speak on their own behalf in court and could not have jury trials. In effect, an arrest amounted to a conviction in many cases. Years earlier Harriet, like many other white people, especially in Cincinnati, had hired as a servant an African American woman she later learned was a runaway slave and then helped her to escape. Now the penalty for giving any help, even food or shelter, to an escaping slave was a fine of up to $1,000 and up to six months in prison. The people to be put in charge of enforcement, known as commissioners, would be paid ten dollars for sending a slave back, but only five dollars if they discovered the accused had a right to freedom. In some northern cities, commissioners simply refused to cooperate; in others, no one could be found for the job.

In frustration that the bill had been passed and that she could not preach against it, and that President Fillmore, a Northerner, was doing nothing to stop the spread of slavery, Stowe found herself almost immobilized with rage. As a woman of letters she knew that ultimately she would have to express her outrage in a significant and public way, but could not at first see what that might be. At the time she kept busy writing for periodicals, primarily for the money. Isabelle Hooker Beecher resented her own helplessness but, as she wrote Harriet, "If I could use a pen as you can, I would write something that will make this whole nation feel what an accursed thing slavery is." Her brother Henry Ward let Stowe know his plans for how he would preach and act against slavery. When Henry visited her in Brunswick, Maine where Calvin taught for a short time, Stowe confided to her brother that she had been thinking of writing something on the subject of slavery. "Do it," he urged.

That same winter, while still in Brunswick, Stowe sat in church while she thought over exactly how she would write about the great wrong she saw slavery to be. As she reflected she experienced something like a dream in which she watched characters she had never seen while she heard their words. At home she wrote frantically to get down on paper what she had "seen," going so quickly that she ran out of paper and had to keep writing on brown wrapping paper. Then she set it aside, not sure of what to make of the odd spiritual experience. That spring when Calvin Stowe returned from a long absence, he found his wife's pages, including the brown paper, as he unpacked and rearranged papers of his own. What he read

Culver Pictures

Harriet Beecher Stowe felt the North was complicit in the evil of slavery, and sought to touch the nation's conscience by writing Uncle Tom's Cabin.

recounted a strongly emotional scene set on a plantation in the South near a swamp. A slave named Tom was being beaten severely and viciously by his master and two helpers. But the beating was not taking place outside. Calvin Stowe asked his wife to tell him more about what she had in mind. As he listened he had ready advice. "You must make up a story with this for the climax. The Lord intends it so."

From the kind of writing she had been doing just before that time, Stowe was in contact with the editor of the *National Era,* considered an antislavery publication. She wrote him that she was planning a story about slavery that would require three or four installments in his magazine. The editor accepted the proposal from an experienced writer he knew would deliver on her promise and offered her $300 for the entire work. From the outset the Stowe family knew that this slavery story would require more of its author's time than the essays she had been turning out. Catherine Beecher decided to move in and take over the household to free her sister from any domestic responsibilities. With time to concentrate and to write, Stowe watched her story grow to something that required far more than a few installments. The first episode appeared in the June 5, 1851 issue of the *National Era* and kept going in weekly issues until April 1, 1852. Readers could barely wait for the next number to follow the thrilling lives of the strongly portrayed personalities.

After its serial publication, *Uncle Tom's Cabin* was published in book form and amazed everyone. While Harriet Beecher Stowe knew of her own personal conviction against slavery, she had not expected the story it inspired to be a national phenomenon as it had to be called. The publisher had three presses running around the clock and consuming the output of three paper mills to satisfy orders from booksellers. For a time the book sold 10,000 copies per week.

In more than one way the book about a slave had meant liberation for its author. The emotions and sense of uselessness that had plagued Harriet had now found their way out. She had used words to tame their force and to inspire courage in other people who had felt the same torment. As a Northerner Stowe had shown the South what their practices looked like to an outsider, and had also made Northerners think about their own racism. Southerners found the book wrong-headed and its author a meddlesome prig. One Southern reader anonymously sent Stowe what he thought she deserved: a human ear, a black ear. While it was true that slavery existed only in the South, many Northerners also looked at Africans as brutes and found slavery horrible and harmful to the republic because it had brought so many Africans to America. In her book Stowe confronts Northerners with their bigotry by making the worst offender, the infamous Simon Legree, a New Englander who had grown rich through the use of slaves at the time of the nation's expansion.

That powerful insight, that slavery and westward expansion had to be seen as related elements in a huge national problem, helps explain the impact of Stowe's book. She had already analyzed and understood something that people were only starting to think about. Her own family had gone to Cincinnati and found racial and social problems they had never seen in the East. In Cincinnati the theology students of Lyman Beecher had made trouble by working as equals with the freed blacks of that city. Beecher's opposition to their social work had cost him and his family a great deal in material terms. A benefactor of Lane, Arthur Tappan, sided with the students and withdrew important financial support.

Lyman Beecher had not adjusted to Cincinnati as a new social world but his daughter gradually understood why African Americans and the West belonged to the same changes brought by growth. It was westward expansion that created the demand for more slaves. With so much good land suddenly available, people saw huge opportunities if they could get enough cheap labor. The demand for slaves skyrocketed in the years the Beechers were in Cincinnati and that demand sent the price for slaves higher than ever. Southerners who had formerly seen their own slaves as a good source of labor now saw them as valuable assets to enhance and to be bred for profit, like livestock. This shift from exploitative to totally dehumanized thinking coincides exactly with the opinions and actions of characters in Stowe's book. One slave dealer thinks of a sale to a good customer who "buys up handsome boys to raise for the market." As that expansion continued and more states were organized, the political debate centered on which of the states would be free and which would be slave states. As slave states gradually urged the repeal of the Missouri Compromise, the disagreement moved from debate to the open conflict that brought on the Civil War. When, years later, Harriet Beecher Stowe met Abraham Lincoln at the White House, he is reported to have asked, "So this is the little lady who made this big war?" Her book had changed slavery from a growing national concern into the only national concern.

Royalties of $10,300 in the first three months meant that Harriet Beecher Stowe's life had changed in a profound way. After many years of being poor and living with the unrelenting struggle of finding as much money as she had already spent, Stowe was rich for the first time, a change she had not seen coming. When she published *Uncle Tom's Cabin* as a book, she had hoped that if sales were good she would be able to buy herself a new silk dress.

So many Americans read the book and loved its message that they wanted reminders of it around them. Characters such as Uncle Tom, Little Eva, and Topsy became wildly popular with illustrators who sold lithographs and prints that people framed and displayed at home. The characters and scenes from *Uncle Tom's Cabin* decorated every kind of household object including tea towels, dishes, calendars, and advertising. The long and dramatic story also lent itself to stage presentations which sometimes changed the morally noble main character into a comic figure. (Whites, not blacks did the acting.) These stage plays, far more than the novel, promoted the pejorative character of "Uncle Tom," the cliché that came to symbolize an African (later, any downtrodden person) who cooperates in his own exploitation. No such degradation belongs to the world view of Harriet Beecher Stowe. Her book did preach, she thought, and showed how much Tom resembles Jesus Christ, the suffering hero who will not be diminished by hatred for those who persecute him.

Harriet Beecher Stowe continued to write novels that preached her clear moral vision to Americans. When the Kansas-Nebraska Act threatened to insure the spread of slavery, she used family connections and every form of privilege available to help move religious leaders to oppose it. In disgust at their impotence and over the Supreme Court's infamous *Dred Scott* decision of 1857, she wrote *Dred*. This antislavery novel was most interesting to modern readers for its heroine, a thinly disguised version of Sojourner Truth, the African American prophetess who stunned the Beechers when she invited herself to Lyman's eightieth birthday celebration. In *The Minister's Wooing*, Stowe wrote to expiate her own pain at losing her son, Henry, who drowned during his freshman year at Dartmouth. In *Poganuc People*, she wrote about Maine where she had spent some of her happiest times. But no book ever repeated what she achieved at the age of forty-one with *Uncle Tom's Cabin*.

No book by her or by any other author would approach *Uncle Tom's Cabin* in touching on a raw nerve for the entire country. The fame brought her by that novel made her an international celebrity. When she toured England, where she had sold one million books in the first year, and earned not one cent because of cranky copyright laws, Stowe declined preaching or even speaking to the audiences who turned out to see her. Still inhibited about her right to speak in public, she could not bring herself to preach directly; her book had done that work. Back in America, only gradually did she start to write in newspapers to tell women to break their silence, as she did against the Kansas-Nebraska Act. The growing strength of the upholders of "Woman's Rights," particularly after the Civil War when these rights were pushed aside in favor of "Negro Rights," inspired other Beecher women to begin to speak, but Stowe remained a product of an earlier way of thinking. She wrote in favor of universal suffrage, seeing all questions of women's rights in the context of the Reconstruction not of the South, but of American society.

Uncle Tom's Cabin, or *Life Among the Lowly* now feels dated because its language strikes modern readers as sentimental, integrates an analysis of an economic system and the dissection of a moral evil. Slavery uses people not for capital but as capital. From her upbringing and her training in Christian theology, Stowe knew that the dignity of every individual exists because every human being was created in God's likeness. How could there even be a debate about a system that reduces a person to a thing, able to be bought or sold? Slavery is only about gain. Her novel showed a profoundly Christian man, an African, who transcended every degradation by accepting the loss of his own life, a Christ-figure teaching loss as a means of gain. A carefully brought up New England lady, the daughter, sister, and wife of preachers had written America's first important novel of moral outrage and protest.

Harriet Beecher Stowe lived to the age of eighty-five, spending her later years in a splendid house she built in Hartford near a neighbor who also wrote about the South—Mark Twain.

QUESTIONS FOR THOUGHT AND DISCUSSION

1. Why was Harriet Beecher Stowe's move to Cincinnati, Ohio, with her father in 1832 so fateful to her eventual fame?

2. Why was the Northern public so overwhelmed by the publication of *Uncle Tom's Cabin?*

3. How did *Uncle Tom's Cabin* reflect Stowe's Christian beliefs?

4. At a time when women were still very much second-class citizens in the United States, how was Stowe able to achieve such notoriety and acclaim?

SUGGESTED READINGS

Cott, Nancy F. and Elizabeth H. Pleck, eds. *A Heritage of Her Own.* New York: Simon, 1979.

Hedrick, Joan D. *Harriet Beecher Stowe: A Life.* New York: Oxford UP, 1994.

Rugoff, Milton. *The Beechers: An American Family in the 19th Century.* New York: Harper, 1981.

Wilson, Forrest. *Crusader in Crinoline.* Philadelphia: Lippincott, 1941.

17

Annie
Turner Wittenmyer

The Old World concept of wealth as an assurance of leisure may have crossed the Atlantic, but could not survive on the frontier. The huge and continued influx of millions of European immigrants in the nineteenth century made it possible for enterprising merchants in the midwest to work hard and thrive. But they kept on working long after they succeeded. Before Chicago had established itself as the new center of commerce and transport, Mississippi River ports such as Keokuk, Iowa let men get rich selling supplies to the arriving hordes who needed everything before they set out to cross the plains.

Annie Wittenmyer's fortune, from her husband's good sense and good luck as a Keokuk merchant, could have given her a comfortable and tranquil life, yet her education, sense of duty, and athletic energy inclined her to a life of effort against huge resistance. Not a shy woman, Annie Wittenmyer confronted generals during the Civil War, listened courteously, and then graciously gave orders. Toughened but not hardened by life on the frontier, she radically changed conditions in battlefield hospitals, at a time when she served the apprenticeship of her important public career.

THE EXPANDING BORDERS of the United States in the nineteenth century changed the demographic profile of Americans. The center of the country moved far to the west, to places not settled by English seekers of religious freedom. The frontier, which had been the edge of English America for the first two centuries of settlement, came more and more to represent American life. For women, especially for those who moved from eastern cities with more refined culture—by American standards—life on the frontier presented physical hardship but, just as difficult, the prospect of isolation, loneliness, and in most cases a permanent separation from family members. But those same deprivations prepared women for the added trial of losing the help of husbands and sons when the Civil War took so many men away from home to fight. Annie Turner Wittenmyer became an early woman executive and reform organizer and an extraordinary example of a woman from the frontier who invented ways of distinguishing herself to help others.

Annie Turner, from an old Louisville family, claimed descent through her mother from the famed explorer John Smith of Virginia. Her family later moved to Adams County, Ohio where she was born on August 26, 1827. Because of the advanced thinking of both her parents, she was better educated than was typical for women at the time. They saw to it that her studies continued through the completion of training at an Ohio seminary for women. Even as a young girl she showed a literary side and published her first poem at age twelve; as an adult she made a name as the author of hymns.

At age twenty she married William Wittenmyer, considerably older than she was, with whom she moved to Iowa. Their new home, the "Gate City" of Keokuk, thrived because of its location as a Mississippi River port, as it grew commercially important for the transport of supplies to the west and the arrival point for new settlers. Married to a rich businessman, the young Mrs. Wittenmyer found ways of applying her wealth to make social changes, without being asked. In Keokuk, she saw school-age children who roamed the streets, a commonplace sight when public education was not free and not compulsory. So she started a school for excluded children, a private school in her own home. Over time this school expanded and was moved to a larger building, a warehouse, where it grew to have 200 students. Her interest in children remained a lifelong focus in her charitable work, a poignant fact since of her own four children, only one lived beyond infancy.

A combination of talent and circumstances allowed Annie Turner Wittenmyer to distinguish herself when the great test of the Civil War began. A natural leader whom other women asked for help, she spoke effectively and persuasively in public, an ability which allowed her to raise money for a local group of women who intended to help Iowa's soldiers. She also wrote so well that she could persuade political, and later military leaders, to take her seriously. People living in and near Keokuk understood the effects of the war in human terms: new recruits were shipped out from there on their way to fight, and barges of wounded men returned to the same port after battles. When her elderly husband died, Wittenmyer found herself a well-off widow with only one small child. Her own mother and sister were willing to care for the child, which meant that at the war's outbreak she was free to travel to field hospitals and see the wounded. Added to this experience, her good analytical mind let her see problems clearly and imagine practical solutions. Transporting fresh eggs to soldiers, for example, could not be achieved easily because cornmeal, the usual packing materials, heated up and ruined the eggs. Oats, Mrs. Wittenmyer directed, would work.

In 1861 when the Soldiers' Aid Society of Keokuk held its first meeting, everyone could see the need for help. Men at the front needed material support of the kind that women back home could provide: bandages, blankets, and, as the women soon learned, pillows, sheets, and lightweight clothing to replace heavy army uniforms. What Annie Wittenmyer understood from her experience as the first executive secretary of the group, on her first visit to a field hospital, was the equally acute need on all sides for information. (Only when she went to St. Joseph, Missouri to help the wounded of the Second Iowa Infantry, for example, did she learn that they were not there and that she would have to follow them to St. Louis.) People at home needed to know exactly what the men lacked and where they were; the army needed to know which groups were able and ready to provide which kinds of help. Reports had come back of excess food going unused in one hospital while men nearby went hungry, and of clothing being abandoned because no one was there to wash it. Charitable organizations also needed to know about the work of other similar groups. The general public wanted to help, but needed to know exactly how to send their donations. Publicity was primitive. At least one large event, a sanitary fair, was organized for which no one made posters. A Keokuk newspaper appealed to local women for aid, then added: "Papers throughout the state please copy."

Frontier life had not given Iowa women experience in organizing themselves in any way, a lack which could have been disastrous. Annie Wittenmyer began regular visits to field hospitals to see what was needed most acutely. On one visit she found that her own sick sixteen-year-old brother, Davis C. Turner, in a hospital bed had just refused the same unhealthy breakfast being served all wounded men: one piece of bacon floating in its own grease, a slab of bread, and a cup of black coffee. By speaking with the men and questioning officers, she learned that wounded men were fed exactly the same diet as men in combat. Rather than find a way to improve food at that one hospital, Annie Wittenmyer organized a system to see that Iowa men everywhere received adequate food. She understood that a wounded man's chances of recovery could be improved if he ate well, although this was an idea that the Army could not "sell" Congress. Early in 1863 the Senate looked at a proposed law that would provide each Army unit with a professional cook, grant ten dollars per month for matrons in hospitals, and change the ration by adding tobacco, sold to the men at cost. In its debate of the bill, the Senate spent most of its time discussing the moral aspect of promoting the use of tobacco. But after it passed the Senate, the bill never left the House, proof that the health of the Army did not concern political leaders.

Problems in the field did not stop with diet. Field hospitals were not antiseptic because the concept did not exist yet. While the notion of public health had begun to make inroads since the Mexican War of 1846–1847, young and progressive physicians who accepted modern beliefs were not in the field at the beginning of the Civil War. Only later, after huge losses of life from disease and infection, did the new thinkers come to positions of influence. Men as young as Wittenmyer's own sixteen-year-old brother often fell ill from exposure to childhood diseases such as mumps and measles, an acute problem for men from the sparsely populated frontier who had not developed immunities to sicknesses which rapidly spread from living crammed together in camps.

Mrs. Wittenmyer may not have known how vulnerable her brother was: the rate of death from disease was forty-three percent higher among Union soldiers from places west of the Appalachians than among easterners. Everyone understood that the fact of being in a hospital put a man's life in danger. As the war went on she became more active in writing letters to intercede on behalf of ailing and wounded men to have them sent home on furlough where they might recover, a less likely outcome in a military hospital. In a later report Annie Wittenmyer described the strain she experienced as an observer not only seeing but also hearing wounded men. To their groans was added "the drip, drip, drip of leaking vessels," part of the improvised technique of placing pans over the heads of the worst wounded so that falling drops of water would keep the bandages cool.

The same lack of organization that had made her efforts necessary in the first place also made them unappreciated or misunderstood. Funding, like other aspects of war relief work, had no systematic organization to begin with. No umbrella organization existed to direct smaller, local efforts. As early as April 1861, Mrs. Wittenmyer was writing to a woman in Iowa to report on her visit to Iowa regiments, a visit she had undertaken without prompting. In order to get herself to such sites, Annie Wittenmyer advanced her own money rather than wait until funds could be approved, a process which could not have gone smoothly and quickly. Later, she was reimbursed for part of her expenses, but rumors eventually started that she had financed her activities by buying supplies and then selling them, making a profit for herself. In fact, early in the war, she did purchase vegetables to distribute because Governor Kirkwood of Iowa directed her to do so. He did not know the men could not buy anything because they had not been paid. Understandably Mrs. Wittenmyer gave away what she had paid for, yet found herself accused of cheating. She denied all such charges, explaining that at times she had bought supplies with her own money and then sold them to surgeons in charge of hospitals, but she had no "proceeds" from such sales because there were none.

Although she did have the official title of State Sanitary Agent, she met resistance from the Army. Iowa had two such agents named by the Governor; the General Assembly in a special session passed a law which said it was the Governor's duty to appoint two or more such agents, one of whom, the law specified, should be Mrs. Annie Wittenmyer. In the beginning, there had been conflict among the Iowa State Sanitary Commission (her group), the Iowa Sanitary Commission (a group unfriendly to her), the United States Sanitary Commission, and the Army Sanitary Commission. Worse, corruption complicated the divided territory. After she created a rigorous protocol of systematic written reports from her aides (weekly, observing detailed guidelines), Wittenmyer found out that at one hospital the surgeon in charge insisted on the odd practice of saving used coffee grounds and drying them out. By investigating further, she learned that the dried grounds were mixed with "log wood" (bark and wood) to give it color, which the used coffee lacked. This dubious drink was reserved for wounded men so that the surgeon could sell for his own profit the coffee that they should have been given. When Wittenmyer learned the name of the surgeon, she reported him to General R. C. Wood in Louisville and insisted that he be dismissed and, if she had her way, "be hung higher than Haman." General Wood began a military investigation of the charges, but before its conclusion the surgeon resigned.

Because of her experience in organizing groups and in managing information, Wittenmyer understood publicity better than some officers she confronted. In August 1861, for example, a visit to Helena, Arkansas made her threaten to expose what she found. More than 2,000 men lay wounded in the sweltering southern heat of late summer. Because they were camped near a swamp, insects carried disease, adding malaria to their ailments. The only available drinking water came from the sun-warmed Mississippi and stood in barrels in the sun growing warmer, while a barge of ice stood tied at the river's edge. In the line of Army authority, no one present had the right to order the ice distributed. But Annie Wittenmyer had money to buy it, which meant that she had it put in the drinking water. When she finally reached the general in charge—he was absent because of illness—she left him little leeway in deciding what to do. Four steamers, she told him, should be brought as soon as possible to remove the wounded men from "that death trap." Even the general's agreement did not satisfy her. "I want the order issued before I leave this office." Not entirely convinced that she could count on prompt cooperation, she reminded the general of how she might follow through. "Remember. I have no other appeal but the newspapers and the great, generous people of the North who sustain them, if you fail."

Whether or not they liked her methods, officers as well as soldiers appreciated Wittenmyer's efficient help at the front, something they knew the Army could not always deliver. To a considerable extent, political complications, which Wittenmyer and some of her aides ignored, could slow down the good intentions of Army leaders. Near the foot of Lookout Mountain in Tennessee, for example, men were freezing to death for lack of fuel at a large field hospital, where the wounded slept in tents with no floors. A nurse, not a general, acted decisively. Mary Bickerdyke ordered men helping her to remove logs from a nearby Confederate fort that had surrendered. The surgeon present reminded her that she acted illegally, in effect stealing government property, because she had no order to help herself to the wood. The nurse, knowing that men would die before any order could be arranged risked defending her decision later, something the surgeon did not dare.

The Army in the 1860s faced structural problems in the assuring of medical care. First of all, it could not easily recruit the best surgeons because there could be no promise of promotion or advancement. The recent and horrible experience of the Crimean War in Russia (1853–1856) had shown the disaster of medical men attempting to give orders to officers who refused to obey anyone of lower rank. In the Civil War, politicians persisted in holding a low opinion of surgeons. A project for better training of army surgeons, for example, got nowhere. When he heard the proposal that surgeons be enabled to upgrade their skills by attending evening classes, Secretary of War Edwin M. Stanton refused the idea because he was sure that the young students would skip off to attend the theater rather than go to class. The result was that army surgeons improved their skills on the battlefield.

Her willingness to travel sometimes exposed Mrs. Wittenmyer to as much danger as the Army surgeons she helped. At Vicksburg as she talked to a surgeon inside a tent, she could not understand why she saw grass outside moving and bending, an odd sight on a hot and still June day. As she tells the story in her book *Under the Guns*, she was seeing movement caused by bullets, as the surgeon let her know. Only a few days later when an officer sat where she had been, in the same chair, bullets killed him. Because a Union hospital had been set up under the guns of both sides during the siege of Vicksburg, Annie Wittenmyer sent supplies to it. The surgeon who received these believed that a visit from her would do the men more good than the food and supplies alone. He offered a horse if she would accept. She rode on a cavalry saddle, even crossed a canal on horseback, as mortar shells from both sides exploded. When she reached the men she experienced not relief but outrage at the wounded being kept near constant noise. The following morning she presented herself to General Grant and told what she had seen. Instantly the General sent his order to move the men that night to a hospital twenty-five miles from where they were. She served with remarkable physical stamina at Shiloh where she worked tirelessly without even stopping to eat for over twenty-four hours.

Thanks to her talents and her persistence, Wittenmyer succeeded in creating as many as 100 diet kitchens in military hospitals. She sent two women to be in charge of each kitchen with written, very explicit instructions on their duties and comportment in seeing to the dietary needs of wounded men, always following the directions of the surgeon in charge, and always giving comfort to the wounded. This last recommendation brought some of her aides into conflict with surgeons who saw the women merely as cooks, that is, servants who belonged in the kitchen. In some cases, therefore, their written instructions from Mrs. Wittenmyer went against the directions of the officer to whom her aides were assigned. A related unforeseen problem arose from Wittenmyer's choice of women. While another energetic worker in the war relief effort, Dorothea Dix, enlisted the help of "homely" women, making sure to avoid the presence of attractive women among soldiers, Annie Wittenmyer saw no reason for such a superficial criterion. She advised her workers to dress plainly and always to comport themselves in a "Christian" manner, but never refused the help of a woman on the basis of physical appearance. Conflicts of this order continued to distract but not impede her efforts.

While carrying on her field work, letter writing, and fund raising efforts, Wittenmyer continued her pre-war efforts to help children. Now, the direction of her work changed slightly. She appealed to the state and to the Army to take responsibility for the care of "war orphans." By this she did not mean children who had lost both parents in the war, but children without fathers. Wittenmyer understood that only in the rarest cases could a woman with small children and without a husband provide for their well-being. In a farm state the hardship of keeping a family going burdened widows excessively.

At the end of the war, Wittenmyer continued to protect the interests of the people who had helped her. Some of the women who had given their services for the entire war found themselves in need yet excluded from any kind of war pension because of a bureaucratic technicality: they had not formally enlisted. In a campaign of letter writing and personal advice and intervention, Wittenmyer made sure that her helpers received the twelve dollars per month that was designated for Army nurses. Her own pension never reached her until decades after the war in 1898, in the amount of twenty-five dollars per month.

Many American women thought that the trials of the Civil War entitled them to compensation after the war in the form of acknowledgment for their work. The reaction that they found from other Americans left them disappointed. The abolitionists, in particular, let it be known that the end of the war brought, as Frederick Douglass put it, "the Negro's hour." In other words, the women would have to wait. One effect of this refusal was to keep alive the spirit of solidarity that women had experienced as helpers in hospitals. Keeping their habits of communication intact, women recognized a new problem, one directly related to the war. Of the men who survived the horrible battles and returned alive from armed conflict, many had learned to drink heavily in their years away from home. Drunken husbands did not give the relief and help that their wives and families counted on with the war's end.

Their reaction was forceful and better organized than the early struggle to make sanitary commissions. No one expressed surprise that the Women's Christian Temperance League, an anti-drinking organization, elected Annie Turner Wittenmyer as its first president when it met in Cleveland on November 18, 1874 and re-elected her without opposition in 1875 and 1876.

Wittenmyer wrote persuasively about the problem of alcohol, which she had the courage to say was not an exclusively male vice. A far worse problem, in her eyes, came from the growing numbers of women who drank, creating even more of a social threat. Alcohol made mothers unable to care for their own children. Wittenmyer recognized that the nature of women's drinking went unnoticed because of a social difference. Women bought their alcohol less openly and could because they were turning not to whiskey but to patent medicines which were marketed primarily to women. These elixirs first exposed then addicted mothers to alcohol in

State Historical Society of Iowa, Des Moines

Annie Turner Wittenmyer expected her orders to be respected by everyone, even General U.S. Grant.

many cases. Such remedies often contained only spirits and sweeteners but produced the same result as hard liquor.

As a temperance leader, she continued lecturing energetically, sometimes giving six public talks in one week. Her wartime habit of travel in the name of a cause continued, with the difference that she could now travel even more freely because the war had ended and because the railroad joined both coasts. Her travels covered the continent, from Maine to California. Not content with writing letters to officers and senators, Wittenmyer worked systematically as she started two papers, *The Christian Woman*, which continued for eleven years, and later *The Christian Child*. It was in her late sixties that she wrote her own book about the Civil War, *Under the Guns* (1894), which recounts her battlefield experiences and shows that on unofficial assignments, Wittenmyer served as America's first woman war correspondent. The widow of General U.S. Grant wrote an introduction to the remarkable book. Writing at a time when the country was disinclined to pensions, she intended the book, probably in part at least, to clear her own name from the malicious and unproven accusations made by her enemies during the war years. At her seventieth birthday in 1897 she was honored by congratulations and gifts from all over the country. She died on February 2, 1900 at her home in Sanatoga, Pennsylvania, where she had returned after giving a lecture in nearby Pottstown earlier in the day.

QUESTIONS FOR THOUGHT AND DISCUSSION

1. Why do you think Annie Turner Wittenmyer was so driven to bring assistance and comfort to the Union soldiers during the Civil War?

2. What does Wittenmyer's experience with the military suggest about how Civil War soldiers were regarded by Congress and much of the military brass?

3. How did Wittenmyer's principal activities in the years after the Civil War reflect a continuity with her wartime concerns?

4. Do you find Wittenmyer a worthy role model or not? Explain.

SUGGESTED READINGS

Adams, George Worthington. *Doctors in Blue: The Medical History of the Union Army in the Civil War.* New York: Schuman, 1952.

Clinton, Catherine. *The Other Civil War: American Women in the Nineteenth Century.* New York: Hill, 1984.

Flexner, Eleanor. *Century of Struggle: The Woman's Rights Movement in the United States.* Cambridge, Mass.: Belknap of Harvard UP, 1959.

Fullbrook, Earl S. "Relief Work in Iowa During the Civil War." *Iowa Journal of History and Politics.* Vol. XVI. April 1918, pp. 155–274.

Gallaher, Ruth. "Annie Turner Wittenmyer." *Iowa Journal of History and Politics.* Vol. 29, No. 4. Oct. 1931, pp. 518–569.

_____. "The Wittenmyer Diet Kitchens." *The Palimpsest.* Vol. XII, No. 9, Sept. 1931.

Riley, Glenda. *Frontierswomen: The Iowa Experience.* Ames, IA: The Iowa State UP, 1981.

18

Abraham
Lincoln

The rapid development of what were increasingly two very different sections of the United States, the North and the South, had already begun by the time Abraham Lincoln was born on the frontier in 1809. A new breed of American, restless for more land, unafraid of wild animals and clashes with native Americans, and proud of his own free labor and opposed to slavery, was moving into the Old Northwest. Whole towns sprang up overnight along the rivers—the Ohio, the Wabash, and the Mississippi—that provided cheap transportation through New Orleans to European markets. By the late 1820s, thousands of immigrants came each year by canal and Great Lake steamer, lured by some of the deepest topsoil in the world.

Abundant non-slave labor and opportunities converged to make the American dream of going from poverty to wealth in a single generation nowhere more possible than in the thriving new towns of the American interior. A revolution in transportation linked the heartland with the East as well as foreign markets, and provided the crops and raw materials that made the United States the breadbasket of Europe by 1860. Increasingly, the North followed a separate industrial and agricultural pathway into a future out of synchronization—and out of patience—with the old slave-labor South. North and South were on a collision course as plain-spoken, fearless freesoilers rallied around a new political party and its spokesman, Abraham Lincoln.

FOR THE FIRST nineteen years of his life while he was growing up on the Midwestern frontier, Abraham Lincoln never saw a slave. He had come to know hard work early; he even knew hardship, but he and his family had always been free, over and over again exercising their independence by moving farther west to find better land and a surer income. Then, at nineteen, Lincoln, standing six feet four inches tall and powerful from years of splitting logs and plowing fields, built his own flatboat, loaded it with farm produce, and poled it down the Mississippi River through the Deep South to New Orleans. What he saw for the first time was not only the world beyond his all-white frontier community but something that transformed him into a man of political action. For most of the rest of his fifty-six years, he never escaped from wrestling with the question of slavery and what he should—and could—do about it.

Abraham Lincoln's first American ancestor, Samuel, emigrated from Hingham, England to Hingham, Massachusetts in 1636, at the time of the Anne Hutchinson sedition trials. Like Christopher Columbus, Benjamin Franklin, and Andrew Carnegie, his father was a weaver, a skilled, hardworking artisan with a portable craft. Samuel Lincoln's son, Mordecai, continued the family tradition of pulling up stakes in search of opportunity: he moved to New Jersey. Subsequent generations migrated to Pennsylvania, and then Virginia. The Abraham Lincoln who was the grandfather and namesake of the sixteenth President owned a farm in Rockingham County, Virginia, during the Revolutionary War serving in the Virginia militia. Moving in 1782 with his wife and five small children to the Native American hunting grounds of Kentucky, he settled in present-day Larue County, where he was shot and killed by a Native American while plowing a field. His Virginia-born son, Thomas, the father of the President, was a farmer and carpenter who fought the Indians as a Kentucky militiaman.

President Lincoln's father was illiterate. He could only sign his name. His mother, Nancy Hanks, was illegitimate and illiterate, a bright, although uneducated and extremely pious woman. They lived in Elizabethtown, Kentucky, for eighteen months after their marriage in 1806. Their first child, Sarah, was born in 1807. Thomas moved again, buying a farm on the Nolin River near Hodgenville, where Abraham Lincoln was born on February 12, 1809. The next year, they moved ten miles away to clear a 230-acre farm on Knob Creek. The Lincoln family was not poor; the log cabin where Lincoln was born was typical of the homesteads of thousands of Americans. If it was crowded, there was plenty of food, clothing, and wood for the fire.

Time after time, the Lincolns had trouble getting clear title to their land, so in 1816, only two years after Tecumseh died in the Battle of the Thames, Thomas Lincoln decided to move to southwestern Indiana, the farthest American frontier, settling on land he could buy directly from the Federal government. Thomas Lincoln did not believe in slavery, which had taken root in Kentucky; in Indiana, slavery was illegal. Loading their possessions onto a wagon, the Lincolns were ferried across the Ohio River, traveling through thick forests to Spencer County where they began transforming 160 acres of wilderness into a farm. Seven year old Abe helped his father build a 360-square-foot log cabin that was his home for the rest of his childhood.

When he was nine, the death of his mother shattered young Abe, who helped his father fashion her coffin from logs left over from making the cabin. The boy whittled wooden pegs to hold the boards together. Abe had been very close to his mother and he missed her terribly. "All I am or ever hope to be, I owe to my sainted mother," he once said. When his father quickly remarried a widow with three children, Abe drew close to her. Sarah Bush Johnston Lincoln was kind to the tall, lanky, somber boy, encouraging him to read and learn.

His silent father could rarely spare Abe from the drudgery of clearing an eighty-acre plot, plowing it, planting, and then threshing the harvest that it took to feed the eight people now living in the unpainted cabin. Abe and his sister Sarah occasionally attended a one-room schoolhouse where they learned the rudiments of reading, writing, and arithmetic. His erratic education—a few months each fall for four of the seven years between ages five and thirteen—was typical of the time. Young Lincoln read voraciously, not only dipping regularly into the family Bible but devouring *Pilgrim's Progress, Robinson Crusoe, Aesop's Fables* and his favorite biography, Parson Mason Weem's fanciful *Biography of George Washington*. Years later, in a speech before the New Jersey Senate, Lincoln asked to be:

> pardoned if, on this occasion, I mention that, away back in my childhood, the earliest days of my being able to read, I got hold of a small book, Weem's *Life of Washington*. I remember all the accounts there given of the battlefields and struggles for the liberties of the country ... and you all know, for you have all been boys, how these early impressions last longer than any others.

Books and paper were scarce on the frontier. Abe fashioned his own arithmetic workbook. He worked out problems on a board, then shaved it clean with a drawknife and used it over and over. He became legendary for walking great distances to borrow books. He read the Bible frequently and, from age fourteen, went with his parents to the Pigeon Creek Baptist Church. However, he never formally joined any church because he loathed the rivalries that wracked the evangelical churches of the time.

Unlike many frontier boys, Lincoln preferred reading to hunting. Bears, panthers, and other wild animals still roamed the forests and preyed on the Lincoln's hogs, but he detested hunting.

Life on a farm was dangerous enough. Shortly after his ninth birthday, Abe was kicked in the head by a horse and was momentarily thought to be dead. As he became more skilled with ax, plow, and sickle, his father rented him out to other farmers. After a day's back-breaking farm work, he liked nothing better than to sit before the fire and read. "My best friend," he later said, "is the man who'll git me a book I ain't read." It was a good thing he decided to educate himself. As Abe later wrote, the education he could expect on the frontier was haphazard at best. "If a stranger supposed to understand Latin, happened to sojourn in the neighborhood, he was looked upon as a wizard. There was absolutely nothing to excite ambition for education. Of course, when I came of age, I did not know much."

Before he was twenty, Lincoln reached his full height, a full head taller than most men. Thin and awkward, rawboned and strong, he had powerful arms, a homely face, dark skin, and coarse black hair that stood on end. His wild look was quickly forgotten when he began to talk. Even as a boy, his innate speaking ability emerged as he did sidesplitting imitations of preachers and politicians for people gathered at the nearby general store. He had no trouble making friends or finding work, cutting vast amounts of firewood, cutting and husking corn, and flailing wheat. The first money he kept he made from tugging at the oars as he ferried passengers out to steamboats on the Ohio River. The river tugged powerfully at him. At nineteen, he made his first flatboat voyage with Allen Gentry to New Orleans—and after fighting off a gang of seven black men who tried to rob them, brought his wages back to his father.

When Lincoln was twenty-one, his father decided to move west again, this time into Illinois. Relatives there had sent back word of rich, deep topsoil. Abe decided to stay with his family only one more year, help them build a cabin, fence their land, put in the first crop, and then go on his own. That autumn of 1830, he gave his first political speech, in favor of improving navigation on the Sangamon River, during a campaign rally in Decatur. The next spring, the twenty-two-year-old Lincoln, with a cousin and a stepbrother, signed aboard a flatboat carrying corn, live hogs, and barrels of pork to New Orleans. Its master, Denton Offutt, hired him, when they got back, as the clerk in his new store in New Salem, Illinois, twenty miles northwest of Springfield. He lived for six years in this raw village of dirt streets and cabins around a mill, cooperage, wool-carding shop, and a few small general stores. He began to read the plays of Shakespeare (his favorites were *Macbeth* and *Hamlet*) and the poetry of Robert Burns. He earned little money, living in a tiny rent-free room behind the store and depending on the kindness of his neighbors for invitations to occasional dinners and help with mending his clothes. Lincoln was well-liked in New Salem, becoming widely known for his honesty and uproarious stories.

It wasn't long before the store failed. Young Lincoln would have been unemployed if the Black Hawk War hadn't broken out. The Sauk and Fox Indians, who were relocated from Illinois to Iowa in 1831 by the federal government, came back across the Mississippi. Several hundred warriors, led by Chief Black Hawk, were trying to retake their tribal lands around Rock Island. When the governor called out the militia, Lincoln joined the company from New Salem and was elected its captain. This first acknowledgment of Lincoln's talent for leadership "gave me more pleasure than any I have had since," said President Lincoln thirty years later. Popular, and admired for his strength and skill as a wrestler, Lincoln was no soldier. Captain Lincoln marched his company of militia to the mouth of the Rock River and joined a force of regulars under Colonel Zachary Taylor. Twice in the next month he was reprimanded, first for failing to restrain his men for getting drunk on stolen liquor, and a second time for discharging a firearm in camp. Never fired at, he only waged "bloody struggles with the mosquitoes." When his month's enlistment as captain expired, he re-enlisted as a private, joining a company of mounted Independent Rangers. When this twenty-day hitch ended, he re-enlisted again for thirty days as a private in the Independent Spy Corps, which failed to track down Black Hawk. In all, he served slightly less than three months without seeing combat, his total military experience in life.

Out of the militia and out of work, Lincoln heeded his friends' advice to run for the state legislature. He only arrived home from the war two weeks before the election. While New Salem gave him 277 of its 300 votes, Lincoln lost his first election at age twenty-three. He wanted to study law but he had no money and little education. When he was offered a chance to buy a New Salem store on credit, he entered a partnership that proved disastrous. The store quickly failed, leaving Lincoln deep in debt. And when his erstwhile partner died, he assumed all the debts of the partnership, refusing to go into bankruptcy and earning the nickname "Honest Abe." Again, Lincoln's popularity rescued him. In May 1833, he was appointed New Salem's postmaster and then deputy county surveyor (even though he knew nothing about surveying). Studying hard and working hard, he managed to make a living.

Lincoln was less lucky in love. He seems to have been quite fond of a petite, blue-eyed blonde girl named Ann Rutledge whose father owned a tavern in New Salem. He often visited her family, but there is no proof he ever proposed marriage to her or that she ever reciprocated his affection. He grieved deeply when she died of typhoid fever in 1835; some authorities believe he contemplated suicide for several days after her funeral. In 1837, he proposed marriage to Mary Owens, whom he had courted before he met Ann Rutledge. After Mary visited her sister in New Salem, she went back to her father's farm in Kentucky, where she gained considerable weight and lost some teeth. Considering herself a refined young lady, she frequently criticized Lincoln for his coarse backwoods manners. When Lincoln saw her again, he wrote to offer her the opportunity to break off their relationship. She never answered. He later wrote satirically about the affair, depicting her as an ugly, toothless hulk who was older than she admitted: "Nothing could have commenced at the size of infancy and reached her present bulk in less than thirty-five or forty years."

It was several years before Lincoln again considered marriage. He plunged into the study of law even as he ran successfully for the state legislature, and was elected for the first of four two-year terms in 1834. A Springfield lawyer, John T. Stuart, offered to lend him lawbooks and Lincoln came twenty miles from New Salem to borrow them. "Sometimes he walked," Henry Dummer, Stuart's law partner, wrote. "He was the most uncouth looking man I ever saw." He had little to say at first, but he soon gained his confidence and charmed the lawyers with his witty conversation, demonstrating a mind that "surprised us more and more at every visit."

Shortly after receiving his law license, Lincoln moved to Springfield, his home for the rest of his life. He became junior partner to Stuart: the partnership lasted four years. Then Lincoln became junior partner to the noted lawyer Stephen T. Logan for three years. By that time, Lincoln was ready to set up his own firm, Lincoln and Herndon, which thrived for the sixteen years until Lincoln became President. Practicing before justices of the peace, the state Supreme Court, and in the federal courts, Lincoln prospered.

As a freshman Illinois legislator, Lincoln's quick wit and debating skill brought him to the forefront. In his second term, he became Whig Party floor leader, taking a leading role in establishing the Bank of Illinois and in planning a statewide system of railroads and canals. He campaigned successfully to move the state capitol to Springfield. In 1837, when the legislature passed a resolution condemning abolition societies, Lincoln made his first public antislavery statement, protesting that, while Congress had no power to interfere with slavery in states where it existed, the Illinois Assembly was committing an "injustice" by failing to call slavery evil. Lincoln and colleague Dan Stone declared that "the institution of slavery is founded on both injustice and bad policy" and condemned lynch mobs that terrorized blacks and abolitionists alike.

Like his neighbors, Lincoln had grown up believing that blacks were inferior to whites, unfit to vote, serve on juries, or marry outside their race. Like other young frontiersmen, he had once made blacks the butt of his jokes, calling grown black men "boys" and telling crude stories involving "darkies," "niggers," "Sambos," and "pickaninnies." In 1846, at age thirty-seven, when he made a steamboat trip on the Ohio River from Louisville to St. Louis, Lincoln still had ambivalent feelings when he saw on the same ship a cargo of slaves "chained six and six together, strung together precisely like so many fish upon a troutline." It pained him to see them "being separated forever from the scenes of their childhood, their friends, their fathers, and mothers." Yet at the time he thought they were "the most cheerful and apparently [sic] happy creatures on board" who "fiddled" and "cracked jokes" and "played various games with cards." But the image of those shackled men kept coming back, Lincoln later said, "a continual torment to me which has, and continually exercises, the power of making me miserable." On many occasions, Lincoln said, "I am naturally antislavery. If slavery is not wrong, nothing is wrong."

He again made a prominent antislavery stand in 1841, in an appeal before the Illinois Supreme Court in *Bailey v. Cromwell*, he argued successfully that a promissory note written to buy a slave was legally void in Illinois due to antislavery strictures in the Northwest Ordinance of 1787 and the state constitution. Lincoln's early record on slavery as a lawyer would seem equivocal because, while he consistently denounced the institution, upholding his lawyer's oath he insisted on upholding the law. In 1837, he argued that "the promulgation of abolition doctrines tend rather to increase than to abate [slavery's] evils." In 1847, Lincoln, representing a slaveowner, argued that a slave family brought from Kentucky to do seasonal farmwork on Illinois soil were not state residents and so were not freed by Illinois antislavery laws. Lincoln was overruled, and the slaves were freed.

Lincoln's developing knack for the barbed word and the thigh-slapping joke were making him popular in the rough-and-tumble politics of the time. Yet he very nearly got into a duel when he published a series of letters mocking Democratic State Auditor James Shields, who challenged him and gave him his choice of weapons. Lincoln chose broadswords. When Lincoln explained the letters were purely political, not reflections on Shields' honor, Shields backed down.

Shortly after Lincoln moved to the new capital at Springfield, he met twenty-one-year-old Mary Todd, a Lexington, Kentucky banker's daughter. Raised as a refined Southern belle, she spoke French and had studied dance, drama, and music. More vivacious than beautiful, she was quick-witted and popular. She had come to live with her married sister in Springfield after quarreling with her stepmother. Sister-in-law of a wealthy Whig legislator, she met Lincoln, ten years her senior, at a dance. After a sporadic two-year engagement, they married on November 4, 1842, in the parlor of her sister's Springfield mansion, and then moved into a furnished hotel room. When their first child was born ten months later, they moved into a rented cottage. In May 1844, they bought the house at Eighth and Jackson Streets where they lived until Lincoln became President.

Always politically ambitious, Lincoln unsuccessfully sought the Whig nomination for Congress in 1843 but worked hard to win political allies. Winning the Whig nomination in 1846, he called for united support for the Mexican War, and was easily elected to Congress. The Whigs were beginning to inject wealth and class into campaigning as Andrew Jackson had before them. In a debate with Lincoln, the incumbent Democrat made the mistake of accusing the Whigs of foppery. Lincoln walked across the platform, pulled open his opponent's coat and pointed out his ruffled silk shirt, velvet vest, and kid gloves. Lincoln was wearing his favorite campaign costume, a flatboat deckhand's trousers reaching only mid-calf—"my only pair of breeches," he assured the guffawing crowd, "shrinking for years whilst I was growing taller … If you call this aristocratic, I plead guilty."

The Lincolns with two small sons moved to a Washington, D.C. boarding house. He was not a successful Congressman. The United States had already won the lightning Mexican War by the time Lincoln was sworn in. Although Lincoln had proposed unity behind the war effort as a candidate, his doubts about the war became clear once in Congress. Serving on three committees—War Department Expenditures, Post Office, and Post Roads—he presented resolutions requesting President James K. Polk to tell the House to point to the spot "where the war with Mexico began," whether it "was or was not on Mexican soil:" the Whigs blamed Polk for illegally starting the war. "The blood of this war, like the blood of Abel, is crying to heaven against him," Lincoln declared, attacking Polk's war policy on the House floor. Yet he refused to abandon American troops in Mexico by cutting off supplies, and voted to re-equip them.

During his two years in Congress, Lincoln saw slave auctions for the first time in the capitol itself. He was disgusted by the sight of African American men, women, and children being treated "precisely like droves of cattle." Lincoln gave notice that he intended to introduce a bill in Congress to free the slaves in the District of Columbia, but he apparently had little Congressional support and never followed through. Instead, he made known his antislavery views indirectly by supporting the unsuccessful Wilmot Proviso, which would have banned the extension of slavery into any territory conquered from Mexico. He voted to exclude slavery from new federal territories and abolish the slave trade in Washington, D.C., but he did not speak out in Congressional debates on slavery. By the time he returned to Illinois, he had learned how deeply rooted it had become. "This is a world of compensation," he wrote, "and he who would be no slave must consent to have no slave." After Mary and the boys went to Kentucky to stay with her father, Lincoln haunted the Library of Congress. He spent his days reading the books once owned by Thomas Jefferson and when the Library closed at night, he invoked his Congressional privilege to carry the books in a red bandanna on a cane over his shoulder back to his boardinghouse, where he read late into the night.

Lincoln believed that a Congressional seat should rotate, and not be claimed consecutively by one person, so he did not stand for re-election. Yet he wanted to stay on in Washington. He unsuccessfully sought appointment as Commissioner to the Land Office. He was not just seeking a federal job: he turned down the Taylor Administration's offers to appoint him as secretary, then governor, of the newly-annexed Oregon Territory. His interest in politics cooled after he campaigned on the stump for Taylor but was denied the Land Office job. Before leaving Washington in March 1849, he made his only appearance before the U. S. Supreme Court, appealing a circuit court ruling applying the Illinois statute of limitations to non-resident's lawsuits. He lost. He also applied, this time successfully, for a patent on an ingenious hydraulic invention that could raise steamboats in shallow water.

He decided to return to Illinois to practice law. His practice was highly successful and increasingly lucrative. Over the next twelve years, he represented railroads and businesses, which were taking an ever more important role in Illinois. As one of the state's leading lawyers in the 1850s, he rode circuit twice a year, trying cases over a 400-mile swath in eight counties that kept him away from home twelve weeks every spring and fall. An ardent supporter of his old commanding officer, he was chosen to deliver the eulogy for the thirteenth President in Chicago in July, 1850. When Henry Clay died in July 1852, Lincoln again was chosen to give his eulogy at the state capitol.

His oratory brought him into prominence just as his interest in politics was rekindled by Congressional passage of the Kansas-Nebraska Act of 1854. Re-elected to the state legislature, he declined the seat to be eligible to run for the U.S. Senate against Stephen A. Douglas, author of the Act. The Kansas-Nebraska Act shattered the 1820 Missouri Compromise and allowed slavery into federal territories by Douglas's doctrine of popular sovereignty. When the Illinois legislature met in caucus to elect a U.S. senator in February 1855, Lincoln, now known as the leader of Illinois anti-Nebraska Act free soilers, led Douglas on the first ballot but, as his support dwindled, Lincoln threw his support to an anti-Nebraska Act Democrat, Lyman Trumbull.

The old Whig party he had supported for thirty-four years was dying. In February, 1856, Lincoln attended a meeting of anti-Nebraska Act newspaper editors who called for a convention to organize a new national free-soil party. Lincoln attended this convention, too, and took part in the founding of the Republican Party in May 1856, stirring the delegates with his rhetoric. That June at the first Republican National Convention in Philadelphia, he received 110 votes from eleven state delegations on the first ballot for the vice-presidential nomination. In the ensuing presidential campaign, he made more than 100 speeches throughout Illinois. Lincoln emerged as the man most prominently opposed to the spread of slavery into the West.

A gradualist on abolishing slavery, Lincoln had long believed that abolitionism was the wrong course to follow, that a sudden break with the past would endanger the Union. Yet the Kansas-Nebraska Act, followed by the *Dred Scott* decision of 1857, added urgency to his long-held belief that slavery was evil and should be eradicated. He was alarmed that federal opposition to slavery was now breaking down. For Americans to allow this, to look on with indifference as slavery continued to spread, "deprives our republican example of its just influence in the world" and allowed the enemies of democracy worldwide "to taunt us as hypocrites." Vowing to oppose this spreading "cancer" of slavery, when Douglas's Senate term expired in 1858, Lincoln sought and won the Republican nomination to run against him. His firebrand acceptance speech was an unequivocal antislavery pronouncement that became immortal: under the Kansas-Nebraska Act, agitation over slavery had "not only not ceased but has constantly [been] augmented." Reminding his audience of the civil warfare that had broken out in Kansas, Lincoln declared that:

> A house divided against itself cannot stand. I believe this government cannot endure, permanently half slave and half free. I do not expect the Union to be dissolved—I do not expect the house to fall—but I do expect it will cease to be divided. It will become all one thing or all the other. Either the opponents of slavery will arrest the further spread of it, and place it where the public mind shall rest in the belief that it is in the course of ultimate extinction, or its advocates will push it forward till it shall become alike lawful in all the States—old as well as new, North as well as South.

After a few more speeches on July 24, 1858, Lincoln challenged Douglas to a series of debates. Douglas, the leading spokesman of the national Democratic Party, accepted and designated seven sites for debates that campaign summer and fall.

Widely covered by the nation's press, these debates focussed on the slavery controversy's impact on law, politics, and government. Lincoln became a national political figure, arguing repeatedly that the Supreme Court had, in the *Dred Scott* decision, opened the way for slavery to enter all of the territories. For his part, Douglas defended his Kansas-Nebraska Act policy with a clear eye to his Presidential candidacy in 1860.

The most memorable debate took place on August 27, 1858. Lincoln arrived in Freeport, a Republican stronghold of 7,000 near the Wisconsin border, on a special train filled with his supporters. A booming cannon salute and a crowd greeted him. By noon, 15,000 enthusiasts surged into a vacant lot, planting themselves on the makeshift stage and on the few benches reserved for politicians. Lincoln made a theatrical entrance in a horse-drawn Conestoga wagon flanked by an escort of "old-fashioned farmers." Banners bobbing above the stage proclaimed the opposing viewpoints: "All Men Are Created Equal," "Lincoln the Giant Killer," "Douglas and Popular Sovereignty," and "No Nigger Equality." The contrast between the two speakers was made even plainer by their attire. Douglas was dressed in a rich ruffled shirt, a trim-tailored blue coat with shiny buttons, and a plantation-style wide-brimmed soft hat; Lincoln in his usual well-worn stovepipe hat (which his law partner, William Herndon, said always looked as if a cow had just licked it), a coarse coat with sleeves far too short, and baggy trousers so truncated they showed his rough work boots.

In a three-hour debate, Lincoln cleverly asked Douglas how he could reconcile his doctrine of "popular sovereignty" with the *Dred Scott* decision. "Can the people of the United States [territories] in any lawful way, against the wishes of any citizen of the United States, exclude slavery from their limits prior to the formation of a state constitution?" Douglas, who had long ducked this issue to avoid losing Southern support, was forced to admit that, under popular sovereignty, any territory's legislature could exclude slavery simply by refusing to enact local police laws that sustained a slave code. Douglas, who at one point had to duck a melon rind, did little for his popularity in Freeport by scornfully commenting that, the last time he had been in town, he had seen black abolitionist Frederick Douglass daring to ride alongside white women in a carriage driven by a white man. "What of it?" someone in the crowd shouted back.

Douglas's damaging admission, forced upon him by Lincoln, that he had no real objections to a ban on slavery in the West, helped to kill Douglas's chances of winning the Presidency in 1860. The admission deprived him of Southern votes, even if, in the meantime, he was able to thwart Lincoln's bid for the U.S. Senate seat by appealing to moderate Illinoisans who considered Lincoln and his supporters too vehemently antislavery. But Lincoln had succeeded in delineating the sharp difference between his newly minted Republican party and Douglas's old-fashioned Democratic position: where Lincoln considered slavery, as he said at Quincy on October 13th, "a moral, a social and a political wrong," Douglas managed to evade the moral issue. Lincoln still avoided what he considered too radical a public stance: at Charleston, Illinois on September 18th he rejected black equality with whites. Lincoln narrowly won the popular election for the Senate but failed to carry the state legislature, where the vote was 54–41. Ironically, except for Illinois and Indiana, the Republicans carried every Northern state in the off-year Congressional election of 1858.

But Lincoln had emerged as a popular Republican spokesman. By early 1860, when he made a fund-raising tour of New York and New England on his way to visit his son, Robert, in school at Exeter, New Hampshire, he was considered a presidential contender. At the Cooper Union in New York City, shortly after John Brown was hanged in Virginia for leading an abortive slave insurrection, Lincoln ended a ringing speech, "Let us have faith that right makes might, and in that faith let us to the end dare to do our duty as we understand it." He spoke to large, enthusiastic crowds as he toured New England.

In May, 1860, Lincoln captured the favorite-son nomination for Presidential candidate at the Illinois state convention. The chairman announced that an old Democrat wished to make a contribution. At that, John Hanks, Lincoln's cousin, walked down the aisle toting two old fence rails with a sign proclaiming:

> The Rail Candidate for President in 1860. Two rails from a lot of 3,000 made in 1830 by Thomas Hanks and Abraham Lincoln, whose father was the first pioneer of Macon County.

In the ensuing pandemonium, Lincoln admitted that he had "split a great many better-looking ones" and the jubilant delegates cheered, "Three times for Honest Abe, our next President." Republican newspapers retold the fence-rail story; Horace Greeley's *New York Tribune* ran a feature story on the "Rail Splitter."

When the Republican National Convention met in Chicago on May 16th 1860, Lincoln stayed home but sent his managers. They hired two Chicagoans known as "shouters" to lead the cheers whenever Lincoln's name was mentioned. When they learned that front-running candidate William O. Seward's backers had cornered most of the admission tickets, they printed duplicates while Sewardians were out parading. Seward's people returned too late and found the Wigwam Convention Hall packed with Westerners shouting for Lincoln. A few hours later, when Lincoln's name was placed in nomination, the Lincoln shouters were ready. As one eye-witness recalled the sound, "Imagine all the hogs ever slaughtered in Cincinnati giving their death squeals together, a score of big steam whistles ..." Lincoln clinched the nomination on the third ballot. A friend telegraphed Lincoln, "Abe, we did it. Glory to God!" Amid the crowd's cheers, Lincoln only said, "There's a little woman down at our house [who] would like to hear this. I'll go down and tell her."

Like other presidential candidates up to that time, Lincoln thought it undignified to campaign, and remained in Springfield as an unprecedented four parties contended. Douglas had angered pro-slavery Southern Democrats: the majority party split, Northerners nominating Douglas, and Southerners backing Vice President John C. Breckenridge. A fourth party, the Constitutional Union Party, dominated by Virginia and opposing secession from the Union, put up John Bell of Tennessee. It was a virulent campaign where even Lincoln's looks and speech were used against him. Lincoln still spoke with a twang, saying "thar" for "there," "git" for "get," and "Mr. Cheerman" for "Mr. Chairman." The Albany, New York, *Atlas and Argus* called Lincoln a "slang-whanging stump speaker," and The *New York Herald* called him "a fourth-rate lecturer who cannot speak good grammar." Southern reaction was even more hostile. The Charleston, South Carolina, *Mercury* called him a "horrid-looking wretch," "scoundrelly" and a "lank-sided Yankee of the uncomliest visage and of the dirtiest complexion." The Houston, Texas, *Telegraph* mocked his "most ungainly mass of legs and arms and hatchet face." Lincoln never responded, but an Illinois friend may have been quoting him when he said, "If all the ugly men in the United States vote for him, he will surely be elected."

Lincoln's candidacy sparked anti-Northern sentiment in the South. Amid rumors of town burnings, of John Brown-style slave revolts, and of slaves stockpiling strychnine to poison water supplies, Southern militia units drilled in case the "black-hearted abolitionist fanatic" Lincoln was elected. When Stephen Douglas broke with tradition and launched the first nationwide presidential campaign speaking tour, Southern Democrats asked him to withdraw from the election in favor of Breckenridge. Lincoln's supporters fanned sectional hostilities by asserting slavery would never survive his presidency. Lincoln himself still believed that Southerners had "too much good sense and good temper to attempt the ruin of the government."

On election day, November 6, 1860, Lincoln's name did not appear on the ballots of ten Southern states. More Americans voted against Lincoln than for him. Lincoln won with only forty percent of the popular vote, but he received 180 votes in the Electoral College, fifty-seven more than the total of all his opponents, carrying the most populous states—all in the North. The day after the election, an effigy of Lincoln was hanged in Pensacola, Florida. On December 20, 1860, Southern leaders who had threatened secession from the Union if Lincoln was elected began to withdraw their states: South Carolina was the first to pass an Ordinance of Secession. "The election of Abraham Lincoln," declared the Richmond, Virginia *Dispatch*, [has] put the country in peril." "The south should arm at once," advised the Augusta, Georgia, *Constitutionalist*.

On February 11, 1861, Abraham Lincoln, one day short of fifty-two years old, paid farewell to his Springfield home for the last time. "Here I have lived for a quarter of a century and have passed from a young man to an old man. Here my children have been born, and one is buried. I now leave, not knowing when, or whether ever, I may return, with a task before me greater than that which rested upon Washington." Lincoln planned to stop at many major Northern cities on his long train trip to Washington, to allow as many people as possible to see the man they had elected President. Lincoln had looked forward to giving a Washington's Birthday speech at Independence Hall, but by the time he reached Philadelphia, he was warned of an assassination plot. Adapting a phrase from Jefferson's Declaration of Independence, Lincoln told the packed hall "that all men should have an equal chance." Twelve hours after the speech, Lincoln slipped into a disguise in a Harrisburg hotel: a large overcoat and a soft felt hat instead of his famous stovepipe. He already looked somewhat different from the man elected three months earlier. At the suggestion of a little girl, Grace Bedell, of Westfield, New York, he grew a beard that changed his appearance. Pulling up his collar, tugging his hat brim down, Lincoln, escorted by two heavily-armed bodyguards, took a special single car night train to Washington.

Inaugurated sixteenth President on March 4, 1861, Lincoln denied any desire to interfere with slavery in states where it was protected by the Constitution, but he vowed to preserve the Union, warning he would use the full power of the Presidency to "hold, occupy, and possess" all "property and places" belonging to the government—including federal forts and arsenals inside the seven states that had already seceded to the Confederate States of America. He appealed to "the mystic chords of memory, stretching from every battlefield and patriot grave to every living heart and hearthstone all over this broad land." Chief Justice Roger Taney, a slaveowner himself and author of the *Dred Scott* decision, administered the oath of office.

Lincoln's thought processes as he watched the South try to dissolve the Union remain mysterious, but William Hernden, his longtime law partner and close friend, shed some light on how his mind worked in a crisis. The man who remained "a riddle and a puzzle" even to most of his neighbors was, according to Herndon, "a close, cautious, persistent, profound, terrible thinker." A slow, penetrating analyst, he had a mind "like polished steel," said longtime friend, Joshua Steel. "A mark once made upon it was never erased." Lincoln continually surprised people with his mental capacity, his memory for names, dates, facts, and long passages of poetry he had read only once. As the inevitability of war overtook him, he devoured books on military science at the Library of Congress.

Yet Lincoln as President would never again immerse himself in books. He believed in reason, common sense, foresight, and relying on his own judgment and intuition. As President, he followed his habit of isolation on the eve of important decisions. "He would withdraw himself from society," wrote a law colleague. "But once he made a decision, he became inflexible." Lincoln believed that if North and South were allowed to divide, neither could survive, and if the American experiment in popular self-government failed, the world would have proof that democracy did not work, that people were not capable of ruling themselves, and that aristocrats must rule them. To Lincoln, no less than the fate of democracy worldwide was at stake in resisting the breakup of the Union.

As Southern states seceded in the months after Lincoln's election, they seized most of the forts inside their borders. Lincoln had to decide whether to resupply the few remaining in government hands. Fort Sumter, in the harbor of Charleston, South Carolina, came to symbolize the Union. If Lincoln withdrew its garrison, he would begin his Presidency in a storm of Northern criticism. To reinforce it was regarded as an act of war by the Confederate States. Lincoln decided to attempt a compromise. He advised South Carolina that he only intended to resupply the fort's garrison with food and water. South Carolina still regarded this as a hostile act and demanded the fort's surrender. On April 12, 1861, Confederate artillery opened fire. The Civil War had begun.

Lincoln responded decisively. With Congress in adjournment, he asserted extraordinary war powers as the Commander-in-Chief. Calling up 75,000 militia from the governors of each state to suppress this "insurrection," he exceeded the congressional troop limit. Rather than wait for Congressional appropriations to supply the military, he called on each state legislature to pledge a regiment of troops and financial support. He ordered a naval blockade of all shipping in and out of Southern ports. To blunt the influence of Southern sympathizers in border states who could obstruct the war effort and cut off the nation's capital from the North, he ordered federal marshals to round them up and imprison them—in all, he would order 14,000 arrests in the course of the war. And then he suspended the writ of *habeas corpus* (allowing for the release of prisoners until they were tried and convicted) in areas such as Maryland and Delaware where Southern support was concentrated. Many critics, especially Chief Justice Taney, protested that he was usurping powers beyond Constitutional limits. When Congress reconvened in July 1861, Lincoln, responding in particular to criticism over suspension of *habeas corpus*, asked Congress, in a special message, "Are all the laws but one to go unexecuted and the government itself go to pieces lest that one be violated?"

By that time, a Federal army had assembled near Washington. Across the Potomac River, an equal Confederate force believed that a single victory would prove decisive. A returning Congress demanded action. Although the Union Army was ill-trained and poorly organized, Lincoln, yielding to Congressional pressure, ordered General Irwin McDowell to march into Virginia as newspaper headlines cheered him "On to Richmond." The first Battle of Bull Run on July 21, 1861, was a clear rout of Union forces. As Lincoln called for 250,000 fresh troops and began his long search for a capable Army general-in-chief, Northerners began to realize they faced a long war. Lincoln's next choice as Union commander, George B. McClellan, proved a good logician and was popular with his troops, partially because he repeatedly shied away from taking the initiative. A full year dragged by before the main campaign of 1862, the Peninsular Campaign aimed at the Confederate capital of Richmond, ended in disaster when Confederate General Robert E. Lee repeatedly beat back Union attacks, further humiliating Northern forces at the Second Battle of Bull Run. Only a fluke, the loss of a set of Lee's plans for invading the North when a Confederate staff officer dropped the cigar case that contained them, prevented a major Confederate victory at Antietam on September 17, 1862. Yet McClellan failed to pursue Lee. Lincoln removed him from command. In this single deadliest day of the war, 23,000 were killed and wounded.

On the advice of Secretary of State William O. Seward, Lincoln had been waiting for a significant Union victory before calling for a change of national policy on slavery. He had carefully kept the survival of the Union, not emancipation of the slaves, the rationale for war against the South. Lincoln also believed it crucial to keep the border slave states of Missouri, Kentucky, Maryland, and Delaware in the Union. But by the fall of 1862, Northern morale was flagging and recruitment dropping off sharply. Moreover, European nations appeared to increasingly favor the South as the defender against an aggressor North. But many Europeans condemned slavery as evil and stopped short of openly supporting the Confederacy. In the North, as the war dragged on and Southern forces, supported by slave labor, fought doggedly on, there was growing political support for shifting the focus of the war to an all-out attempt to stamp out the institution of slavery.

Lincoln reasoned that, not only would a proclamation of emancipation of the slaves give the North the moral high ground but would allow freed slaves to serve as soldiers in Northern armies, something Lincoln believed the South dreaded.

The Bettmann Archive

A practical joker and brilliant trial lawyer, Abraham Lincoln predicted his own assassination.

Lincoln seems to have made the decision alone, advising but not seeking the advice of his Cabinet. Lincoln called in Congressmen from the border states three times in the spring and summer of 1862, appealing to them to endorse a plan for gradual emancipation. They bristled, objected, and refused. In July, Lincoln summoned the Congressmen again to the White House: "The unprecedentedly stern facts of the case" called for immediate emancipation of the huge Southern slave labor force that had freed one million white men to fight the North. Lincoln's limited war had become a total war; pressure to make it a war of total abolition had mounted. If the border states did not decide "at once to emancipate gradually," Lincoln warned, slavery in their states "will be extinguished" by the "mere incidents of the war." Again, they refused by a caucus vote of twenty to nine. Angry, Lincoln decided to embrace abolitionism, that very evening determining to issue an emancipation proclamation. Lincoln later wrote, "I struggled nearly a year and a half to get along without touching the 'institution' ... I gave a hundred days' fair notice ... to all the States and people. They could have turned it wholly aside by simply again becoming good citizens of the United States. They chose to disregard it." He made the Emancipation Proclamation, he added, on "military necessity."

In June 1862, Lincoln called Vice President Hannibal Hamlin into the library of the Soldiers Home, where he went to escape the pressures of the White House, and read him a draft of the proclamation that would free many of the nation's slaves. Two weeks later, Lincoln revealed his plan to individual Cabinet officers. At a Cabinet meeting, Secretary of State Seward urged Lincoln to be cautious and wait for a major Union Army victory so that the proclamation did not seem a sign of desperation. Lincoln reluctantly agreed.

On August 14, 1862 he invited a delegation of free blacks to the White House and disclosed his thinking. Blacks were suffering "the greatest wrong inflicted on any people." Lincoln had considered colonization of blacks to Africa or Haiti, because he feared white hatred was a "fact" that resulted from the presence of blacks in America. "Our white men [are] cutting one another's throats ... But for your race among us there could not be war .... It is better for us both, therefore, to be separated." Lincoln's confidential briefing only angered black abolitionist Frederick Douglass. Lincoln's "tone of frankness and benevolence which he assumes in his speech is too thin a mask not to be seen through. The genuine spark of humanity is missing in it." Another black delegate, Isaiah Wears of Philadelphia, thought it unconscionable "to be asked, after so many years of oppression and wrong" to "pull up stakes;" to be forced to leave the U.S. was "unreasonable and anti-Christian." Wears added that "It is not the Negro race that is the cause of the war, it is the unwillingness on the part of the American people to do the race simple justice."

As criticism mounted, Lincoln isolated himself. He wrote privately that he was trying to puzzle out "the will of God." When news reached him in the White House that the Union had finally won a major victory at Antietam, Lincoln summoned his Cabinet and read the proclamation declaring freedom to all slaves inside Confederate lines on January 1, 1863. When Frederick Douglass heard the news, he proclaimed that the Civil War had suddenly become "invested with sanctity."

The Emancipation Proclamation seemed to breathe new life into the Union cause. In his annual message to Congress, Lincoln declared: "In giving freedom to the slaves, we assure freedom to the free ... The world will forever applaud and God must forever bless." One result of the Proclamation was that 180,000 blacks, fully ten percent of all Union forces, would enlist before the war's end. Another result was that, more than ever, it became a fight to the finish for the Southern way of life, a fight in which most of the good generals seemed to be on the Confederate side. Lincoln's generals with few exceptions seemed incompetent. Lincoln replaced the procrastinating McClellan with Ambrose E. Burnside. In his debut at Fredericksburg, Virginia, on December 13, 1862, with 113,000 troops against

Lee's 75,000, Burnside ordered his troops up a bluff fourteen times into withering Confederate fire, causing 10,884 Union casualties, more than double Southern losses. The latest humiliation came only two weeks before the Emancipation Proclamation took effect. On January 1, 1863, Lincoln declared all slaves still in areas of rebellion "then, henceforward and forever free."

As black men—"in vast numbers—an army in themselves"—fled plantations and flocked to the Union standard and died in battle from Fort Wagner, South Carolina to Nashville, Tennessee, Lincoln dropped forever his ideas of deportation and colonization and praised the black men who "with silent tongue and clenched teeth and steady eye and well-poised bayonet have helped mankind on to this great consummation." By August, 1863, when the Union Army had organized 50,000 black soldiers, Lincoln declared in a public letter that "the emancipation policy, and the use of colored troops, constitute the heaviest blow yet dealt to the rebellion."

Lincoln was spending more and more time away from his family—in the telegraph office of the White House, and at Cabinet meetings. Poet Walt Whitman, a volunteer nurse at the Soldiers Home, treating the wounded brought by train from the front, recorded in his diary that Lincoln went back and forth every day escorted by twenty-five or thirty cavalrymen "with sabres drawn and held upright over their shoulders." There seemed little but grief for Lincoln at the White House. His oldest son, Robert Todd, was away at Harvard through most of the war; his favorite son, William Wallace, "Willie", had died in early 1862, leaving his mother and his father inconsolable. Mary Todd Lincoln turned to mediums, holding seances in the White House. She was already disliked and distrusted by many Union leaders because she had brothers-in-law and cousins fighting on the Confederate side. When her brother-in-law, Confederate General Ben Helm was killed at Chattanooga, Mary's half-sister, Emilie, came to stay at the White House, despite mounting criticism. It was often eleven at night before Mary saw the President— "my tired and weary husband."

There was little privacy at the White House. There were Indian treaties with chiefs who came from the plains of Minnesota where warfare had broken out. Lincoln refused to attempt Indian talk even as he smoked the calumet and attempted to crack jokes. When he met with a large delegation of chiefs in the East Room on March 27, 1863, an Indian named Laughing Water was introduced as Minihaha. Then he met Crying Water and quipped, "I suppose your name is Miniboohoo?" Amid the dark days, Lincoln tried to make people laugh. He permitted P. T. Barnum to arrange a wedding reception for the enormously popular midget "General Tom Thumb" (Charles S. Stratton) and his bride, Lavinia Warren. Lincoln gravely presented the couple to Mary Lincoln, who shed her mourning clothes for the first time in a year.

But only news of Union victories could mitigate Lincoln's growing melancholy. A fresh Union disaster at Chancellorsville, Virginia, in May 1863 meant a fresh change in command. Lincoln appointed General George G. Meade to replace the inaptly named F. J. "Fighting Joe" Hooker. Even the greatest mistake of the Confederacy— Lee's invasion of the North in July 1863 and his bloody repulse at Gettysburg—did not end the awful struggle. It was not until April 1864, after three full years of civil war had killed nearly half a million men, that Lincoln was able to find a general, Ulysses S. Grant, who agreed with him on how to end the war—one year of total war.

In his message to Congress in December 1861, after the first season of war, Lincoln had deplored the possibility that the conflict might "degenerate into a violent and remorseless revolutionary struggle." In his own mind, Lincoln was a moderate who did not want to destroy the South, only to keep it in the Union. In three years he had metamorphosed into Lincoln the Revolutionary, advocating a total, crushing warfare, giving Grant one year to obliterate Lee and his army. They were the enemy; to defeat Lee was to break the South's will to fight on, wherever they were. With unrelenting, unprecedented fury, Grant and his former second-in-command, William Tecumseh Sherman, attacked the South. Their sudden if bloody victories, ironically ending the chances for a negotiated peace, swept Lincoln, who pledged total war until the unconditional surrender of the Confederacy, to re-election in November 1864. In April 1865, exactly one year after assuming command, Grant forced Lee to surrender at Appomattox Courthouse. In all, 620,000 Americans had been killed.

In a few short, awful years, Abraham Lincoln had presided over the destruction of not only the institution of slavery but the rural Southern plantation way of life. He had, as Mark Twain said of the Civil War itself, "uprooted institutions that were centuries old, changed the politics of a people, transformed the social life of half the country, and wrought so profoundly upon the entire national character that [his] influence cannot be measured." America was forever transformed. As Lincoln put it many times, "Broken eggs cannot be mended." Not only had slavery, the basis of the South's social and economic order, been eliminated, but the South's place as the most prosperous region per capita in the nation was lost. More than half of the South's farm machinery and two-fifths of its livestock were destroyed. One quarter of its white males of military age (the best age for production of any sort) were destroyed, killed, or seriously wounded, a higher proportion than any European country suffered in either World Wars I or II.

Abraham Lincoln, a man who started out deploring violence, who had said so often that "right makes might," finally turned these words inside out and accepted war as the only way to win to save the Union. By April 1865, the Union had the largest army and navy, the most railroad trackage, and the most advanced industrial economy in the world. The old Democratic Party, the party of Jefferson and Jackson, was also destroyed. In its place stood Lincoln's Republicans. The party of Lincoln passed the most sweeping agenda of changes since the first American Revolution: a higher protective tariff, a homestead act that provided land for millions of veterans and European immigrants, a land-grant college act, a transcontinental railroad act that funded an overland route to the Pacific, a national banking act that accompanied the introduction of "greenback" paper currency and war bonds that helped to finance the war, and an Internal Revenue Act that imposed progressive income taxes for the first time. Most of all, Lincoln ended the old agrarian order in America and helped usher in a new industrial age. As he told Congress in December 1862, "The dogmas of the quiet past are inadequate to the stormy present. As our case is new, we must think anew and act anew."

Certainly not every American agreed with him or even was willing to acquiesce in the transformation. Lincoln did not outlive his revolution from the top down by a single week. On the Good Friday evening of April 14, 1865, after he received a standing ovation from the packed crowd at Ford's Theater in Washington, D.C., and as his wife looked on, he was killed by a single shot in the head by a twenty-seven-year-old Maryland-born white supremacist, Shakespearean actor John Wilkes Booth. One week later, Booth himself was hunted down and died after being dragged from a barn set afire by Union soldiers. Booth's last words were "Tell mother I die for my country."

QUESTIONS FOR THOUGHT AND DISCUSSION

1. The life of Abraham Lincoln is often treated in history as a sacred legend of log cabin to White House. What does Lincoln's rise to the presidency suggest about nineteenth century society and politics?

2. What would you define as the best and worst aspects of Abraham Lincoln? Would you consider him heroic? Why or why not?

3. How did Lincoln's opposition to slavery develop, and how did it serve to lift him to the presidency?

4. Was the Emancipation Proclamation a significant turning point in the Civil War? How did it reflect a change in Lincoln's own thinking about the war and the status of African Americans in the United States?

SUGGESTED READINGS

Baker, Jean H. *Mary Todd Lincoln*. New York: Norton, 1987.

Donald, David Herbert. *Lincoln*. New York: Simon, 1995.

Douglas, William O. *Mr. Lincoln and the Negro: The Long Road to Equality*. New York: Atheneum, 1963.

Holzer, Harold, ed. *The Lincoln-Douglas Debates*. New York: Harper, 1993.

Kunhardt, Philip B., Jr. et al. *Lincoln: An Illustrated Biography*. New York: Knopf, 1992.

Lincoln, Abraham. *Speeches and Writings, 1832–1865*. Ed. by Don E. Fehrenbacher. 2 vols. New York: Library of America, 1989.

McPherson, James M. *Abraham Lincoln and the Second American Revolution*. New York: Oxford UP, 1991.

_____. *Battle Cry of Freedom*. New York: Ballantine, 1988.

_____. *Ordeal by Fire*. New York: Knopf, 1982.

_____. *The Negro's Civil War*. New York: Ballantine, 1991.

Neely, Mark E., Jr. *The Last Best Hope of Earth: Abraham Lincoln and the Promise of America*. Cambridge: Harvard UP, 1993.

Nichols, David A. *Lincoln and the Indians: Civil War Policy and Politics*. Columbia: UP of Missouri, 1978.

Oates, Stephen B. *With Malice Toward None: The Life of Abraham Lincoln*. New York: Harper, 1977.

Williams, T. Harry. *Lincoln and His Generals*. New York: Knopf, 1952.

19

Robert E. Lee

As the nineteenth century opened, few Americans could foresee the survival of slavery. Even as European immigrants surged west seeking cheap and abundant land, slavery was proving less profitable. In 1807, the year Robert E. Lee was born, Congress outlawed the slave trade with Africa. The corrupt bargain at the heart of the Constitutional debates of 1787— to table Congressional debates over slavery for twenty years—had expired. It seemed a needless gesture; every state except South Carolina had banned the odious traffic.

But the invention of machines to "gin" cotton ended the time-consuming labor of hand-picking stubborn seeds from sticky cotton. Eli Whitney's invention came just a few years before the nation's land area was doubled by Thomas Jefferson's Louisiana Purchase. Machines could work sixteen hour days at high speed without tiring. Southerners kept pace with the new textile machinery by breeding more slaves to cultivate more land. Cotton culture boomed as the new lands west of the Mississippi filled with plantations. A war with Mexico, the nervous neighbor of the sprawling American giant, gave Americans their first experience of foreign conquest and Southerners the prospect of vast new plantations. It also produced a generation of confident, seasoned, professional officers, most notably Robert E. Lee. A dozen years of sectional strife over the expansion of the slavery culture led to the war nobody seemed to want, the Civil War.

UNQUESTIONABLY THE greatest Confederate general of the Civil War and probably the greatest hero of the Old South, Robert E. Lee was the son of a Revolutionary War hero and he himself married into the family of George Washington, becoming the executor of Washington's estate. He came from one of the most distinguished Anglo-American families—and that may have been not only his good fortune, but his curse. While his fame relies on his superb military achievements (and his spectacular failures) in the face of overwhelming odds, he was widely respected for generations for his selflessness. There has never been a question whether he fought for personal gain. So admired was he in defeat that Union General Ulysses S. Grant, who finally forced Lee to surrender to him, would write that "there was not a man in the Confederacy whose influence with the whole people was as great as his."

The man who personally and publicly took on the mantle of Washington and defended the slave plantation social order of the Old South considered slavery evil and had freed his own slaves. Lee's name became synonymous with honor, duty, and futile courage in the South. Sitting stoically in his gray uniform with his gray beard on his gray horse, Traveller, this prematurely old man on a charger symbolized Southern resistance to the juggernaut Union armies, unflinchingly facing the Industrial Revolution as it mowed down his beloved, old fashioned, country gentry way of life. Yet few in the South or North during the Civil War or for generations afterward knew just how much, most of his life, Lee silently suffered as the poor relation of an aristocratic family. In fact, Robert E. Lee wanted to become a doctor. He never wanted to become a soldier. He only went to West Point because West Point was tuition-free. That was the only way he could afford to go to college after his famous father squandered the family fortune.

Robert Edward Lee was born on January 19, 1807, in Stratford Hall, near Montross, Virginia, in a baronial brick mansion, a generous gift built as thanks to the Lee family by Queen Caroline of England after the original house burned down. Lee's royalist English roots ran back to the Norman Conquest. Two of his relatives signed the Declaration of Independence. His father, Henry, had become famous during the Revolutionary War as he led "Lee's Legion" on daring cavalry raids and scouting missions. But his father was equally reckless in peacetime, speculating wildly and unsuccessfully in Western lands. By the time Robert was two, his father was in debtor's prison, and two years later his humiliated mother, Ann Carter Lee, daughter of an even richer Virginia family, had to move her children into a small rental house in Alexandria, Virginia. There, Robert grew up, living largely on the proceeds of selling off the family furniture.

Lee's father spent time in and out of debtor's prison until he was offered a fresh command when the War of 1812 came and the United States fought England a second time. One day in July 1812, Henry, also known as Light Horse Harry, rode off to nearby Baltimore, Maryland to visit the Federalist printer Alexander Hanson, an old friend who opposed the war. A mob thought Hanson was disloyal and attacked the paper. Lee knew how to handle a mob, he thought; he fired his pistols in the air. The crowd attacked anyway. Before he could be dragged by militiamen to the city jail for his own protection, Lee had been clubbed and stabbed. He never completely recovered. Brought home more dead than alive, Lee, now fifty-four, turned down a commission as a major general and instead decided to leave his family behind and book ship's passage for Barbados. Robert was seven when he last saw his father, who drifted from island to island for six years while his family lived on the proceeds of selling family heirlooms.

Living virtually in the shadow of Mount Vernon, Lee was raised on frequent visits to wealthy relatives and his mother's lectures on frugality, duty, honor, and loyalty. Somehow this only made him worship his profligate absentee father more even as everyone else said Light Horse Harry had abandoned his family and disgraced it. He lived for the occasional letters from his father. "Self-command is the pivot upon which the character, fame, and independence of us mortals hang," his father wrote. "Fame in arms or art, however conspicuous, is naught unless bottomed on virtue." To his mother, his father wrote, "Robert, who was always good, will be confirmed in his happy turn of mind by his ever-watchful and affectionate mother."

Leaving the plantation to move into town turned out not to be entirely a bad move. Receiving the best education the town had to offer at Alexandria Academy, Lee especially enjoyed studying classical Roman and Greek history, literature, and mathematics. Between parental homilies and school lessons, Robert, during his three years at the academy, grew to five-feet-ten and a half, tall for his time. Handsome and serious, he assumed more of the burdens at home as his mother and older sister became invalids. He took over running the house, the garden, and the stable. He became a fine horseman and learned to fish and to hunt with his hounds. His oldest brother, Carter, went off to Harvard and his brother, Sidney, went off to sea as a navy midshipman. Robert, aware that there was no money left for his college education, decided to seek a commission to West Point. He liked scientific studies, and at West Point he could become an engineer.

There was, even then, stiff competition for admission to the U.S. Military Academy, which accepted only 250 students each year based on academic merit and political influence. With a strong recommendation from his school for mathematics and his "gentlemanly deportment," Lee made his first frontal attack on Washington, D.C. He hoped to receive a presidential appointment to West Point if he could secure an endorsement of his nomination by the Secretary of War, John C. Calhoun. The seventeen-year-old Lee personally delivered his application to Calhoun, who strongly recommended him. Appointed in March 1824, he had to wait in line for a full year, since so many were admitted that year from Virginia.

Beginning four years at the austere military academy on the bluffs overlooking the great bend of the Hudson River, Lee learned to live according to the book— which banned smoking, drinking, gambling, public displays of affection, reading novels, or keeping a horse—Congress would not pay to feed Army horses for another decade until Plains Indians shamed it into establishing a cavalry. Lee is still remembered for a flawless record at West Point. He never received a single demerit for an infraction of the rules. His academic record was equally impressive: he was made a math instructor in his second year as well as class staff sergeant, the highest honor available to a yearling, or second-year man. Named one of four assistant professors, he taught mathematics and studied the strategy and tactics of the recent Napoleonic Wars. He also proudly read a new addition to the curriculum, his father's *Memoirs of the War in the Southern Department*, introduced as a textbook study of the American Revolution. During his final year, he was named assistant to the commandant. He was graduated with highest honors in 1829—only weeks before his mother died. He arrived home just in time for her death.

The life of a newly commissioned Army engineer promised low pay and very slow promotion. The United States was at peace from 1815 to 1846. Virtually all there was to occupy a young officer was desk work or fort-building. Lee was sent off to strengthen Fort Pulaski on mosquito-infested Cockspur Island off the Georgia coast for seventeen months. In 1831, he was transferred closer to home to work on Fortress Monroe, a giant new artillery installation aimed at preventing an enemy from sailing right up to Washington, D.C., as Robert had seen the British do in the War of 1812.

This assignment brought him closer to home, making possible more frequent visits to a young woman, Mary Anna Randolph Custis. He had decided he would like to marry her. Mary was the great-granddaughter of Martha Washington: she lived in a stately, Greek-columned mansion her father, George Washington Parke Custis, had built high above the Potomac River at Arlington, just across the Potomac from Washington, D.C. The stepson of President Washington, Parke, as he was known, was always Washington's favorite stepchild, and he had built Arlington as a shrine to the Founding Father. Lee loved to visit the house. He was so like Washington had once been, an impecunious young officer seeking the hand of a woman far wealthier. Mary Custis would inherit Arlington, its hundreds of acres, and its slaves. It would take two years of besieging him before Custis decided that the penniless if handsome and ramrod-straight Lee was good enough to marry his only daughter. On June 30, 1831, Robert and Mary were married at Arlington, and Lee moved into the shrine to Washington's memory.

They were to be apart more than they were together. Mary could have children—the first of seven was born the next year—but she developed a recurring pelvic infection that kept her bedridden for a year and then she could only walk with a cane. When he was promoted and transferred in 1835 after three years at Fortress Monroe to a desk job in Washington, D.C., Lee decided to commute every day on horseback. Two years later, after Mary recovered sufficiently to spare him, he accepted his first trouble-shooting assignment to St. Louis, Missouri. The Mississippi River, constantly changing, was cutting a new channel into the Illinois shore that was leaving St. Louis's waterfront silted, high and dry, and useless for steamboats. Lee changed the course of the river with an assortment of dikes, new channels and underwater jetties that saved the port city from economic ruin and earned Lee promotion to captain. He was away from home almost constantly now. The vagabond life of a peacetime military engineer next took him to New York City to construct Fort Hamilton. The assignment lasted five years. There were now six children on a captain's meager pay.

Lee was deciding whether he could afford to go on or should become a civilian engineer, the course most West Pointers he knew had followed, when war with Mexico broke out. Nearly forty years old and after twenty-one years of military life, Lee jumped at the chance for active duty and requested transfer to the war zone. Stopping off at Arlington to visit his wife and children, he drew up his will, and then boarded a steamboat crammed with Army officers and men. He arrived in San Antonio, Texas in time to join General John Wool on an overland expedition into northern Mexico. Lee was assigned the task of building bridges.

Soon transferred to General Winfield Scott's expeditionary force attacking the key port city of Vera Cruz, Captain Lee went ashore in the same launch with four other West Pointers of the First U. S. Engineering Battalion. He would get to know them much better in the Civil War: George McClellan, George Meade, P.G.T. Beauregard, and Joseph E. Johnston. In the long march through mountains overland to Mexico City, Lee used his knowledge of horses and terrain on a daring one-man reconnaissance mission to find the safest possible route for the 10,000-

man American force to thread its way through deserts and over mountains to attack Mexico City. Wounded once by a Mexican sentry's fire as he escaped at dawn from an enemy camp, he was several times reported "missing in action." Three times, he trudged alone across the Pedregal dry lava beds, five miles of jagged rock that looked like frozen ocean waves, as he led the Americans on what was supposed to be a surprise attack that only his tireless reconnaissance kept from becoming a Mexican surprise attack. Six other couriers had been lost. Only Lee got through in what General Scott described as "the greatest feat of physical and moral courage of the entire Vera Cruz campaign." Promoted twice, Lee was singled out as one of the heroes of the brief, bloody war. Scott pronounced his own "success in Mexico was largely due to the skill, valor and undaunted courage of Robert E. Lee, the greatest military genius in America."

Peace brought three years of dull duty at Fort Carroll in Baltimore Harbor before Lee was appointed superintendent of West Point, one of the Army's highest honors, in 1852. Improving the buildings and the academic courses, Lee was remembered as a fair and compassionate commandant who spent much of his time with the cadets, especially his son, Custis, ("Boo," he called him). Another cadet in particular caught his attention: J. E. B. Stuart would one day become his favorite cavalry officer. At West Point, too, Lee became an Episcopalian. Each year, he was becoming more deeply spiritual. He had been horrified by his first glimpses of battle in Mexico. "You have no idea what a horrible sight a field of battle is," he had written to his son.

After three years on the Hudson, he was assigned to duty as lieutenant colonel of a new cavalry regiment posted to San Antonio on the Texas-Mexican frontier. It was here, protecting settlers from raids by Apache and Comanche Indians that Lee spent the last six years of relative peace before the Civil War broke out. It was the longest period he was away from his now-invalid wife; it was also during this tour of duty that Lee's father-in-law died, leaving him master of Arlington. He took leave and hurried home.

As executor of the Custis will, it was Lee's duty to carry out Custis's wish to free all of his 280 slaves within three years. He found the Arlington estate in disrepair and its fields lying fallow. He rented out some of the slaves for cash, and put the others to work planting new crops of wheat and corn that would produce an income and plenty of food and require less labor in the future. With Arlington restored, he found jobs and homes for the slaves before manumitting them. "I have always been in favor of emancipation," he would testify before Congress after the war. Denouncing slavery privately as "a moral and political evil," Lee believed slavery had an evil effect on master as well as slave.

With a guerrilla war raging over the westward extension of slavery into lands conquered in the Mexican War, with Southerners threatening to secede from the Union to which he had sworn his undying allegiance as a West Point cadet, Lee was in agony. "I wish to do what is right," he wrote to his son, Custis, "urging this young officer to make up his own mind where his duty lay." To his cousin, Markie, he wrote:

God save us from our folly, selfishness and shortsightedness ... What will be the result, I cannot conjecture. I only see that a fearful calamity is upon us, and fear that the country will have to pass through for its sins a fiery ordeal. I am unable to realize that our people will destroy a government inaugurated by the blood and wisdom of our patriot fathers that has given us peace and prosperity at home, power and security abroad.

But he had decided what he would do: if Virginia, which he considered his home country, seceded, he would resign his Army commission. He would only take up arms if Virginia were attacked:

I wish to live under no other government, and there is no sacrifice I am not ready to make for the preservation of the Union save that of honor. If a disruption takes place, I shall go back to my native state, and, save in her defense, there will be one soldier less than in the world now.

Lee resented what he considered the self-righteousness of abolitionists who lumped all Southerners as evil: he believed that extremists from North and South were pushing the nation into civil war. He felt that his state was more moderate and responsible, that Virginia was protecting the liberty, freedom, and constitutional rights and principals for which George Washington, his father and so many of his forebears had fought. Just as Washington, an Englishman, had been willing to leave his allegiance to the Great Britain of his ancestors, Lee was willing to leave the Union to fight in what he and many Southerners saw as the second war for their independence from a tyrannical government.

To fight against his home country, his neighbors, and his family was unthinkable. To his sister, he wrote:

In my own person I had to meet the question whether I should take part against my native state. With all my devotion to the Union, and the feeling of loyalty and duty of an American citizen, I have not been able to make up my mind to raise my hand against my relatives, my children, my home. I have therefore resigned my commission in the army, and, save in defense of my native state—with the sincere hope that my poor services may never be needed—I hope may never be called upon to draw my sword.

Colonel Robert E. Lee's last official act as an American army officer had been to lead Marines who put down John Brown's attempted slave revolt at Harper's Ferry in 1859. An armed attack on Virginia by abolitionists convinced him of the inevitability of a civil war. When Texas seceded from the Union in 1861, Lee left his post at Fort Brazos, and was recalled to Washington, D.C. to await further orders. Offered the field command of all Union troops by his old commander, Union General of the Armies Winfield Scott, Lee resigned his commission. He crossed the bridge to Arlington, ending thirty-six years as a U.S. Army officer.

The new President, Abraham Lincoln, ordered the resupply of the harbor at Fort Sumter in Charleston, South Carolina. Virginia now seceded and joined the Confederacy. Lee accepted a commission as a full Confederate general and became Confederate President Jefferson Davis's chief military adviser. That autumn, he led Virginia troops in halting a Union attack from western Virginia, then took charge of the fortification of the South Carolina seacoast. Returning to Richmond, the Confederate capital, he organized Confederate forces, then under the command of his old comrade from the Mexican War, Joseph E. Johnston. When Johnston was severely wounded, Lee was placed in command of Virginia

The Bettmann Archive

Offered the command of both Union and Confederate forces in the Civil War, Robert E. Lee saw his first duty to Virginia, home of his elite family.

forces on May 31, 1862. In his first Special Order, he named the Army of Northern Virginia, which was to become the most famous Confederate Army, under his command. Thwarting the first major Union attempt to seize Richmond in the

Peninsula Campaign, in his first month of command he humiliated the Union commander, another old comrade, George McClellan. Outnumbered two-to-one, Lee inflicted two-to-one casualties, fighting almost every day and launching a surprise attack on Union forces at the Second Battle of Bull Run that routed the Army of the Potomac and cleared Virginia of the hated Union bluejackets.

But the South simply could not afford to lose one man to every two Northerners. The North could put six men into the field for every Southern soldier and soon would add black troops, 180,000 of them, to its ranks, something the South refused to do, even when a desperate Lee urged it late in 1864. Lee ultimately failed because he changed from defending the South to seeking ways to inflict losses on the North. Instead of wearing down the enemy, as had his model, George Washington, only striking selectively, he insisted on keeping to a bloody initiative, repeatedly sacrificing his dwindling manpower. As historian James B. McPherson put it, "The qualities most honored by the South since his death ruined the Confederacy: devotion to the offensive, daring, combativeness, audacity, eagerness to attack, and taking the initiative." Lee could have afforded to lose most of the battles and still won the war; because he tried to win every battle, no matter the cost, and never called retreat, Lee, and the South, lost.

Had Lee not rallied Confederate forces in the summer of 1862, Richmond and the Confederacy probably would have fallen, forced to return to the Union. Ironically, had this happened, slavery would have survived indefinitely, but by fighting doggedly on in one of history's most brilliant and sustained defenses, Lee assured that slavery would be abolished. He fought on, so threatening the Union that Lincoln declared his Emancipation Proclamation.

Lee won virtually every battle he fought in defense of his beloved Virginia. Only when he left Virginia and took the offensive—at Antietam in September 1862, at Gettysburg in July 1863—did he fail spectacularly. Lee fought on in the hope that his relentless bloodletting of the North would erode Northern enthusiasm to fight on and lead to negotiations that would restore the pre-war status quo. But he fought an old-fashioned, outmoded form of war, wasting thousands of lives in futile attacks against better-armed, better-fed Union forces until he came up against a Union general, Ulysses S. Grant, as determined to fight every day to the death as he was. With only 6,000 starving men left out of his proud Virginia legions, Lee, in his finest dress uniform, handed over his sword to the slouching, cigar-chomping Ohioan, in his mud-spattered private's uniform. The war had lasted exactly four years and cost 620,000 lives, worse than the loss of life in all other American wars combined.

When it was all over, Lee chose to live out his life as president of a small college in Lexington, Virginia, now named after himself and the man whose mantle he had assumed. At Washington and Lee College, he tried to set an example for other Southerners. "Make your sons Americans," he urged. Applying for a complete pardon, he sent in his application without the required oath of allegiance. He sent in the oath a little later, but a clerk in a Washington office misplaced it and Lee was not pardoned. More than a century after Robert E. Lee died of a stroke on October 12, 1870, the oath turned up in the National Archives. In 1975, his citizenship was restored by Congress.

QUESTIONS FOR THOUGHT AND DISCUSSION

1. Contrast Robert E. Lee's background to that of Abraham Lincoln.

2. Why did Lee, who thought slavery was evil and who opposed secession, lend his support to the Confederate cause, becoming its greatest general?

3. How was Lee able to win so many battles against usually greater Union forces throughout much of the war? Why was Lee ultimately unsuccessful in bringing about a Confederate victory?

4. Although his property was confiscated, Lee was not otherwise punished for leading the Confederate forces in the Civil War. Should he have been hanged for treason? Why, or why not?

SUGGESTED READINGS

Connelly, Thomas L. *The Marble Man: Robert E. Lee and His Image in American Society.* New York, 1977.

Freeman, Douglas Southall. *Robert E. Lee.* 4 vols. New York: Scribners, 1934–5.

_____. Lee. New York: Scribners, 1961.

McPherson, James M. "How Noble Was Robert E. Lee?" *New York Review of Books.* November 7, 1991, pp. 10–11.

Miers, Earl Schenck. *Robert E. Lee: A Great Life in Brief.* New York: Knopf, 1956.

Nolan, Alan T. *Lee Considered: General Robert E. Lee and Civil War History.* Chapel Hill: UPof North Carolina 1991.

Sears, Stephen W. "Getting Right With Robert E. Lee." *American Heritage.* May, 1991, pp. 58–60.

Thomas, Emory M. *Robert E. Lee: A Biography.* New York: Norton, 1995.

20

Charlotte Forten

$\mathcal{T}$he American War of Independence, as the British called the Revolutionary War, claimed to "dissolve the bonds" that joined the mother country to her transatlantic colonies. Politically, the war achieved its end. But language and genes stubbornly endure. In the early nineteenth century, Great Britain and the United States developed in ways that continued their old relationship. Outstripping the size of its mother, the United States soon had enough territory to show strong regional characteristics as different areas imitated different strains of British culture. The North, with more concentrated population centers, had an economy increasingly based on trade and manufacturing and higher literacy, and resembled the England of the Industrial Revolution. The North emulated just as closely the reformist spirit that sprang up in England to defend humanitarian values. The same outlook that campaigned for improved conditions in factories and mines in England found expression in the abolitionist journalism of the North.

Another strand of English consciousness turned away from grimy factory towns and consumptive children to contemplate the tranquility of a romantic past, made newly and immensely popular by the novels of Sir Walter Scott. In the United States, Southerners esteemed these novels as ennobling and as upholding the legitimacy of the rural, agricultural way of life.

In the small territory of the British Isles, partisans of the two views had to make accommodations, had to practice cohabitation in their philosophies. The luxury of abundant space in North America for decades allowed each side to claim its own considerable turf, but Northerners of the reformist frame of mind saw a new enemy on this side of the Atlantic. Northern abolitionists in particular, the most zealous human rights activists up to the civil rights movement of the 1960s, saw the enemy as fellow Americans who owned slaves. Southerners saw them as trouble-making meddlers. The conflict became bitter beyond the possibility of compromise because it opposed two positions based first of all on belief, but then reinforced by people's experience, by an economy and by a way of life. Black Americans, excluded from participating in most civic activities, found themselves *largely excluded from the debates and discussions of their treatment and of their future. But there were notable exceptions.*

A PRECOCIOUS young woman with an aptitude for literary studies, the shy Charlotte Forten energetically attended public talks and literary gatherings organized in Salem, Massachusetts and even in Boston in the 1850s. Coming from a well-to-do family, she met people only under close supervision, the usual plan for young ladies being prepared to be New England leaders. But she must have stood out every time because, unlike most proper young Massachusetts women, Charlotte Forten was black. A modest and valuable witness to the atmosphere of women's education in New England, Charlotte Forten recorded in her diary the inner life of a person she saw with disturbing objectivity, as if she were outside herself at times. Not for one minute, it seems, did she forget that people pointed to her as evidence that black Americans could be made literate.

While she received an excellent education in Salem, her family had stayed in Philadelphia, where they were well-known and respected both for their consider-able wealth (her grandfather, James Forten, had made a fortune on an invention to ease the handling of sails on ships) and because of their active and generous par-ticipation in civic causes. The Fortens worked to help end slavery but also to win equal treatment for women at a time when those causes were still linked.

Although he could have afforded to send his daughter to a private school in Philadelphia, Robert Bridges Forten chose not to use that easy denial of a legalized injustice: no public school in Philadelphia would admit a black child. After her mother died in 1840 when Charlotte was three, her father had arranged to educate her at home by engaging private tutors. Through his strong association with New England antislavery groups, however, Robert Forten learned about the good inte-grated public schools in Salem, Massachusetts. When he sent his daughter off to Higginson Grammar School in Salem, Robert Forten did not know, perhaps, that she would keep a diary of what she experienced, and he could not have known that because of that diary her reputation would endure.

Charlotte Forten's journal begins in 1854, shortly after the sixteen-year-old moved to Salem, to a radically different climate and culture, far from her family. Yet New England in the mid-nineteenth century could not have been a better place for a young woman of her temperament and interests. A serious commitment to the abolition of slavery impassioned many leaders in Massachusetts. From her own home in Philadelphia, a home to which African American leaders had always been welcomed, Charlotte saw only people like her educated family members intent on opposing the South, but in Massachusetts antislavery feelings permeated the entire society. While the South had viewed slavery as a necessary economic solution to the problem of running plantations, it was becoming, in the eyes of Northerners, a morally outrageous arrangement and a reason to despise its practi-tioners and upholders.

The rhetoric of the publications of antislavery groups at the time, including *The Liberator*, equated the South with a rising tide of despotism. To end what they saw as the evil and unequal treatment of "Negro Americans," the abolitionists intended to destroy the South by taking away its moral ground, by exposing slavery as absolutely indefensible. Their cause did not stop in North America. When Great Britain ended slavery in 1834, abolitionists everywhere felt heartened. In 1840, the World Antislavery Convention met in London. Among the most impressive speakers was Robert Purvis, who married an aunt of Charlotte Forten. At that same meeting Charles Lenox Remond rejected the seating plan which segregated no one by race but put women in the gallery upstairs. Remond gave up his place on the main floor to sit with women in protest. He belonged to the circle of educated African Americans who frequented the prosperous Forten home when Charlotte was born on August 17, 1837.

To be an abolitionist in Massachusetts could not be called a position as much as it was a way of life. In her diary, Charlotte Forten notes the numerous lectures she attended that abolitionists sponsored, sometimes a series or "course" of lectures, sponsored through the Salem Female Antislavery League, which she officially joined in 1856. Besides the public lectures there were fund raising society benefits such as the annual Antislavery Bazaar in Salem, and another in Boston. The abolitionists lived by their own calendar which honored such dates as the twentieth anniversary of the end of slavery in England and the anniversary of the day a crowd chased William Lloyd Garrison, editor of *The Liberator,* through the streets of Boston with a noose on his neck.

Women played a central role in this network and understood that they must draw audiences of both sexes. Such intelligent and imaginative women as Mary Shephard, principal of the Higginson Grammar School, understood that to draw a large crowd they needed not just competent, but famous speakers. Ralph Waldo Emerson accepted their invitations to speak as did the "Poet Laureate of Abolition," John Greenleaf Whittier. Charlotte Forten sometimes attended several such talks enhancing her knowledge of politics and of Boston society. People must have known her by sight, but her diary gives no hint at how people reacted to a cultivated, well-brought-up, black woman who lived at the Salem home of C. L. Remond. Her writing reflects her intellectual maturity, the result of her considerable self-discipline, developed through study and also from separation from her family. But when the diary begins, Charlotte was just sixteen, an age at which few young people can bear to describe, let alone describe how people react to them.

Circumstances suggest that this motherless, isolated girl must have suffered from loneliness. But more than any self-indulgent sentiment, a sense of duty drove her, according to what she wrote. She saw herself as owing her race a great deal. Because she had the good fortune to study at a fine school, she felt obliged to prove that a black student is as capable as a white of "self-improvement." We know that in the student body of two hundred she was the only black, but she does not say so. In fact, when she mentions people, in Salem or in Philadelphia, she does not identify them by race. Even when she feels contempt for a group, she does not use racial words to characterize them. "The military" she views with great contempt when she sees soldiers guarding an escaped slave, a fugitive caught on the streets of Salem "as if he were a criminal." In rage, in her one outburst, she refers to the soldiers as "doughfaces," the one nearly explicit antiwhite term she ever uses.

In Charlotte Forten's record of her energetic pace in the name of education—so many public talks, discussions, poetry readings, and regular contact with the Female Antislavery Society—we read between the lines that no young women or men make efforts to befriend her. Older people recognized her exceptionally stalwart personality—her principal becomes a lifelong friend, John Greenleaf Whittier, the poet, takes pains to help her—but few bonds link her to other adolescents. Forten talks about her studies as "my best friends" while at school, as the diary hints at how hard she worked. In one manuscript of the diary, a list was found of the books she read in one year, a list that ran to 100 titles.

If anyone in Salem had not noticed Charlotte Forten when she started to attend Higginson, no one could ignore her at graduation. All the students were invited beforehand to submit a hymn, one of which would be chosen for the students to sing at the ceremony. On that day, Miss Forten hesitated to acknowledge to the public that the poem chosen was hers.

The record of her work habits shows how greatly it mattered to Charlotte Forten not only to pass in school but to excel. Studying harder than any student needed to, she worked to teach herself German, after she learned French and Latin at school. On her own she produced a translation of a French novel which she eventually published. Obviously, her efforts did not belong to a plan to win credentials and start a career. Far beyond practical aims, she believed that her academic success would help remove the question of whether a black person could stand up to the rigors of scholastic work and, thereby, improve herself. Proving that fact to herself explains in part the existence of the diary. Early in her diary she writes that she intends to record her thoughts over a long enough period of time so that she might see improvement in her way of reasoning. Knowing that aim, readers may find it odd that her way of expressing herself does not change markedly from 1854 to 1864, not because she did not develop but because she began as such a skilled writer and clear thinker.

After graduation from Higginson Grammar School in 1855, Charlotte Forten enrolled in the Salem Normal School, the next step for women hoping to teach. After completing the equivalent of modern high school, young women usually studied for three terms before being allowed to teach young children. In exchange for free tuition, graduates promised to teach in Massachusetts public schools. In their year of advanced study they took one course on methods of teaching, but the accent fell on proper language. The typical curriculum included: arithmetic, algebra, geometry, geography, spelling, reading, etymology, critical study of English authors, history of English literature, English grammar, art of reasoning, rhetoric and composition, Latin, and theory and practice of teaching.

Not long after graduating from Salem Normal School, Forten found a good position in Salem, at the Eps Grammar School. Before her, no African American person had ever been a teacher in Salem, Massachusetts, a fact which Forten's diary does not mention. She stayed in Salem until her health forced her to leave in 1857. She returned to Philadelphia and then went back to Salem, always trying to stay in touch with the community where she had come of age.

While she was back in Salem, John Greenleaf Whittier suggested that she look into a new kind of teaching in which he thought she would excel. The Civil War had broken out and offered Charlotte an unusual opportunity. As part of a "social experiment" teachers were going south to Port Royal, a settlement off the coast of South Carolina captured by Union soldiers in 1861. The experiment meant testing the hypothesis that not just blacks but former slaves could be educated. Teachers went down from northern cities to work at teaching this population to read and write. When she applied from Boston Charlotte Forten was turned down, supposedly because she was a woman, even while other women were being sent. After this refusal, Forten went home to Philadelphia in order to reapply from a different city. The Philadelphia Board accepted her and she went to the island of Saint Helena in late 1862. The record shows that of the teachers who arrived from the North with her she was the only black, though her diary does not refer to the racial make-up of her group. When Charlotte Forten arrived full of good will she experienced culture shock. Among the freed slaves she found it quite difficult to understand their speech. Her diary records her embarrassment when she could not decode the words of the songs they sang. We can guess that she had not heard such an accent before from her practice of writing down the sound of slave speech in 1862, years before Mark Twain attempted to reproduce it in the pages of *Tom Sawyer*. Because she had spent so much time in Salem, Charlotte Forten had acquired the sensibilities of an educated New England woman. She describes the costumes at slave weddings that took place—sometimes as many as six at a time—as comical.

Probably the most moving entry in the entire diary occurs on January 1, 1863, while she is still in the South. Without explanation she begins by calling it "The most glorious day this nation has yet seen, I think." Before Charlotte Forten had left for the South, President Lincoln had announced in late September that on January 1 the Emancipation Proclamation would take effect. Forten reports on the ceremony at Camp Saxton and tells how everyone present felt touched when a group of freed slaves started to sing spontaneously, "My country 'tis of thee." She remained at Port Royal until 1864 when her old respiratory ailment ("lung fever" in the language of the times) bothered her, not long after the death of her father. When she returned North, an old friend bowled her over with a proposition.

The well-respected and well-connected poet John Greenleaf Whittier, still interested in Charlotte's career, asked her to write up her experiences at Port Royal for the *Atlantic Monthly*, already a prestigious journal of the New England literary establishment. When he forwarded her work to the editor, he added a brief note which appeared in the magazine after the title of the article, "Life on the Sea Islands." The note said:

> The following graceful and picturesque description of the new condition of things on the Sea Islands of South Carolina, originally written for private perusal, seems to me worthy of a place in the "Atlantic." Its young author—herself akin to the long-suffering race whose Exodus she so pleasantly describes—is still engaged in her labor of love on St. Helena Island. —J.G.W.

In her article, which ran in two parts, May and June 1864, Forten described in slightly expanded form her arrival and working in South Carolina. White readers could respect the emotion she mentioned on her way to work among the "freed people" as she repeatedly called the former slaves: "We thought how easy it would

Moorland-Spingarn Research Center, Howard University

Charlotte Forten enjoyed all the benefits of a solid liberal arts education — except easy acceptance in educated society.

be for a band of guerrillas, had they chanced that way, to seize and hang us; but we were in that excited, jubilant state of mind, which makes fear impossible, ..." Her readers also understood, even if Forten did not make it explicit, that if a band of Confederate guerrillas had found her and the other black teachers on their way to the settlement, the teachers might have been enslaved and never heard from again.

When Forten's article described the great day of Emancipation, as her diary noted, she treated it as a fact well-known in the South. *Atlantic* readers of May,

1864 may have believed her, but in fact Abraham Lincoln, at that time, pondered anxiously what he saw as the failure of his Proclamation. Lincoln feared for slaves more than ever because he saw how weak his chances grew for re-election. Without him the Proclamation would be withdrawn and slavery would continue. In any case, Lincoln knew that slaves were not making a mass exodus out of Confederate territory, which his Proclamation said they had to do in order to be liberated.

To try to understand why this was not happening, President Lincoln spoke with his respected advisor on all questions related to slavery, Frederick Douglass. The black man saw an explanation that Lincoln had not counted on in the deceitful behavior of slaveowners. Probably a great many slaves had never even heard of the Proclamation, Douglass reasoned, because their "masters" had made sure that they did not find out that anything had changed. Together, Lincoln and Douglass worked out a plan for sending undercover agents to the South to make sure the news was spread, a plan that never had to be used because the Union Army started winning battles and helping Lincoln's chances for re-election.

In many ways, Forten's article could not have been more timely. Racism, not just slavery, divided voters in an election year. Lincoln spelled out for voters that to be against emancipation meant being against a victory for the North, in other words, being against the Union. At the time of the election, it helped Lincoln's Republicans tremendously to see that three-quarters of the absentee votes of soldiers were on their side after a campaign to get soldiers to "vote as they shot."

In her article Forten spoke about her tremendous admiration for Colonel Robert Shaw and his soldiers. *Atlantic* readers did not need a note from the editor to explain why the schoolteacher should talk in such an admiring and moving way about that officer in particular. Shaw had led a brigade that had already become famous, the 54th Massachusetts Infantry. Shaw, a white officer, led that black brigade in July 1863 in its attack against Fort Wagner, the Confederate defense at the entrance to Charleston harbor. The famous black regiment led by Shaw, from an important Abolitionist family, fought ahead of others in the capture of the fort. Almost half of the regiment died in that assault, among them Shaw himself, who was found shot through the heart. Some Massachusetts readers no doubt knew that when his family had asked for the return of their son's body, a Confederate officer was said to answer, "We have buried him with his niggers."

The attack on Fort Wagner quickly became for black Americans the equivalent of Bunker Hill for patriotic families of Massachusetts, a day with which descendants proudly claimed a connection. Other readers would have known that at the very same time as the fighting at Fort Wagner, New York City had witnessed draft riots because so many white Americans, recent immigrants from Ireland in particular, refused to join up and risk their lives for slaves, blacks whom Charlotte Forten knew had already been Americans for generations.

Forten's excellent diary stops in 1864, so that our knowledge of her subjective experience does not continue past her teaching days. After Emancipation Forten worked in Boston for the New England Branch of the Freedmen's Union Commission. From 1865 to 1871 she served as the link between teachers of freed slaves in the South and the teachers and other Northerners who wanted to help them. After teaching in Washington, D.C. for a short time she worked as a clerk (her rank was first-class clerk) at the Treasury Department. Charlotte Forten kept her federal job until 1878 when she met the man she would marry.

In 1878, at age forty-one, Charlotte Forten married Francis Grimké who was a student at Princeton Theological Seminary and thirteen years younger than she. Her husband's upbringing showed none of the same wealth and privilege of his wife's distinguished family. Although he was the nephew of the well-known abolitionist Angelika Grimké (the son of her uncle), she did not know they were related for many years. In fact, Francis Grimké had been a slave partly through the treachery of his white half-brother who sold him. Great physical courage and intellectual stamina distinguished Francis Grimké who escaped, eventually graduated from Lincoln College in Pennsylvania (as class valedictorian), and studied law at Howard University before turning to theology at Princeton.

At age forty-three Charlotte Forten had her only child, who died as an infant. Although she did not enjoy strong health for much of her life, she lived to the age of seventy-six. For the last year of her life, Charlotte Forten was an invalid, always cared for devotedly by her husband. They worked together to provide every kind of support to former slaves. She died in Washington on July 22, 1914.

QUESTIONS FOR THOUGHT AND DISCUSSION

1. Did Charlotte Forten pay a price for being a prominent black woman in Salem, Massachusetts in the 1850s? How did the social climate for African Americans in Salem compare to the situation in her native Philadelphia?

2. Why do you think Forten virtually ignores racial descriptions in her diary entries? Do you think race was irrelevant to her, or did she seek to overcome its importance by not mentioning it in her diary?

3. In what ways did Forten find living among the newly freed slaves in Port Royal, South Carolina a culture shock?

4. What do the lives of Annie Turner Wittenmyer, Harriet Beecher Stowe, and Charlotte Forten suggest about opportunities for women in nineteenth century America? Would you regard them as early feminists? Why, or why not?

SUGGESTED READINGS

Billington, Ray Allen, ed. *The Journal of Charlotte Forten: A Free Negro in the Slave Era.* New York: Norton, 1953.

Forten, Charlotte. "Life on the Sea Islands" in *Atlantic Monthly.* May 1864, pp. 587–596; June 1864, pp. 666–676.

Kunhardt, Philip B., Jr., Philip B. Kunhardt, III and Peter W. Kunhardt. *Lincoln: An Illustrated Biography.* New York: Knopf, 1992.

McPherson, James M. *Battle Cry of Freedom: The Civil War Era.* New York: Ballantine, 1988.

Smith, Jessey Carney, ed. *Notable Black American Women.* Detroit: Gale Research, 1992, pp. 358–364.

Stevenson, Brenda, ed. *The Journals of Charlotte Forten Grimké.* New York: Oxford U., 1988.

Index